QUIXOTE'S GHOST

Quixote's Ghost

The Right, the Liberati, and the Future of Social Policy

DAVID STOESZ, Ph.D.

OXFORD
UNIVERSITY PRESS

2005

OXFORD
UNIVERSITY PRESS

Oxford University Press, Inc., publishes works that further
Oxford University's objective of excellence
in research, scholarship, and education.

Oxford New York
Auckland   Cape Town   Dar es Salaam   Hong Kong   Karachi
Kuala Lumpur   Madrid   Melbourne   Mexico City   Nairobi
New Delhi   Shanghai   Taipei   Toronto

With offices in
Argentina   Austria   Brazil   Chile   Czech Republic   France   Greece
Guatemala   Hungary   Italy   Japan   Poland   Portugal   Singapore
South Korea   Switzerland   Thailand   Turkey   Ukraine   Vietnam

Published by Oxford University Press, Inc.
198 Madison Avenue, New York, New York 10016

www.oup.com

Library of Congress Cataloging-in-Publication Data
Stoesz, David.
Quixote's ghost : the right, the liberati, and the future of social policy /
David Stoesz.
p. cm.
Includes bibliographical references and index.
ISBN-13 978-0-19-518120-3
ISBN 0-19-518120-4
1. United States—Social policy—1980–1993. 2. United States—Social policy—1993–
3. Public welfare—United States. 4. Conservatism—United States.
5. Liberalism—United States. 6. Right and Left (Political science)
7. United States—Politics and government—1989–   I. Title.
HN59.2.S75   2004
361.6'1'0973—dc22   2004019754

1 3 5 7 9 8 6 4 2

Printed in the United States of America
on acid-free paper

Para Julio,
todos niños son
una promesa

CONTENTS

QUIXOTE'S GHOST

INTRODUCTION

The enemy isn't conservatism.
The enemy isn't liberalism.
The enemy is bullshit.
LARS-ERIK NELSON

THIS IS A MEDITATION on the ascendance of conservatism as public philosophy and its impact on social policy—an inquest, if you will, into social epistemology. An open society is subject to alterations in how public affairs are conducted, as well as the ends to which they are put. It follows that a nation's social infrastructure evolves over decades, its irregularities a product of changes in public philosophy. This has certainly been the case for the American welfare state, which has been ongoing for almost a century. Sustained by liberalism and the Democratic Party, federal social programs have been so enduring that they have come to consume over half of the federal budget, 61 percent in 2002.[1] Yet, a conspiracy of circumstance suggests that this legacy will not be sustained. This reflects a wholesale revision in public philosophy, a remarkable transformation that has occurred during the past three decades. Essentially, Americans have become receptive to a different understanding of social policy than one dominant only a generation ago. The evidence of philosophical realignment is obvious: Conservatism is ascendant while liberalism has faltered; the Republican Party is triumphant while Democrats founder. On May 14, 2003, that bastion of progressive preferences, the *New York Times*, reported that more Americans (53 percent) perceive the Republican Party as offering "a clear vision for the country" compared to Democrats (40 percent).[2] Conceding the Right's influence in public affairs, the following year the liberal *New York Times* appointed a journalist to cover the conservative beat.[3]

Most remarkable about the rightward vector in social policy is its increasing radicalism. Not content with holding social programs in check, conservatives have engineered a series of tax cuts that, combined with the Medicare reform of 2003, effectively preclude future initiatives. As preemptive fiscal strikes on the domestic front, the tax cuts have momentous implications for the American welfare state: A nation confronted with $44.2 *trillion* in future deficits will be hard-pressed to provide the Social Security and Medicare benefits to which baby boomers are entitled much less mount new programs without driving the federal budget into precipitous deficit. The fiscal consequences of Bush tax policies have stunned even veteran Republicans. Peter Peterson, Secretary of Commerce during the Nixon administration and current Chair of the Federal Reserve Bank of New York, has decried the "tax-cut theology" of George W. Bush's presidency, noting that it carries with it "$25 trillion in total unfinanced liabilities" for Social Security and Medicare.[4] The tax cuts redistribute massive amounts of income to wealthier Americans, leading Kevin Phillips to characterize the emergence of a second gilded age of American capitalism that dwarfs the income disparities between rich and poor evident in the nineteenth century.[5]

There is an indirect purpose to the tax cuts, of course. Unable to reduce the scale of popular social entitlements through political means, conservatives are cranking hard on the spigot, cutting off vital revenues for social programs that sustain the welfare state. Because the deficits range from 4.2 percent of the national economy in 2004 to an anticipated 1.7 percent in 2008,[6] they are not so large as to impair economic performance, yet they do set the stage for a political reckoning. Economist Paul Krugman has averred that "the administration was deliberately setting the country up for a fiscal crisis in which popular social programs could be sharply cut."[7] The 1996 welfare reform may be prophetic in this regard. The family cash entitlement was converted to a discretionary program and devolved to the states as a block grant. Five years later, welfare rolls had been halved, many welfare recipients were working, and conservatives claimed their first triumph in reforming a liberal social program. Public assistance programs targeted for the poor have always been more vulnerable than the more popular and better defended social insurances designed for the middle class. After its Medicare reform victory, the Right is well-positioned to forge ahead and privatize Social Security. Thus, the interaction of fiscal insolvency and the inundation of retiring baby boomers will presage the restructuring of the social insurance programs. Either taxes will have to be doubled to provide Social Security and Medicare benefits to the next generation of retirees or these programs will be retrofitted as welfare so that benefits can be reserved for the needy.

As a cautionary note, when I offer my social policy students (virtually all card-carrying liberals) this choice in a hypothetical 2020 presidential election, they consistently prefer the candidate who would convert social insurance programs to welfare. While their vote for a conservative Republican may be counterintuitive, my students explain that they expect to have made provisions for their own retirement needs; besides, they wonder, "Who knows if Social Security will be around anyway . . . ?" When conservatism has so influenced the next generation of human service professionals, the integrity of the American welfare state is suspect, to say the least.

In retrospect, a conservative tilt in social policy is not so surprising. The ideological lurch to the Right brings to fruition the advocacy of conservative intellectuals, who, smarting from the licking that Barry Goldwater received in 1964, became intent on rolling back liberalism as public philosophy. Stymied from using the universities as their base of operations, the Right invested in a network of think tanks—private organizations that explored alternatives to liberal social programs—marketed them to the public via the media, and saturated Congress with their proposals. While conservatives went about subverting the American welfare state, liberalism split into two disparate camps. A cadre of policy analysts continued the Progressive tradition by providing sophisticated evaluations of existing programs. Holding senior appointments at select universities and think tanks, these analysts applied the methods of the social sciences to assess the impact of public policy. Their analyses were notable in two respects: They were so arcane as to be undecipherable to the public, and they were reluctant to venture beyond the limits of their data to suggest future policy prescriptions. An altogether different camp forsook empiricism altogether and, taking the expansion of the Welfare State for granted, flirted with a series of intellectual fads under the guise of postmodernism. Having secured tenured positions in the academy, the Liberati—leftist intellectuals who rejected empiricism in favor of identity politics—waxed enthusiastic for European social philosophy, which denigrated science as an institution that contributed to the patriarchal and colonial tendencies of predatory capitalism. The Liberati challenged the idea that the Welfare State was a logical progression in industrial development, contending that it was actually an oppressive institution facilitated by an array of professions. This bifurcation of liberalism allowed conservatives strategic openings in the social policy debate. The obtuse research of program analysts was characterized by the Right as self-serving and antipopulist; the Liberati's romance with postmodernism was criticized for being anti-American. Upon reflection, the Right's dominance in social affairs could be attributed as much to the esoteric research of liberal policy analysts and the intellectual dalliances of a university-based Liberati as the sophistication of conservatives in marketing their ideas.

The triumph of conservatism in social policy underscores the importance of knowledge in public affairs. This relationship has been the subject of scholarly interest since the dawn of history, but more so with the modern era when it became evident that humans could fashion society toward predetermined ends. To be sure, the result could prove contradictory—unprecedented prosperity coupled with unimaginable horrors—but the deliberate shaping of social institutions would be ubiquitous. A postindustrial era, driven by information technology, the commercialization of experience, and the globalization of culture, promises to accelerate this trend, though in ways that would not have been anticipated by the educated elites of the modern era. During the twentieth century, a mature industrial order exacerbated extant social problems (such as poverty, illness, illiteracy, and racism), fostering the liberal belief that these could be mitigated through the welfare state and the myriad public programs it engendered. In the industrial West, a welfare state consensus evolved that endorsed a primary role of national governments in relieving social distress. Despite some variation among governments, a general trend was not only evident, but ineluctable: Expansion of public expenditures for social welfare would be characteristic of future societies. For American liberals, the trans-Atlantic accord on the welfare state justified a dominant role of the federal government in social policy, tempering unrestrained capitalism. Established through the Social Security Act of 1935 and amplified three decades later during the War on Poverty, the American welfare state would, according to liberal expectations, eventually replicate those of northern Europe.

There was little that the Right perceived as desirable about expanding social programs. Conservatives objected to the welfare state on several grounds: social programs subverted individual initiative and fostered dependency on government; federal programs usurped the authority of subordinate levels of government; taxes upon which benefits were derived diverted resources from capital formation; a fully articulated welfare state in which government was dominant diminished the role of nonprofit and commercial institutions of the private sector. Ultimately, conservatives wondered, what *was* the end point of liberal endeavors to protect Americans from insecurity? Initiatives proliferating under the welfare state banner addressed a vast array of concerns: housing, health, income, employment, education, mental disorders, urban development, and transportation. The list seemed endless. Did the expansion of social programs that addressed the needs of disadvantaged groups, which, in turn, supported the priorities of the Democratic Party, promise to marginalize Republicans further? By the late 1970s, Right-wing intellectuals concluded that the specter of a welfare state run amok was untenable.

Thirty years later, this question sounds amusingly quaint, and that is because conservatives have assumed command of domestic policy. Their preoccupation about metastatic social programs would eventually result in a paradigm shift in public philosophy, a masterful accomplishment in that it would occur in only two decades and right under the noses of a cadre of well-pedigreed liberal intellectuals. Having realized a strategy for recharting the welfare state, conservatives have been driving social policy ever since, leaving liberals in the dust, slack-jawed and wondering what went wrong. As writers for *The Economist* observed, "the [R]ight has out-organized, out-fought, and out-thought liberal America over the past 40 years. And the [L]eft still shows no real signs of knowing how to fight back."[8]

To be sure, the Right's designs on domestic policy have provoked a firestorm of criticism from the Left, much of it empirically substantiated. The gender gap remains high, leaving women at a comparative disadvantage to men in the labor market. Jobs for low-income workers continue to be inadequate to sustain the typical family. Economic policies that concede globalization of markets encourage the hemorrhaging of jobs overseas. Such staples of the liberal Left lose their edge when conservatives rebut them with countervailing data showing that the gender gap has virtually disappeared among young women who avoid family obligations, that low-wage workers experience substantial upward mobility over time, and that globalization optimizes the deployment of productive capacity and accelerates the development of the Third World. Thus, conservatives have not only challenged the liberal Left for the high moral ground of public policy, but, in so doing, have sometimes based their claims on grounds of social justice.

As conservatives refuted liberalism as desirable public philosophy, they eroded its political viability. "By the mid-1980s," Barbara Ehrenreich acknowledged at the beginning of the first Bush presidency, "liberalism appeared, for all practical purposes, to be dead."[9] For many liberals, the Clinton presidency promised to bring the nation back in line with its moral precepts; yet the sum total of two terms of a Democratic president was a record that was at best diaphanous. "Once in office [Clinton] acted on the assumption that the country had run out of enthusiasm for doing good and wanted to taste the pleasures of doing well," reflected Russell Baker. "Nudging Democrats off their traditional left-of-center ground, he moved them into the vacant trenches formerly occupied by 'moderate' Republicans, a nearly extinct species, thanks to the conservatives' efforts to purge the party of impure ideas."[10] Despite the interregnum of a Democratic president whose policy agenda mirrored that of a moderate Republican, conservatism remained regnant in domestic policy, generating sufficient electoral support to control both houses of Congress and the White House. The liberal loss of electoral support is of structural import. In a comparative analysis of western welfare states, Peter Lindert concluded that the most compelling factor in their expansion was the endorsement of voters: "The Americans paid less in taxes for social transfers because fewer of them voted. The Democratic Party has long rued the fact that a small share of its registered partisans actually show up at the polls, whereas registered Republicans show up more regularly."[11] The liberal basis of public philosophy has lost its credibility with voters, leaving conservatives dictating the terms of social policy.

Conservative dominance in social policy has manifestations that liberal intellectuals have been loathe to appreciate fully. Any ideological triumph falls under the province of normative theory, the deployment of institutional resources, and processes toward objectives engineered by particular parties. For example, the liberal Left's caricature of the Right typically indicts avaricious capitalists who exploit vulnerable minorities through massaging popular opinion and manipulating representative government. This simplification is a cognitive cartoon. As such, it fails on several counts: It denies the centrality of markets through which most

Americans receive goods and services; it denies the multiple, sometimes tragic, failures of social programs; and it dismisses the Right's appeal to voluntarism as a basis of social provision. Given these outcomes, one might think it time for liberals to begin a thorough and merciless inventory of their precepts; but that does not seem forthcoming anytime soon—much easier to cling to the moral high ground, even if the purchase is increasingly tenuous. Too late, liberals are just now coming to appreciate that conservatives did their homework, having developed theories and applied data in their critique of the welfare state.

In explaining the fate of the American welfare state, a disclaimer on theory is warranted. Classically, theory would mean a logically deducible system of abstract propositions;[12] but, this usage is certainly too rigid for a subject as fluid as social policy. Terry Eagleton's suggestion that "theory means a reasonably systematic reflection on our guiding assumptions"[13] is more apropos of the subject matter. More loosely, postmodernism uses Theory (capital T) to refer to a diffuse collection of artifacts and motives, the presentation of which is dictated by ideology and is often opaque. My preference is for "theories of the middle range," a strategy attributed to one of the leading welfare philosophers of the twentieth century, T. H. Marshall, who advocated "stepping stones in the middle distance."[14] Later, Robert K. Merton adopted the idea to advocate those theories that avoid the pretense and finality of grand theory, yet are useful in explaining social events as people experience them.[15] The middle range represents a tactical and prudent choice on the part of the theoretician. "To concentrate solely on the major conceptual scheme for deriving all sociological theory is to run the risk of producing twentieth-century equivalents of the large philosophical systems of the past, with all their suggestiveness, all their architectonic splendor and all their scientific sterility," cautioned Merton. "To concentrate solely on special theories is to run the risk of emerging with ad hoc speculations consistent with a limited range of observations and inconsistent among themselves."[16] Stripped of pretense then, middle-range theory might be aptly described as bourgeois philosophy. In advocating theoretical pluralism, Merton crafted a scholarly concept that was particularly apropos of a democratic society: a civil order that provided sufficient space for multiple actors and agendas.

Pluralism in American culture has been favored by conservatives while liberals have enlisted stratification to advance their ends. In the competition within what Oliver Wendell Holmes called the "marketplace of ideas," conservatives have been adroit at churning out social policy prescriptions that reify the American melting pot and appeal to mainstream voters, while liberals remain largely wedded to an explanation of social problems focused on stratification along race, income, gender, and more recently sexual orientation. In the theoretical dispute between pluralism and stratification, ironies abound. This is evident when liberals criticize Republicans over tax policies that favor the rich, prompting the Right to accuse the Left of "class warfare," as well as when liberals steal a page from the conservative's facility to leverage campaign contributions by establishing special interest 527 committees to fund anti-Republican broadcasts in battleground states. As amusing as these anecdotes may be, they are embedded in the nation's political economy; democratic capitalism invariably generates a dynamic in which the economy that produces prosperity and inequality is subject to correction by a representative polity.

The fortunes of political parties have varied with respect to their ability to exploit opportunities over time; they use public policy as a means to embellish institutions with which they are aligned, while disparaging those of their opponents. Liberal Democrats used their faith in government—and their apprehensions about capitalism—to justify a welfare state under the province of the federal government. Subsequently, conservative Republicans have denigrated federal social programs—while lauding the virtues of markets—as a competing vision. This dynamic invites networks of influence to emerge that shape public policy according to their affluence and agility. At the end of the day, the victor will have established an institutional edifice that cannot be challenged by its opponents. The welfare state was such an edifice, established by liberal Democrats to protect Americans from the ravages of poverty, illness, unemployment, and other misfortunes. Their preferred solution was to deploy a public utility model in social policy, a solution that enjoyed success for decades. Since the 1970s, however, conservatives have directed withering fire at the poor performance of the public utility model, targeting particularly welfare, education, and housing.

The transformation of an institution on the scale of the American welfare state is momentous, of course, entailing the welfare of millions of beneficiaries, the expenditure of billions of dollars, and the job security of thousands of employees. The future configuration of social policy, and therewith the welfare state, will be an indicator of the comparative success of various networks and their ability to market ideology. In this major reorientation of social welfare in the United States, conservative think tanks have been central because they *control the means of analysis*. The jockeying of networks as they attempt to bring social policy in line with their preferences is undertaken by *structural interests*, groups that are symbiotically dependent on the welfare state and seek to exploit the public policy environment. Upward on the social stratification, more consequential networks become *industrial complexes*, configurations that shape major aspects of social policy. The role of health corporations, public officials, and lawmakers in Medicare reform illustrates this. On the lower registers of our stratification are *networks of negligence*, linkages that provide inferior services to struggling Americans. Such networks are sustained by trade associations, public administrators, and professional schools, often under the guise of public welfare. Thus, power is stratified, the outcome elaborating Murray Edelman's contention that politics redistributes tangible awards to elites, but symbolic awards to mass publics.

An idiosyncrasy of American social welfare is that Washington, D.C., has become the site of overlapping *networks of negligence*; public agencies providing housing, child welfare, mental health, and other essential services have been placed under court supervision because of gross discrepancies between their mandated missions and routine performance. Thus, lawmakers who converge on the nation's capitol from other regions of the country are constantly reminded by the *Washington Post* of how odorous things are in the state of welfare. Of course, the institutional inferiority that characterizes the social infrastructure of Washington, D.C., can be attributed to a variety of unusual circumstances, ranging from the corruption spawned by Mayor Marion Barry to the absence of voting representation in Congress. Disclaimers notwithstanding, many members of Congress have come to view the District as a laboratory for everything that could possibly go wrong with social welfare.

That power differentials exist with respect to social policy networks is not to suggest that those brokering major social legislation exercise malevolent influences in public policy any more than it means that welfare workers toiling on the front lines are unable to provide valid assistance to some of the most troubled among us. The analytic problem is one of identifying patterns in decision-making that advance or retard the purpose of social welfare. Having held direct service as well as administrative appointments in public welfare and mental health, I am intimately aware of how difficult circumstances are for human service professionals working in public agencies. Having done so, I am not convinced that maintaining the myth of social service, especially in an era of diminishing public support, ennobles any of the parties involved. It is for that reason that I propose *radical pragmatism* as a basis for future social policy.

The antics of Don Quixote, the Knight of the Woeful Countenance, provide a suitable metaphor for the Progressive predicament in social policy. Cervantes attributed Quixote's escapades to his preoccupation with obscure texts on chivalry, an early illustration of Romanticism, and used them to put him on the road to comic ridicule:

> In short, [Don Quixote] became so caught up in reading that he spent his nights reading from dusk till dawn and his days reading from sunrise to sunset, and so with too little sleep and too much reading his brains dried up, causing him to lose his mind. His fantasy filled with everything he had read in his books, enchantments as well as combats, battles, challenges, wounds, courtings, loves, torments, and other impossible foolishness, and he became so convinced in his imagination of the truth of all the countless grandiloquent and false inventions he read that for him no history of the world was truer.[17]

By modern standards, Quixote would be diagnosed as suffering from delusions of grandeur with obsessive-compulsive features.

Symptomatic of the postmodern disregard for historical authenticity and its preference for entertainment, Americans are more likely to appreciate Quixote through the musical *Man of La Mancha*, recalling the hopeless romantic who is struck by the captivating Dulcinea and steadied by his sidekick Sancho. Significantly, the Broadway incarnation of Quixote bears little resemblance to the original. Despite moments of lucidity, Cervantes's Quixote was certifiably insane, inflicting all sorts of injury on friends and strangers alike. "It is as if those determined to see Don Quixote as some kind of saint or missionary of the spirit had simply closed their eyes to the mayhem and suffering he causes," corrected James Wood.[18]

Much as *Don Quixote* has been misconstrued, many liberals have misunderstood the basis of social policy. While intellectuals of the Right have applied themselves to the empirical task of reversing liberals' designs in domestic affairs, the liberal Left has engaged in Romanticism, proclaiming an ideological nostalgia that is increasingly divergent from the American mainstream. Chivalry is to Quixote as postmodernism is to the Left. Leftist pieties about oppression and social justice, notwithstanding, a social policy agenda that is so out of synch with American voters is fatal in a democratic polity. In a real sense, the Liberati is haunted by Quixote's ghost.

If there is consolation in these events, it is of a philosophical nature. The welfare state was the institutional expression of a singularly American philosophy: pragmatism. As a means for countering the corruption of early industrialization, introducing the professions to advance progress, and fostering unprecedented prosperity, pragmatism proved an admirable success. Yet, pragmatism is a philosophy of process, abjuring ends per se. The genius of pragmatism lay in its capacity to organize intelligence; the supposition was that its application would enhance social welfare broadly understood. Liberals relied on the university as the engine of progress in the end establishing the welfare state as an instrument of social justice, while conservatives have deployed think tanks to deflect the liberal trajectory in domestic affairs. To bolster its credibility, the Right has relied on a stable of old war horses for philosophical justification: John Locke, Edmund Burke, Adam Smith, and more recently Friedrich von Hayek and Milton Friedman. While these provide ample targets for university-based intellectuals from the Left who have relished disparaging them in academic journals and classroom lectures, the Right has accomplished an end run around the academy through the creation of an intellectual network of policy institutes that have routed university-based liberalism. The victory of the Right is ironic insofar as the modern American university was the instrument of pragmatism. Conservatives thus hijacked pragmatism to attain dominance in public affairs. Of course, all of this has transpired in the public arena and is, therefore, subject to reversal. Whether or not the Right continues to shape social policy depends on the ratification of its agenda by the polity as well as the Left's continued adherence to ideological nostalgia. Since 1980, bets have been on the conservatives.

For the same reasons that the Right has commandeered social policy, assiduously critiquing social programs, cobbling together alternatives, and promoting them to lawmakers, Progressives could use the same means to achieve their ends. This is unlikely, however, if they continue to be haunted by Quixote's ghost. As the following chapters illustrate, pragmatism can reassert valid preferences in domestic policy. My accounting includes philosophers and theoreticians that are somewhat out of fashion. Beginning with William James, my points of orientation include John Dewey, C. Wright Mills, Murray Edelman, Robert Alford, and Martha Nussbaum. Americans with a decided appreciation for international events, they provide a native foundation for the discussion, though it is important to note the contributions of Europeans, especially Pierre Bourdieu, George Soros, and Terry Eagleton. This classification will doubtlessly annoy those Americans who consider themselves internationalists and those Europeans who have diligently cultivated American sensibilities, but it serves to underscore the possibility of reasserting a native philosophy for addressing domestic concerns.

As will be evident, I believe E. J. Dionne, Jr., was correct in locating the primary American ideologies (liberalism and conservatism) as well as the dominant political parties (Democrat and Republican) in the industrial era; however, a template for social policy that is congruent with the requirements of a postindustrial milieu imposes different requirements.[19] Addressing those requires rigorous thought and debate, toward which this is intended to contribute.

ACKNOWLEDGMENTS

Colleagues have provided invaluable assistance in the preparation of this manuscript, though they might take issue with some of its conclusions. Years ago, Harris Chaiklin taught a demanding seminar in social theory upon which I continue to reflect; he is a testament to the value of thought in the human endeavor. William Epstein provided a critique of the first draft that more resembled an essay than a review; it was so witty that it was hard not to laugh at his skewering my more preposterous statements. Al Roberts was instrumental in convincing Oxford University Press of the book's merit. A number of reviewers, including Joel Blau and Neil Gilbert, provided valuable suggestions on improving earlier drafts of the manuscript. Kristen Russo proved invaluable in tending to details. To all of them, a heartfelt "Thanks!"

1

PARADIGM LOST

Seeing, therefore, that Arms, like Letters, require intelligence, let us consider now which of the two performs the greatest mental labour, the man of letters or the man of war; for this will be decided by the end and object at which each is aiming—since the purpose which has the noblest end in view must be the more highly valued. The end of the object of learning . . . I am speaking of the humanities, whose aim is to maintain impartial justice, to give every man his rights, to make good laws, and to see that they are kept. That is certainly a lofty and generous aim, and highly praiseworthy, though not so much as the profession of Arms, whose aim and object is peace, the greatest good which men can desire in this life.

DON QUIXOTE

SEPTEMBER 11, 2001, began auspiciously enough. Retrieving the morning paper, I found the day more late summer than early autumn. Over breakfast, I scanned the *Washington Post*, clipping a pair of articles that would be useful for the week's classes. After walking my son to the school bus stop, I began to gather books and papers for work, half-hearing an odd National Public Radio (NPR) story about a plane crashing into the World Trade Center. Driving to work along the George Washington Parkway, which follows the Potomac River just outside Washington, I was enjoying a Beethoven overture when the music was interrupted by an announcement that riveted my attention: *Two* planes had slammed into the World Trade Center. As I contemplated the unlikelihood of this, the traffic began to slow. Then I saw a gray mushroom cloud rising not far up ahead. "Uh, oh," I thought, "that's the Pentagon." The NPR announcer was patched in to a reporter at the Pentagon who stated, improbably, that he was unable to confirm that anything had happened there. A few minutes later my car was parallel to the building, which was framed by a curtain of black, billowing smoke. As if from an old horror movie, men in business suits, their ties askew and jackets aflutter, began to crab their way between the cars, crossing the parkway, working their way away from the Pentagon, furtively looking behind at some menace that had just descended upon them. Within hours, the World Trade Center towers would collapse, marking a new era of American vulnerability and resolve with respect to terrorism.

Only two years later, the response to the terrorist attack would be unmistakable: the nation opted to redouble its efforts with respect to *national* security, even if it would be at the expense of *social* security.[1] If the blowback of September 11 toppled the Taliban in Afghanistan and stirred up a hornets' nest in Iraq, it also effectively finished the end game of liberal Democrats who had struggled to protect social programs from conservative assault. Already, 2001 had been problematic for Democrats. Smarting from a Supreme Court decision that awarded the presidency to George W. Bush despite Al Gore's popular victory, Democrats then failed to counter a massive tax cut engineered by congressional Republicans. Despite a brief respite due the defection of a Republican senator to the Democratic Party, liberals were obviously on the defensive. By late summer, Democrats had crafted their strategy: establish a "lock box" on Social Security in order to protect its surpluses from Republicans who would subsequently be unable to balance the budget without driving the federal government deeply into deficit as a result of their first tax cut. Accordingly, Democrats figured they could corner the Bush White House and congressional Republicans, at the same time protecting liberal social programs; eventually the Grand Old Party would have to concede that it had created a fiscal chasm between social entitlements and Treasury revenues on a scale of the Grand Canyon. Democrats calculated that the White House would have to reverse course.

September 11 put an end to all that.

A watershed in American history, September 11 served not only to veer the nation to the Right, redoubling appropriations for defense, conflating dozens of federal agencies into a new federal security department, sacrificing civil liberties in the name of protecting national security, and providing pretext for a war against Iraq, but also to mark the end of the liberal vector in American social welfare. In consort with congressional conservatives, the Bush White House diverted billions of dollars in future social benefits to current defense needs, attempted to devolve more public assistance programs to the states as discretionary block grants, redefined Medicare and education as Republican issues, and, as a preemptive strike to control spending on social programs, enacted another massive tax cut. Its momentum having been slowed since the Reagan presidency in the 1980s, the American welfare state was being reformed by the Right. Rather than opposing social programs, conservatives were "engaged in a bold experiment: to see whether programs that were created by liberals from the 1930s to the 1970s can be reshaped in a conservative direction."[2]

There is much more to the story of the demise of the welfare state than liberal caviling and conservative triumphalism, of course. Certainly, opportunism has played a central role; the fulcrum for policy change is that moment when politicians recognize the possibility of engineering a political realignment, as Newt Gingrich anticipated so brilliantly in the 1994 mid-term elections. Nor can the symbolism of events be underestimated. Early criticized for attempting to label catsup a vegetable in order to cut funding for the School Lunch Program, Ronald Reagan would sign the 1988 Family Support Act, the first conservative imprint on social welfare legislation. However, it was Bill Clinton who would realize the Right's aspirations in welfare reform, signing the Personal Responsibility and Work Opportunity Reconciliation Act eight years later. Finally, the role of institutions in domestic policy would prove critical in the transformation of public philosophy, although this would escape most Americans. In this case, Progressives who inhabited the institutions that had lain the foundation of the welfare state, denizens of liberal think tanks and university social science departments, assumed that the trajectory of the welfare state, set with the 1935 Social Security Act and amplified during the War on Poverty of the 1960s, was fixed. Meanwhile, intellectuals from the Right, unable to employ the university toward their ends, established a parallel set of policy institutes from which they framed bold alternatives to liberal social programs and used entrepreneurial methods to market them to lawmakers and the public.

Insofar as social policy is more than an amorphous agglomeration of discreet events, theory and philosophy provide not only an explanation to the past but a road map to the future. Had he been willing to dabble in social policy, Thomas Kuhn would have characterized developments of the past two decades as a paradigm shift. A historian of science, Kuhn observed that science did not evolve in a linear manner, each discovery building on the previous, but was typified by fits and starts. As one school ascended due to its ability to explain certain phenomena, it attained dominance and its practitioners engaged in what Kuhn called "normal puzzle-solving science" in order to elaborate the dominant paradigm. But any paradigm has a limited capacity to explain reality, so anomalies become increasingly problematic. Kuhn described how the dominance of certain schools of thought, which controlled the means by which science was conducted, disintegrated as rival cabals pointed out inconsistencies and contradictions in the received wisdom, eventually accomplishing an intellectual coup d'etat, a paradigm shift.[3] If science, noted for its dispassionate regard for evidence, is subject to the politics of knowledge, then how much more so social policy? Shaped by human volition and caprice, buffeted by political and economic forces sometimes unforeseen, and always subject to dispute about its intended aim, social policy is incalculably more fluid by comparison.

Yet many questions remain: What was the regnant paradigm? How did anomalies subvert it? What actors, institutions, and events proved pivotal in the paradigm shift? What theories and philosophies offer some guidance as to how this change occurred, and where it might lead us in the future?

These questions have been brooding for the past quarter century. By the beginning of the second millennium, it is evident that American social welfare has been rapidly morphing from a welfare state toward a future of indeterminate architecture. Since the 1980s, a liberal vision of social welfare, predicated on the replication of a northern European welfare state, has been in retreat, replaced by a dynamic conservatism that has yet to configure a convincing agenda for the requirements posed by the twenty-first century. This has profound implications for social philosophy and analysis, yet the intelligence guiding the nation's social policy remained anchored in industrial-era modernism. Proponents of "convergence theory"[4] hold that industrialization introduced the corporate and governmental bureaucracy as the vehicle for social progress; the welfare state, in its various forms, evolved as an ungainly combination of their varying provisions to reduce human insecurity. However awkward the arrangement, a trans-Atlantic welfare state accord had been achieved during the twentieth century, promising replication of the northern European ideal in the United States. With the elections of Margaret Thatcher and Ronald Reagan, the welfare-state accord began to unravel, and any further momentum was effectively halted by the Third Way initiatives pursued by Tony Blair and Bill Clinton. Subsequently, conservatives and liberals began to pursue divergent vectors: Invoking "compassionate conservatism," the Right advocated strengthening the role of the private sector and sectarian agencies, in the process becoming a credible participant in the social welfare debate. Largely ignoring conservative momentum in domestic affairs, the Left split into two camps: a cadre of think-tank policy analysts preoccupied with sorting through the statistical entrails of existing programs and a university-based Liberati who attained tenure through critiquing Western civilization.

Of the actors who feature prominently in this drama, the Liberati warrant special attention because it was the university-based intellectuals who conceived the burgeoning welfare state of the twentieth century. Instead of continuing the Progressive course in domestic affairs, the Liberati has indulged in a narcissism of political correctness in which aggrieved groups vilify the national culture in order to leverage special concessions, in the process denigrating the rigorous research that has driven the nation's prosperity and the courage that has enlarged its moral purpose. Having secured life-time employment, tenured Leftists have betrayed the university's role in domestic affairs.

In this respect, *Don Quixote* serves as a suitable metaphor.[5] A neglected work of social criticism, Cervantes's biting wit has been defanged so that it is more likely recalled as an insipid musical, *Man of La Mancha*. An accurate reading of Cervantes reveals a Don Quixote submerged in madness, whose escapades invariably damage the unsuspecting and innocent alike. Absent the correction of any regulatory authority, the Knight of the Woeful Countenance is free to indulge himself with his fantasies of knights errant, whose victories of centuries before are revealed only in his collection of spurious historical texts. Though his friends attempt to disabuse him of his follies, even to the point of destroying the ersatz histories, they are unable to avert the ensuing disasters, of which jousting windmills is most affectionately recalled. Less well known are Quixote's appalling indiscretions: refusing to pay an innkeeper for lodging, attacking two flocks of sheep after mistaking them for advancing armies, assaulting mourners carrying a funeral bier, freeing a group of convicts after attacking the guards, ransacking an inn, assaulting a group of holy brothers who insisted that a wash basin was not a helmet, charging into a group of penitents carrying a shrine, and on and on. Forgotten is Quixote's insanity: all of the alleged gallantry is predicated on fictive texts, romanced by the fantasy "Lady" Dulcinea del Toboso whom the knight imagines but has never met, and supported by a manservant whose foibles range from ignoring the needs of his own family to inventing the malapropism.

Cervantes wrote during a transitional period, the decline of late sixteenth- and early seventeenth-century Spain, in which he set Don Quixote loose.[6] As a soldier of several military campaigns, a hostage and slave for several years, and a disabled veteran who would struggle financially in civilian life, Cervantes would have little sympathy for the narcissistic lunacy of Quixote. That a heroic, sentimental Quixote would become an icon of Romanticism is a fate that Cervantes could never have imagined, particularly considering he was writing during the Inquisition when the publication of books without official permission could warrant the death penalty.[7] Much like the transitional Spain that Cervantes knew, America is changing as well, from an industrial to a post-industrial culture. Historical transformation of such magnitude upsets conventional institutional arrangements, leaving people uncertain about the future. Indeed, as America is thrust into the future, its people seem to have diminishing confidence in its social policy. The ideologies that arose from, and were central to, industrialism—liberalism and conservatism—seem to have atrophied, vestiges of a receding age. Not unlike Cervantes's knight errant, passé ideologies appear to be chasing after a culture that has loosed its moorings; in the absence of guidance and discipline, one can only wonder at the opportunities lost, as well as the harm done, through the mismanagement of social affairs.

ORIGINS

To invoke theory is to inquire about how the world works. The most expansive canvases for such explorations have been the depictions of philosophers who have ruminated about ultimate values and the human condition. Since the inception of the written word, various explanations of reality have been posed and with them implied or explicit instructions for navigating the more problematic features of an often hostile environment. The early Greek preoccupation with physical reality and mathematics also addressed human relations and the ideal state. The classical era was eclipsed by the rise of Christian theology, the reaction against which would eventually set the stage for the emergence of the modern era. Pre-modern philosophy scrutinized fundamental and timeless questions about human nature, political organization, and the cosmos—astronomical as well as spiritual—in so doing, affirming the profundity of organized thought. Without a grounding in critical reasoning, Socrates would not have likely concluded that "the life not tested by criticism is not worth living," nor would he have gladly drunk the poison hemlock. Centuries later, Jesus would use the Greek Logos to replace a pantheistic animism with a unified theology and moral code— "And the Logos became flesh and dwelt among us"—the penalty for doing so being crucifixion.[8] It is through philosophy that such courage reverberates through the centuries, animating the human mind and altering the course of history.

The stultifying dogmatism of medieval Catholicism provoked a philosophical reaction well into the seventeenth century that would provide the preliminary template for modern social policy.[9] The Renaissance witnessed a virtual explosion in thought; the philosophers of the Enlightenment posed frameworks for advocating the natural rights of man, the rules for economic markets, and the scientific method. The integration of these themes would allow a sallow European backwater to overtake the richer and more dynamic empires of India and China within a century, eventually securing global dominance.[10] Ironically, the triumph of the West lay largely in its attention to detail, a decidedly empirical predisposition toward reality: "Begin with the unbiased analysis of concrete data and only then reason inductively, and cautiously, to reach general, empirically supported conclusions."[11] Whether man, molecule, or money, the operant unit of analysis was the isolated entity that achieved value as it freely combined with others, completely independent of the sectarian forces that had theretofore defined reality. The rise of democracy, capitalism, and science thus came to amplify the West, providing the bases for a society typified by open civil institutions, economic prosperity, and technological sophistication.

Empiricism accounted for the ascendance of the Occident. Indeed, the Enlightenment proved a startling chiaroscuro to its antecedents, witnessing the eclipse of alchemy by chemistry, astrology by astronomy, monarchy by democracy, aristocratic society by civil institutions. The transition to modernity was, to be certain, not without attendant dislocations. New political forms became dominant, but not after revolutions that toppled kings and clerics alike. Even the physical sciences showed evidences of radical transformation as upstarts with new theories challenged established orthodoxies.[12] Advances in physics and chemistry generated new production processes, and these in turn accelerated industrialization, the expansion of which brought forth enormous plants that employed legions of workers. While the transition into the modern era brought unprecedented prosperity, it also introduced misery on a grand scale: staggering unemployment during periodic depressions, massive slaughters during war time.

The empirical ethos carried along by the marvelous achievements attributed to the scientific method pervaded social affairs as well. Much as the mysteries of the natural world had been deciphered by science, then reordered to human preference, empiricists promised that society could also be analyzed, engineered, and planned according to scientific methods. Toward this end, logical positivism provided the means by which social relations could be understood, manipulated, and perfected. Drawing on the accomplishments of scientists who were exploiting the physical world, positivism sought "a unified view of the world of phenomena, both physical and human, through the application of the methods and extension of the results of the natural sciences."[13] Scholars investigating individual motivation employed experiments to ascertain human behavior, and having done that, fashioned psychology to alter it. Researchers of collective behavior crafted survey methods to capture the experiences of entire populations and used sociology to justify social programs to enhance the public's welfare.

The excesses and omissions associated with scientism introduced a contrasting sensibility: Romanticism. Emerging from the aesthetics of the arts and humanities, Romanticism viewed the world as a totality perceived and experienced by the self. If reality was complex, multilayered, and in many instances sublimely unfathomable, any derivation of truth necessitated an open, impressionistic, and unrestrained approach. The introspective self could uncover the meaning of life and benefit from the epiphany; so also, the collective self could comprehend its social circumstance and reorder it. At both levels, Romantics celebrated the will: "Like imagination, the will too was considered a necessary element in the attainment of human knowledge, a force preceding knowledge and freely impelling man and universe forward to new levels of creativity and awareness."[14] Much as an individual could will a revelation, groups could refashion society by mobilizing the collective will, challenging the tyranny of the status quo, and liberating the oppressed, all in the name of advancing the well-being of the entire population. Romanticism, thus, served as a rationale for the passionate idealism fueling the social reform movements of the nineteenth century:[15] the abolitionist movement, the labor movement, and women's suffrage. A century later, American Romantics relied on similar values to mount the Civil Rights movement, the student antiwar movement, and the women's movement.

Empiricism and Romanticism conflicted sharply in content as well as tone.[16] Romantics had little patience for the empiricist's requirement that knowledge be generated from valid data that were used to test hypothetical propositions. Moreover, Romantics alleged that scientism was responsible for modernity, a malignant social reality that was superficially commercial, insistently conformist, and ultimately dehumanizing. For all the technical advances associated with empiricism, entire spectra of the population remained in subordinate status, denied basic opportunities with respect to political, economic, and social institutions. In the worst instances, these populations were most likely to be ground up by modernist industrial and military institutions that had exploited empiricism so effectively.

Similarly, empiricists had little tolerance for Romantics who were unwilling to produce the evidence on which knowledge was built. A Romanticism derived deductively from metaphysical statements about the dignity of man and human rights was insufficiently specific to produce testable propositions. In fact, there was little evidence that Romantics respected rational thought very much at all, often preferring vainglorious rhetoric over formal reasoning, so amply evident when self-styled revolutionaries took to the streets, spouting Marx. Contravening the lofty ideals professed by Romantics, empiricists contended that revolutionary projects often evidenced excesses that were stunningly horrific, so obvious in the cases of the French and Russian revolutions, which preceded the later horrors of Stalin's gulags, Pol Pot's killing fields, and Mao's cultural revolution. To the defenders of empiricism, the utopian reach of Romanticism simply exceeded its grasp of rationality.

In Europe more so than America, the competing sensibilities of the Enlightenment versus Romanticism were bridged by Immanuel Kant, who reasoned that logic was apropos of different types of knowledge: *phenomena* were suitable for scientific inquiry, but *noumena* were the undecipherables of which civil society was constructed. Kantian dualism thus incorporated, however tentatively, the rival orthodoxies of the period and provided a serviceable template for a rapidly evolving European *bourgeoisie*.[17] This required a reconciliation between individual and society, which Kant achieved by proposing that the good society provided a government within which individuals could realize their potentials freely. "The central problem for mankind is that attainment of a universal system of law for civil society founded not on the relation of ruler to ruled, or force, but on interhuman relationship in which every individual is an end to himself. As a free agent, man participates in a constitution on the basis of laws he helped to develop."[18] Kant provided the foundation for a modern European understanding of social policy, though it would quickly diverge into separate camps: one focusing on legal formalism in order to advance the prudent ordering of social affairs, another seeking the organic principles through which entire societies functioned, and logical positivism, the adherents of which sought to apply the tenets of science to society. The emergent discipline of sociology provided the arena through which these competing explanations were advanced; notably, Max Weber and Emile Durkheim, scholars who explored the relationship between the individual and society.

AN AMERICAN PHILOSOPHY

In the New World, the tension between the Enlightenment and Romanticism was reconciled differently. The Enlightenment provided adequate intellectual grist for a native, emergent aristocracy that would assume governance over the American colonies. While the intellectual founders of the United States depended on the social contract philosophers in justifying a break from the British monarchy—in the process providing *the* case study for Romanticism—the requirements of crafting a new society necessarily reinforced their empirical proclivities. Not that they needed much prodding. As students of the Enlightenment, they acknowledged the philosophical contributions of Adam Smith, John Locke, and David Hume—as is so clearly evident in the enthusiasm of Thomas Jefferson[19] and Benjamin Franklin[20] for all things scientific. Indeed, much of the novelty of the American experiment lay with its application of the very precepts that had illustrated the Enlightenment. Though it would take a Revolution followed by two attempts at drafting a political framework for the new republic that finally culminated in the Constitution, the venture was strikingly ambitious: of the American experiment in democratic governance, Joseph Ellis observed simply, "All the major accomplishments were unprecedented."[21]

In retrospect, the creation of the United States along the ideals so eloquently penned by Jefferson and others was anything but an exercise in celestial harmonics.[22] War with Britain resulted in the sacking of the new capitol; a whiskey rebellion on the frontier was suppressed; friction among the states over the question of slavery intensified; and financial scandal jeopardized the new nation's economy. In various ways, each of these challenged the philosophical basis of the American republic that demonstrated a surprising resilience; for all the strife following independence, the United States endured. Yet, if these events buffeted the nation's Federalist public philosophy, testing its coherence and integrity, the ultimate test would be the Civil War.

In threatening the very essence of the United States, the Civil War struck to the core of the nation's increasingly tenuous philosophical base. Not only were the constitutional mechanics, so carefully drafted decades earlier, suddenly inadequate, but their dismissal resulted in a war of unimaginable carnage—the first application of industrial methods to conflict generated unprecedented destruction in person and property. The blow-back from the bloodbath stained the generation of young intellectuals who struggled to make sense of the trauma. Reflecting on the horror of the Civil War, Oliver Wendell Holmes concluded critically, "Certitude leads to violence."[23] Ultimately, exhortations on the basis of ultimate truth—whatever its validity—precipitate acts that are ultimate in their consequences. In its aftermath, a small group of intellectuals suspected that an explanation for the Civil War rested with the philosophical extremes justified by the absolute truths that had been trumpeted by abolitionists and secessionists alike. The origin of such thinking, Holmes averred, could be found in the social circumstances of the actors themselves: "Man is like any other organism, shaping himself to his environment so wholly that after he has taken the shape if you try to change it you alter his life."[24]

Along with Holmes, William James, Charles Peirce, and John Dewey laid the foundation for a peculiarly American philosophy: pragmatism. By claiming that humans were conditioned by their environment, pragmatists not only distanced American thinking from the trivializing data collection associated with empiricism and the grand utopianism of Romanticism, but they also suggested that ideas were the animating force that inspired people.

> What [the pragmatists] had in common was not a group of ideas, but a single idea—an idea about ideas. They all believed that ideas are not "out there" waiting to be discovered, but are tools—like forks and knives and microchips—that people devise to cope with the world in which they find themselves. They believed that ideas are produced not by individuals, but by groups of individuals—that ideas are social. They believed that ideas do not develop according to some inner logic of their own, but are entirely dependent, like germs, on their human carriers and the environment.[25]

A pragmatism based on the social construction of reality, while useful in explaining historical events, was less satisfactory in proposing a means for establishing truth, however. "Truth *happens* to an idea," contended James. "It *becomes* true, is *made* true by events. Its verity *is* in fact an event, a process: the process namely of its verifying itself."[26] While pragmatism was distinctly American, it nonetheless shared a decidedly Kantian philosophical problem: the plasticity of a civil society that was constantly in flux, and, therein, the absence of absolutes that could provide the foundation for social philosophy.

Pragmatism seemed especially fitting for a burgeoning society propelled by immigration and industrialization, and the new philosophy dovetailed with requirements of the New World. Having rebelled against monarchy and rejected a strong, centralized government, the America chronicled by Alexis de Tocqueville was a land that celebrated individualism, self-sufficiency, and community. Accordingly, pragmatism adapted European preferences to the American context. Kant's categorical imperatives informed Peirce as well as Dewey, who sought to meld individual action, communal morality, and social science. The originality of pragmatism could be attributed to its appreciation for individual psychology and how it could be put to socially desirable ends. Having located individual action within a societal context, pragmatism also resonated with early sociology. Essentially, pragmatists held that society provided the arena for social action by presenting a priori norms. These are taken as axiomatic until their legitimacy is brought into question by doubt, at which point individuals and groups of citizens engage in thought experiments, the results of which vary in their success in resolving the precipitating problem. The winnowing of experiments is constant, the outcome being individual and social improvement. Thus posited, pragmatism placed the individual as engaging in a continuous experiment of trial and error; the community enhanced with the accretion of knowledge derived from successful experiments. Pragmatism, so conceived, appealed directly to individualism, empiricism, and progress. Indeed, Dewey would effectively institutionalize the philosophy, arguing that a modern society required special organizations that would conduct social experiments toward social betterment, the American university. By situating rationality within individuals who enjoyed their liberty as members of a free society, pragmatism was as explicitly democratic as it was suspicious of aristocratic elites.[27]

Dewey understood that public policy could amplify social welfare, a realization that came from his experience with Hull House, the Chicago settlement established by Jane Addams and Ellen Starr. A founding trustee of Hull House while he taught at the University of Chicago, Dewey was attracted to Addams's sense of organizational experimentation as well as her respect for moral philosophy. "Hull House was soberly opened on the theory that the dependence of classes on each other is reciprocal," explained Addams, "and that as the social relation is essentially a reciprocal relation, it gives a form of expression that has peculiar value."[28] With Dewey's assistance, Hull House would prove a remarkable institution, becoming a magnet to young Progressives who used their residence to gain firsthand knowledge about social conditions of the disadvantaged and experiment with strategies of social change. The tenants of Hull House would account for much of the vision and leadership of the New Deal: Edith Abbott participated in drafting the Social Security Act while her sister, Grace, organized the first White House Conference on Children and later directed the U.S. Children's Bureau; Julia Lathrop, visionary of the first juvenile court and first child mental health clinic, became the first director of the U.S. Children's Bureau; Florence Kelley was central to several national advocacy organizations for children and workers; and Frances Perkins would serve as the first Secretary of Labor. Addams, a national figure in her time, would receive the Nobel Peace Prize in 1931.[29]

Reaching its intellectual maturity during the heyday of the industrial era, pragmatism proved the consummate, if sometimes unprincipled, instrument for a cadre of idealistic reformers who sought to perfect society. Accordingly, the Progressive Era witnessed the rise of a professional class that, armed with pragmatism, sought to reform society by investigating and altering its basic institutions. Given the despair, debris, and corruption spawned by an industrialization exacerbated by immigration and urbanization, the Progressives certainly had much to do, and pragmatism served them well: public health professionals cleaned up the meat-packing industry; teaching professionals modernized public education;

political reformers rooted-out corrupt officials; welfare professionals standard-ized services and benefits for the needy; economists oversaw the implementation of the income tax, unemployment insurance, and the inception of the Federal Trade Commission, as well as the Federal Reserve Board.[30] Such reforms often put Progressives at odds with those who had generated unprecedented wealth and influence. Indeed, the excessive wealth and sheer power exercised by the titans of industry offended even Theodore Roosevelt (hereafter, TR), a Republican presi-dent who advocated federal regulation of trusts: "The vast individual and corpo-rate fortunes, the vast combinations of capital, which have marked the develop-ment of our industrial system, create new conditions, and necessitate a change from the old attitude of the State and the Nation toward the rules regulating the acquisition and untrammeled business use of property."[31] As the nation's most prominent Progressive, TR argued that wealth was inversely related to social wel-fare: "The man who wrongly holds that every human right is secondary to his profit must now give way to the advocate of human welfare, who rightly main-tains that every man holds his property subject to the general right of the com-munity to regulate its use to whatever degree the public welfare may require it."[32]

Through reformist efforts to establish "good government," pragmatism actually attained a touch of panache that complemented the boisterousness of the period. Responding to a newspaper story by muckraker Lincoln Steffens chronicling po-litical corruption in New York, a Tammany Hall crony, George Washington Plun-kett, complained: "Steffens means well, but like all reformers, he don't know how to make distinctions. He can't see no difference between honest graft and dishon-est graft and, consequently, he gets things all mixed up."[33]

If Plunkett provided comic relief to the Progressives' intent on eliminating the miasma of urban America, others questioned the motive and methods of social reformers. Baltimore newspaperman and critic H. L. Mencken made a career out of spoofing meddling do-gooders, often reserving his invective for social workers.

> The social worker, judging by her own pretensions, helps to preserve multi-tudes of persons who would perish if left to themselves. Thus her work is clearly dysgenic and anti-social. For every victim of sheer misfortune that she restores to self-sustaining and social usefulness, she must keep alive scores of misfits and incompetents who can never, for all her help, pull their weight in the boat. Such persons can do nothing more valuable than dying.[34]

In railing against self-righteous Progressives, Mencken helped popularize social Darwinism, a theory that complemented America's embrace of its frontier ethic as well as its enthusiasm for laissez-faire capitalism. "It seems hard that widows and orphans should be left to struggle for life or death," intoned the social philosopher Herbert Spencer. "Nevertheless, when regarded not separately but in connexion [sic] with the interests of universal humanity, these harsh fatalities are seen to be full of beneficence—the same beneficence which brings to early graves the children of diseased parents, and singles out the intemperate and the debilitated as the victims of an epidemic."[35] Social Darwinism would reach its apogee in the eugenics movement, a misguided application of science that would not only lead to the involuntary sterilization of thousands of poor, mentally impaired Americans but ultimately a doctrine of racial superiority which presaged the Holocaust. Eugenicists included not only esteemed Americans such as Oliver Wendell Holmes and Margaret Sanger, but also counted on the institutional support of major foundations such as the Carnegie Institution and the Rockefeller Foundation.[36]

Progressives effectively countered the pseudoscience of social Darwinism by wedding their reformist ethic with an empirical method for purposes of advancing a humane form of social betterment. The result was social engineering that became integral with the emergent social sciences. That the Progressive movement would ultimately become so influential in domestic affairs could be attributed to the failure of two prominent institutions to address adequately the dislocations attendant with industrialization. For a century, the American *polity* had arbitrated differences through the Constitution; but the Constitution was a product of an agrarian society and seemed incapable of negotiating the demands imposed by the new industrial era. Similarly, with industrialization American *commerce* expanded exponentially, generating massive wealth and inordinate poverty at the same time. Progressives stepped into the breach that had formed as a result of an antiquated polity and a runaway economy, proposed scientifically based technological solutions to an increasing number of social problems, and established the American meritocracy in the process. As Progressive initiatives became institutionalized in government, the progressive mood insinuated itself in an emergent intellectual class. "By about 1910, intellectuals were found in many American places," observed John Lukacs. "They were men and women who were less provincial, more bookish, generally more liberal, and more progressive than were most of their neighbors." In fact, the Progressive insistence on the usefulness of good ideas was part and partial to the rise of the American middle class, or at least its more informed strata. "The years 1900 to 1950 were the American bourgeois interlude, the half-century when American civilization was marked by the existence of a largely urban and urbane bourgeoisie."[37]

An expanding middle class pushed to center stage a new American persona, one that combined the culture's traditional respect for native know-how with burgeoning technology: the professional expert. The expert imprimatur proliferated, shaping manufacturing through scientific management, government through the civil service, and local health and welfare agencies via the new helping professions. At the same time, experts worked assiduously to elevate their status while keeping the public from interfering with their work. Professional oligopoly, ascendant during the early twentieth century, served to consolidate a gamut of what would have otherwise remained as occupational guilds. Teachers, nurses, social workers, and city planners established control over the new institutions of modern society, justifying their hegemony on the technical sophistication necessary to introduce scientific methods in social affairs. In so doing, Progressivism served as a beacon for those concerned about the excesses of capitalism, yet did so within the strictures of constitutional democracy.

Certainly, the professionalization of social affairs demonstrated anything but a unilinear progression in societal perfection; it had its skeptics, most vociferously those of a nascent labor movement. Full-blown industrialization that introduced a new class of professionals also catalyzed masses of workers who bore the brunt of economic caprice. Attracted to Karl Marx's economic determinism that depicted human history as a clash between bourgeois capitalists and proletarian workers, laborers worldwide joined unions, advocated collective bargaining, and, when such moderate proposals failed, engaged in strikes to assert their rights. Eventually, Marxist Romanticism would provide the philosophical foundation for anticapitalist revolutionaries who captured national governments, installed command economics, and suppressed dissent. In its ultimate manifestation, Marxism would serve as the justification for Communist tyrannies that spanned entire regions of the globe, or in its more modulated form, a Fabian Socialism that sought economic equality by democratic means.

With the important exception of the Great Depression, Marxism grafted poorly to the American experience. Although the Industrial Workers of the World (IWW) staged a radical Marxist insurgency in the Western states, the American labor movement was ambivalent about using it as a means to leverage social and economic justice for workers. Intellectuals to whom the historical sweep of economic determinism might have appealed would recoil at the misapplication of science, to say nothing of the trampling of human rights that became associated with state socialism. That Communist nations tended to be insular—effectively denying open exchange of information, resources, and the arts—cast them as antithetical to the more open and dynamic nations that evinced political economies that were democratic-capitalist. Arguably the most concise critique of Communism was proposed by Isaiah Berlin, who employed "negative liberty" to question the ability of the state to guarantee freedom while in pursuit of equality.

> Negative liberty was the core of a properly liberal political creed: leaving individuals alone to do what they want, provided that their actions did not interfere with the liberty of others. Positive liberty was the core of all emancipatory theories of politics, from socialist to communist; for all such doctrines wish to use political power to free human beings to realize some hidden, blocked or repressed potential.[38]

Absent a compelling counterpoint to democratic capitalism, the professional meritocracy elaborated pragmatism to ends of social improvement. Indeed, the establishment of the American welfare state through passage of the Social Security Act of 1935 reflected perfectly the accommodations that Progressives were willing to make in their quest for prudent reform: Modeled after private insurance, the social insurance programs were self-financing and provided minimal benefits; the public assistance benefits were dictated largely by the states that had a reputation for benefits that were stingy if not outright punitive. If the American welfare state would prosper in the decades following the Progressive Era, it would not be a result of any implicit Romantic impulse to liberate the masses who had suffered during the Depression, but rather a judicious exercise in policy incrementalism or, as circumstance might dictate, occasional opportunism.

CONCEIVING THE WELFARE STATE

As institutional edifice, the American welfare state was anything but elegant. Launched as a response to the Great Depression, it had a poignant urgency, most evident in a 25 percent unemployment rate that provoked a labor insurgency by the IWW and a financial crisis that threatened to close down the nation's economy, both of which festered while Herbert Hoover minimized the calamity. As it was to materialize six years after the Wall Street crash, the Social Security Act borrowed from an assortment of state welfare plans, omitted entire swaths of the population, provided others with meager benefits, and accelerated the rise of a professional meritocracy. Certainly, the conception of an American welfare state was clouded by contradictions. If a welfare state means a prominent role of the national government in the provision of essential services to vulnerable populations, arguably the first such initiative afforded educational, health, and employment benefits to emancipated slaves under the Freedmen's Bureau from 1865 to 1872.[39] Not long thereafter, benefits to Union Civil War veterans consumed as much as 40 percent of the federal budget.[40] Using these benchmarks, the first unambiguous federal social programs had a common denominator,: war of emancipation. Indeed, the Freedman's Bureau and Union veteran's benefits were both creations of the Republican Party. While important programmatic developments, presaging what would later be understood as a thoroughly liberal and democratic institution, could be traced to Abraham Lincoln, later initiatives bore the imprint of TR. The nation's most prominent Progressive, TR represented those educated conservatives who chafed at the excessive influence and wealth of industrial capitalists, fearing the ascendance of an American aristocracy. Among the issues championed by TR and the Progressives were prohibitions against child labor, regulation of interstate commerce, the institution of health and safety standards in consumer affairs, and the provision of welfare to destitute families. TR introduced the first White House Conference on Children and nodded approvingly as the states established Widows' Pensions, precursors to family welfare.[41]

If, in retrospect, Republicans provided important impetus for federal activity in social affairs, Democrats were less than consistent in their laying the foundation for the American welfare state, the Social Security Act. None other than Franklin Delano Roosevelt (hereafter FDR) was ambivalent about its provisions. On November 14, 1934, speaking before an audience summoned by the White House, at the National Conference on Economic Security, the President noted the implausibility of a healthcare proposal, then surprised everyone by questioning "if this is the time for any federal legislation of old-age security," a comment that sent his aides scrambling to contact the editors of the nation's major newspapers, who promptly published editorials asserting the need for a universal pension program.[42] His commitment subsequently reaffirmed, FDR pursued the endorsement of Southern legislators, eventually agreeing to the most cynical of ploys, deleting from the nation's nascent pension program domestics and agricultural workers, not only assuring the South a supply of cheap black labor, but also denying a generation of low-wage African Americans a retirement program available to other workers. As enacted, Social Security was less than generous to those workers who were eligible for retirement benefits. Contrived so as not to interfere with private pension arrangements established by industry and supported by unions, Social Security paid little better than subsistence benefits for retirees, largely because benefits were derived from a withholding tax that applied to only the lower register of earnings.[43] But Social Security was universal, so it benefited virtually all workers, and later dependents, who had been employed 40 quarters. Subsequently, a trade-off typified social insurance: universal benefits, but of substandard adequacy.

The issue of family welfare was even more problematic. Progressives had promoted a model of the virtuous family in order to leverage passage of state Widows' Pensions, one in which the mother stayed at home and evidenced exemplary behavior. Such state family welfare programs became the precursor to Aid to Families with Dependent Children (much later Temporary Assistance for Needy Families), a state-federal collaboration in which states established eligibility and the federal government paid roughly half of benefits. These parameters exacted a toll on minority mothers who were often excluded from assistance due to discriminatory practices by state welfare officials, particularly in the Jim Crow South. On the eve of passage of the Social Security Act, minority families accounted for only 4 percent of those receiving aid.[44] In this manner, Progressives and New Dealers fashioned a *maternalist* welfare state, one that subordinated women to men, inhibited women's participation in the labor market, and reinforced institutional racism.

Despite its mongrel pedigree and inconsistent provisions, the American welfare state thrived. FDR "seized the Progressives' centralizing agenda, thrust it upon what had been a dourly Jeffersonian party, and used it to weld together the coalition—unionists, farmers, Northern blacks, Southern populists, and urban

liberals—that brought the Democrats to dominance for a generation."[45] Propelled by industrialization and crafted assiduously to avoid conflict with private
sector benefits, Democrats oversaw the accretion of federal social programs and
the institutionalization of the welfare state. The Social Security Act introduced
Social Security, Unemployment Compensation as insurance programs for workers, and public aid for children, the disabled, and the blind. With the Great Society
of the mid-1960s, these were augmented by Medicare, Medicaid, Food Stamps,
and an extensive list of initiatives designed to abate poverty. By 1980, social programs would consume 54.4 percent of the federal budget.[46]

Nowhere was the Progressive imprimatur more evident in governmental reform than through the inception of the civil service. Theretofore, employment
was a spoil that was awarded to cronies of political machines, like Tammany Hall,
which Boss Tweed used to control New York City. Progressives objected on the
basis that such patronage was unfair, but more importantly, because it was inefficient. Optimally, the modern political economy required the knowledge of the
dispassionate expert. Subsequently, the emergence of governmental social programs generated unprecedented demand for professionals to ameliorate social
problems. A burgeoning welfare state only amplified the demand for experts, necessitated by its division of labor (directors, supervisors, case workers), fields of
activity (health, welfare, education), specializations (client service, research, coor-
dination), and various jurisdictions (federal, state, county, city). Often the expertise was quotidian, as in the case of social workers who endeavored to help the
needy in the most professional manner possible.[47] At others, it emphasized the
esoteric, as in computing the distributional formula for Social Security benefits.
The special skills necessary for smooth operation of social programs established
professional education as the means for upward mobility in modern society, and
the welfare state escalated the growth of the full-status professions (law and medicine) as well as the newer semiprofessions (teaching, nursing, and social work).[48]

When combined with the unprecedented prosperity that followed World War
II, the promise of expertise fostered mass consumption that made the middle
class regnant in American culture.

> The devastation of Germany, Japan and the Soviet Union guaranteed Ameri-
> can Industrial preeminence and, with it, rising incomes for blue-collar union
> men as well as the growing army of white-collar executives and profession-
> als. Big government helped too: building the highways that led to suburbs,
> financing home purchases and, for veterans, college educations.[49]

The consumer society, distinguished by extensive affluence and buoyant opti-
mism, not only provided bright relief to the stark and devastating war years, but it
also induced millions of men to establish careers in the professions, the entrance
to which required higher education. A robust economy, in turn, generated in-

creasing employment opportunities and therewith the revenues required for a burgeoning welfare state.

Through the remainder of the twentieth century, meritocracy suffused the welfare state and became a dynamic component of its expansion, justifying the professional credentials needed for its functioning but also reflecting the different benefits that it provided. Between 1970 and 2000, federal social program expenditures rose from $69.3 billion to $1 *trillion*, more than ten-fold; the federal civilian labor force, at its zenith in the mid-1980s, exceeded 3 million workers.[50] Since many social program employees worked for subordinate levels of government, this was only the tip of a very large iceberg. In 1985, 14.9 percent of the U.S. civilian labor force was employed by government, a modest ratio since the more extensive European welfare states in which the number exceeded 20 percent.[51] A swelling civil service staffed the social programs of an expanding welfare state, and, in the process, bolstered the enrollment of university professional schools—the realization of Progressive pieties about good government.

However slow its expansion, the American welfare state gradually extended protection to greater numbers of citizens, at least approximating the outcomes projected by European welfare philosophy. T. H. Marshall had presented an evolutionary scheme in which the eighteenth century was concerned with the establishment of civil rights, including freedom of speech and religion; the nineteenth with political rights through representative democracy; and the twentieth with economic rights through the welfare state.[52] Reprising the thesis during the halcyon years of the War on Poverty, Harold Wilensky and Charles Lebeaux concurred: "Under continuing industrialization all institutions will be oriented toward and evaluated in terms of social welfare aims. The 'welfare state' will become the 'welfare society,' and both will be more reality than epithet."[53] Three decades later, Wilensky would observe that

> the structural correlates of industrialization push all rich democracies toward convergence at a high level of social spending [despite] differences in the power of mass-based political parties as they interact with national bargaining patterns (especially the structure, functions, behavior, and interplay of labor, the professions, management and the government).[54]

Echoing the trans-Atlantic accord on the welfare state, Richard Titmuss enthused that the welfare state ideal was universal and would eventually be realized by a "welfare world."[55] According to welfare philosophy of the mid-twentieth century, the welfare state was emblematic of the good society, an ineluctable outcome of mature industrialization. "The liberal welfare consensus as it became known dominated American life for many years," noted James Midgley.[56] Approaching the end of the millennium, Leon Ginsberg characterized "the welfare state [a]s a phenomenon of the industrialized world."

It is, in many ways, the means that human societies have used to deal with exigencies of the industrial, corporate world, as humans have made the transition from rural, agrarian life to interdependence and complexity in the establishment of cities and the life of manufacturing and automation. For [liberal] thinkers, the development of the welfare state is a natural and parallel outgrowth of the industrialization of the world. Just as physical things became more complicated following the Industrial Revolution, so did social relations. The rise of metropolitan areas, the decline of the extended family, the recurring incidence of economic crises, and the increasing need for objective help from strangers in the form of government, all made the welfare state and its current patterns inevitable.[57]

The belief in an ever-increasing array of social programs was bedrock liberal faith, even if evidence failed to fit the paradigm. Writing in the mid-1980s, historian Arthur Schlesinger, Jr., hypothesized 30-year ideological cycles—the New Deal of the 1930s followed by the Great Society of the 1960s—prophesizing the election of a liberal president in the 1990s who would usher in a third generation of liberal social programs.[58] This projection would become but one of the many casualties of the Clinton presidency.

While the Progressive impulse in social policy emanated from the Republican Party, it would be Democrats, under the leadership of FDR and his New Deal confederates, who would be wedded to the welfare state. Early liberals recognized the political gains implicit in an expanding array of social programs that would appeal to legions of beneficiaries and be operated by battalions of professionals. The political calculus was stated with pithy brevity by Harry Hopkins, social worker and head of the Federal Emergency Relief Administration, an early New Deal work program: "Tax, tax, spend, spend, elect, elect." The logic was as impeccable as it was effective: through progressive taxes, redistribute wealth from the rich to workers by way of government social programs, the workers voting Democratic in appreciation. In the early years of the New Deal, Hopkins, along with other settlement house veterans, cobbled together a list of work programs to put men back to work: the Civilian Conservation Corps, the Public Works Administration, the National Youth Administration, the Works Progress Administration, among others.[59] Although FDR's gestures to African Americans were tentative at best, they were sufficient to pry their allegiance from the Republicans—"the party of Lincoln"—an accomplishment that would benefit the Democratic Party through the rest of the century. With the Social Security Act and the inception of World War II, the temporary work programs were cashiered, but the strategy remained intact.

As victory over the Axis appeared imminent, FDR proposed that "economic security, social security, and moral security" provide the foundation for a Second Bill of Rights. "We cannot be content, no matter how high that general standard of living may be, if some fraction of our people—whether it be one-third or one-fifth or one-tenth—is ill-fed, ill-clothed, ill-housed, and insecure." Much as the First Bill of Rights spoke to political guarantees, the Second identified eight economic and social rights:

- The right to a useful and remunerative job in the industries or shops or farms or mines of the Nation.
- The right to earn enough to provide adequate food and clothing and recreation.
- The right of every farmer to raise and sell his products at a return which will give him and his family a decent living.
- The right of every businessman, large and small, to trade in an atmosphere of freedom from unfair competition and domination by monopolies at home or abroad.
- The right of every family to a decent home.
- The right to adequate medical care and the opportunity to achieve and enjoy good health.
- The right to adequate protection from the economic fears of old age, sickness, accident, and unemployment.
- The right to a good education.

So configured, the Second Bill of Rights would have made the United States a full partner in the welfare state project that would evolve in northern Europe; yet, the template failed to inspire the necessary legislative backing and, despite the legislative and judicial victories of the War on Poverty, future expansion of the governmental welfare state was subsequently held in check by Richard Nixon.[60]

The 1935 Social Security Act included Unemployment Compensation and Social Security, which secured the fealty of workers, much as Old Age Assistance, Aid to Dependent Children, and Aid to the Disabled did for the poor. Immediately following the war, Democrats launched the GI Bill, which afforded millions of veterans entry to the middle class by subsidizing their higher education and home purchases. When the Civil Rights movement highlighted the grinding poverty experienced by minority families, Democrats mounted a War on Poverty that provided health assistance (Medicaid), preschool care (Head Start), nutrition aid (Food Stamps), and a host of other benefits to low-income households. Tucked into the poverty legislation was Medicare, a health insurance program for the elderly; augmenting the Great Society was the Civil Rights Act, which, coupled with presidential executive orders, prohibited discrimination based on race, gender, or ethnicity.

Augmenting the New Deal with the War on Poverty represented a strategic gesture by Democrats to populations that had been given short-shrift by the Social Security Act. "The 'old' New Deal liberalism of the trade unions and their working-class constituency had seemed to offer no new challenges. But with the discovery of poverty, the liberal agenda could be expanded beyond such innocuous postwar goals as 'growth,'" noted Barbara Ehrenreich. "Henceforth, middle-class liberalism had a mission, and a middle-class liberal' could be defined as someone who—however vaguely or remotely—'cared about' the poor and their conditions."[61] With the introduction of a raft of new social programs, welfare liberalism was ascendant. "In the mid-1960s big-government liberalism was in a triumphant mood," reflected contributors to *The Economist*:

> Keynesian economists thought that that they had discovered the secret of economic growth: all you needed to do was adjust a few economic indicators and, presto, the world would go on getting richer. More amazingly still, policy makers thought they had the power to cure social ills, from poverty to prejudice, and most Americans trusted them to do so.[62]

However affirming the War on Poverty would prove to welfare liberals, the transition was not without its detractors. Ominous clouds appeared on the intellectual horizon when Theodore Lowi questioned the provisions of benefits to those not part of the working class.

> Old welfare was a creation of old liberalism, which took capitalism for what it was and sought to treat the poor as the inevitable, least fortunate among the proletariat. It was a good system and was endangered only because of the efforts to make welfare policy do more than it could possibly do. New welfare is a creation of new liberalism, interest-group liberalism. While new welfare defines poverty in simple economic terms, it rejects the notion of poverty as a natural and inevitable sector of economic life.[63]

Despite conservative apprehensions, the expansion of the welfare state during the 1960s was facilitated by several events: a robust economy, a cadre of results-oriented professionals, an increasingly muscular Civil Rights movement, and an enterprising Democratic Party.

In this manner, the Democratic Party attained the allegiance of the large numbers of Americans who desired to improve their circumstances but had found obstructions to their aspirations due to class, race, and gender. The result would arguably be the signal social accomplishment of the twentieth century: the creation of the American middle class. In 1940, almost half of Americans were very poor, and only 10 percent were middle class; by 1990 the ratio was reversed—fewer than 10 percent were very poor while almost half were middle class.[64] Little of this would have happened without the welfare state, the benefits it provided to upwardly mobile workers, the cadre of professionals who monitored its performance, and liberal Democrats who justified its expansion. The welfare state would be a juggernaut that dominated social policy through the middle of the century, overriding conservatives whose natural inclination was to oppose it. Indeed, the American welfare state was so compelling that its largest period of expansion occurred during the presidency of a Republican, Richard Nixon.

The twentieth century thus chronicled the rise of pragmatism as the nation's public philosophy. The infusion of pragmatism into public life by way of an army of professionals who maintained and expanded the meritocracy was gradual, and it was perceived as largely benevolent given the excesses of industrialization and dislocations of immigration. Yet, outside of the academy, few Americans would have appreciated the import of the transformation, no less than a revolution in expertise. Indeed, with the exception of TR's flamboyant embrace of Progressivism through the Bull Moose Party, the pragmatic moment would go largely unnoticed by the public. After all, the openness of American culture provided sufficient space and freedom for emergent social movements focusing on the rights of workers, minorities, and women, events that generated much more noise and dissent. During the twentieth century, the Constitution and the dominant political parties arbitrated a raucous polity, providing a measure of reassurance to an uneasy public while accommodating the demands of marginalized groups, however imperfect those groups might have perceived the outcome. Thus, conflict was presumed to be part of the American experience much as the authors of *The Federalist Papers* had anticipated. Yet, these episodes in social justice continued to be episodic, clearly reflective of Romantic impulses that had amplified the American ethos since its origin, but relatively transient in the nation's evolution.[65] For all the thunder and lightening that accompanied these mini revolutions, the nation's understanding of itself was increasingly dominated by pragmatism, which served to reconcile the major conflicts of the era.

Critical to pragmatism's success was the professional meritocracy which, by the mid-twentieth century, enjoyed hegemony in social affairs. Insulated by the professions, pragmatism "enjoyed a charmed life."[66] Despite the protestations of debunkers such as Thorstein Veblen, whose scathing critique took the form of a formal academic *oeuvre* (*The Theory of the Leisure Class*) or Mencken, who savaged the *booboisie,* pragmatism successfully insinuated itself in government as well as the academy. The governmental meritocracy was staffed by graduates of the nation's expanding universities. Encouraged by the Morrill Act of 1862, which set aside thousands of acres for higher education, states established institutions that largely replaced an aristocratic education in theology, philosophy, Latin, and literature with an applied orientation in science, engineering, and mathematics. In 1890, there were 2,382 graduate students in American institutions of higher education; by 1930, the number had skyrocketed to 47,255; during the same period the number of granted doctorates grew from 164 to 2,024. Concomitant with the rise of graduate education, professional societies were established in history (1884), economics (1885), mathematics (1890), psychology (1892), philosophy (1901), sociology (1905), and political science (1906).[67]

Yet, it would be the post–World War II Servicemen's Readjustment Act of 1944 (the GI Bill of Rights) that thoroughly democratized American higher education. The GI Bill effectively diverted millions of veterans from a saturated labor market that had been artificially "ginned up" by the war to the nation's colleges and universities. The GI Bill of Rights was formatted in the best New Deal tradition: "No means test, no tax credits, and minimal red tape were required to receive an unemployment allowance," observed Milton Greenberg, yet the range of benefits was extensive: "loan guarantees for purchase of a home, a farm, or a business; and educational opportunities—collegiate, vocational, or on-the-job apprenticeships—with tuition, fees, and books paid for, and supporting stipends for living expenses provided, for up to 48 months, depending on length of service."[68] By 1956, the GI Bill had invested $14.5 billion training 7.8 million veterans, of which 2.2 million went to college. The GI Bill not only opened a previously elitist institution to the masses, but in the process afforded African Americans and Jews access to credentials that would have otherwise been denied them. In 1947, veterans accounted for 49 percent of college enrollment. Subsequently, GI Bills for the Korean conflict allocated $4.5 billion for veteran training, sending 1.2 million to college, while services for Vietnam-era veterans cost $42 billion, much of which was to cover the higher education expenses of 5.1 million vets.[69] During the latter part of the twentieth century, higher education would exhibit striking growth. In 1960, 7.7 percent of Americans over age 25 possessed at least an undergraduate degree; in 2000 the number had jumped to 25.6 percent. During the same period, expenditures for higher education would rise from $42. 6 billion to $273.8 billion, a factor of six, almost double the increase of the nation's Gross Domestic Product.[70]

PRAGMATISM AT TWILIGHT

Despite its centrality during the industrial era, by the end of the twentieth century, pragmatism was exhausted as liberal public philosophy. During the 1960s, a Romantically inspired Left voiced apprehensions about the reliance on government as a vehicle for social betterment, especially since the federal government had been reluctant to move assertively to reverse racial discrimination and had prosecuted an unpopular war in Southeast Asia. Having been situated within the university, pragmatism became a target for revolutionary intellectuals who associated it with the status quo. The Left's tactics—civil rights demonstrations in the South, burning draft cards in protest against the Vietnam conflict—revived Romanticism in American thought, highlighting stratification according to class, race, and later gender as the source of the nation's woes. According to Leftists, the nation could not be reaffirmed until the aristocratic white patriarchy was overthrown. Thus, it is no small irony, during the maelstrom of the Civil Rights and anti-war movements, that a second generation of social programs—Medicare,

Medicaid, Food Stamps, Head Start, among others—would be instituted, a major expansion of the American welfare state.

The 1960s were a lightning rod for the Right, especially the upsetting of conventions about marriage, the family, sex, and abortion, the "culture wars." Though the Left would win the culture war, it provoked conservatives who would subsequently win the political war.[71] In their political counteroffensive against the Left, conservatives focused on social programs. Since its inception, conservatives had qualms about the welfare state project, especially the role of the federal government in advancing social and economic equality. Conservative intellectuals argued that the welfare state, an illustration of Berlin's notion of "positive liberty," would invariably lead to an expansion of the state and a commensurate diminution of individual freedom. Subsequently, conservatives targeted the public utilities that had been deployed to enhance social welfare as well as the meritocracy that maintained it. Initially alone, and later under the sponsorship of ideologically oriented policy institutes, conservatives railed at the ineffectiveness and waste that seemed endemic to public provision of services. Rather than providing a solid education for all Americans, public education had become a fiefdom of educational administrators and teachers, both of which seemed indifferent to the horrendous performance of students in urban public schools. Rather than providing shelter for welfare- and working-poor families, public housing had become a haven for gangsters involved in selling illegal drugs. Rather than sustaining families through hard times, welfare fostered dependency on government, contributed to family dissolution, and spiked the incidence of teen pregnancy.

Beset on the Left and the Right, pragmatically minded intellectuals held fast, even if their purchase on social policy was proving increasingly tentative. The more visible disarray in the public sector was paralleled by confusion within the academy. The institutional legacy of pragmatism, American higher education was suddenly confronted with strident Romanticism. Emboldened by victories against segregation and the Pentagon, students moved against the university, in the process denigrating its scholars. Certainly, prominent academics had developed theories that were ripe for deconstruction, as in Talcott Parsons's structural functionalism. Traced to the German sociologist Max Weber, who was recognized for his work on the rise of bureaucratic authority and its influence on modern society, Parsons Americanized Weber, parsing society according to functional units, basic social processes, and unified by "pattern maintenance variables." By the time Parsons was finished, modern society was dissected with a thoroughness that was as formalistic as it was antiseptic. Sociology students of the period struggled to determine what was worse, Parsons's justification of the status quo or his impenetrable prose.

The deconstruction of traditional higher education, begun during the 1960s, would eventually claim many casualties, even scholars whose work was congruent with pragmatic liberalism and incremental expansion of the welfare state. Among the most academic was Robert Merton, an astute theoretician whose observations ranged from mass persuasion to deviance and whose seminal contributions included focus groups, opportunity structures, and the sociology of science.[72] But intellectual discourse was at best secondary to the Romantic's preference for action, so rigorous social analysis gave way to depictions of reality that were the product of dogma and idealism.

In their critique of the status quo, the Left found support in C. Wright Mills, one of the most provocative public intellectuals of the Cold War. Positing the existence of interlocking directorates, networks comprised of leaders representing prominent social institutions, Mills identified the military-industrial complex as not only a manifestation of the Cold War, but a primary source of its propulsion. Mills was a radical in the classic sense—his formulations struck to the core of social reality—but his methods were well within the framework of conventional pragmatism.[73] "The unity of theory and action must be recognized and restored in practice so men may gain a fuller consciousness of the consequences of their acts," concluded Mills's biographer, because "the function of theory was to guide men in changing the world."[74] But the Left was suspicious of empiricism. Accordingly, "praxis"—the integration of theory with method—became a trope of the leftist intellectual, and it soon eclipsed the notion that a logically integrated framework was essential to social analysis, a necessity for Mills. That praxis was running away with theory was nowhere more evident than in the repudiation of the research of James Coleman. In a classic illustration of analysis for purposes of social reform, Coleman undertook empirical studies concluding that family poverty often subverted preschool education for poor children, busing to achieve desegregation hastened white flight from cities, and Catholic education generated better performance and less inequality than public schools. For his efforts, Coleman was roundly vilified by ideologically correct colleagues to the extent that the American Sociological Association almost censored him for "producing subversive sociology."[75]

But it would be Daniel Patrick Moynihan who gained notoriety after being rebuked for failing to adhere to political correctness. Concerned about social consequences of the increasing number of female-headed black families, Moynihan drafted a Labor Department memo in 1965 entitled "The Negro Family: The Case for National Action."[76] The result was wide denunciation of Moynihan. Subsequent accusations of racism effectively removed minority poverty from the academic research agenda. "Indeed, after the furor over the Moynihan Report on the black family, the topic of the values and culture of poor people became virtually off limits for academics, especially white academics, who exercised a form of self-censorship in order to avoid being charged with 'blaming the victim,'" observed a researcher decades later.[77] The consequences of the public humiliation to which Coleman and Moynihan were subjected did not go unnoticed by the next generation of university researchers. As William Julius Wilson later observed, research on minority poverty was deleted from the academic research agenda; a generation of social researchers occupied themselves with other projects at the very moment the black ghetto was imploding.[78] Instead of continuing to supply the raw and distilled intelligence for fashioning social policy, the academy turned its back on one of the most compelling social problems of the time.

Despite the fault lines that were more conspicuous within the pragmatic paradigm, its adherents struggled to shore it up. Two neopragmatists were central to the effort. Drawing from his origins in the American Left, Richard Rorty incorporated the lexicon of postmodernism in advocating a conversational philosophy. "If we see knowing not as having an essence, to be described by scientists or philosophers, but rather as a right, by current standards, to believe, then we are well on the way to seeing *conversation* as the ultimate context in which knowledge is to be understood."[79] But, mapping a conversation that reflected Progressive concerns found Rorty increasingly frustrated with the elliptical ideological orbit of the American Left. "Th[e] Left will have to stop thinking up ever more abstract and abusive names for 'the system' and start trying to construct inspiring images of the country," he wrote, "and to start proposing changes in the laws of a real country, inhabited by real people who are enduring unnecessary suffering, much of which can be cured by governmental action."[80]

Drawing from the Civil Rights movement, Cornel West proposed "prophetic pragmatism" to revive the flagging philosophy:

> [Prophetic pragmatism i]s a form of cultural criticism that attempts to transform linguistic, social, cultural and political traditions for the purposes of increasing the scope of individual development and democratic operations. Prophetic pragmatism conceives of philosophy as a historically circumscribed quest for wisdom that puts forward new interpretations of the world based on past traditions in order to promote existential sustenance and political relevance.[81]

Echoing Rorty, West pleaded for a philosophical revival that would correct the nation's descent into the intellectual mediocrity of ideology. "Prophetic pragmatism calls for reinvigoration of a sane, sober and sophisticated intellectual life in America and for regeneration of social forces empowering the disadvantaged, degraded, and dejected. It rejects the faddish cynicism and fashionable conservatism rampant in the intelligentsia and general populace."[82]

Neopragmatism was essentially a salvage operation, an attempt to rescue the public philosophy from sagging popularity. Always a tentative compromise between the competing vectors of empiricism and Romanticism, pragmatism's ascent was largely due to its programmatic successes. "A difference to be a difference has to make a difference," the pragmatists like to claim, and pragmatism had delivered, providing effective, if sometimes disputed, responses to the demands of modern industrial society. In addition, pragmatism was flexible, demonstrating a surprising and continuous capacity to co-opt the most severe criticism originating from the Left and the Right. Through intellectual triangulation, pragmatism borrowed freely from competing schools of thought, gravitated consistently toward the center, and, however inelegantly by European standards, advanced America forward despite any number of obstacles.

By century's end, however, the liberal justification for the welfare state and the meritocracy that managed social programs were under assault. Two British observers concluded that "*liberalism* as a governing philosophy is dead. The success of American liberalism was based on its ability to solve problems. The New Deal not only tackled the Depression, it created a constituency for activist government." As a result, the United States was diverging from the European welfare state paradigm. "But for the past thirty years this formula has been failing. Americans no longer rally to the standard of activist government, in the way they did in the 1960s, or in the way Europeans continue to do."[83] The philosophical paradigm that had provided the rationale for American social policy during the industrial era was exhausted.

While the momentum of the Progressive pragmatism that had dominated social affairs during the first seven decades of the twentieth century was diminishing, pragmatism of an entirely different orientation was emerging, a regressive pragmatism that viewed the private sector, not government, as the genius behind the American experience. Before exploring the rise of corporate pragmatism, however, it is essential to examine the edifice at which it was deployed—the American welfare state.

2

THE ARCHITECTURE OF ALTRUISM

The truth is that when his mind was completely gone, he had the strangest thought of any lunatic in the world ever had, which was that it seemed reasonable and necessary for him, both for the sake of his honor and as a service to the nation, to become a knight errant and travel the world with his armor and his horse to seek adventures and engage in everything he had read that knights errant engaged in, righting all manner of wrongs and, by seizing the opportunity and placing himself in danger and ending those wrongs, winning eternal and everlasting fame.
DON QUIXOTE

COMPARED TO ITS EUROPEAN counterparts, the American welfare state was, to be certain, an ungainly swan. By definition, a welfare state is established when the national government assures essential goods and services to people as a right of citizenship. By that standard, the American welfare state has lagged behind those of Europe. Several factors contribute to American exceptionalism in social policy. First, a legacy of voluntary activity predated the Social Security Act. By the onset of World War I, most American cities boasted a Charity Organization Society that regulated the provision of alms as well as a Settlement that promoted social change. The organization of charity provided the basis for "friendly visitors," the precursors of professional social work, and sought to address pressing issues, such as neglected and abused children. Settlement houses, most notably Jane Addams's Hull House, promoted community organization as a method to ameliorate the problems experienced by the urban poor. Typical of the period, private agencies often refused to serve Negroes who established their own mutual assistance organizations, such as the Knights of Tabor, the Knights of Pythias, the

Ancient Sons of Israel, and the Grand United Order of True Reform.[1] The voluntary legacy in American social welfare would pose a problem for New Dealers simply because this array of organizations had already been deployed. Indeed, one of the more intriguing events in the creation of the American welfare state was Harry Hopkins's decision to prohibit states from diverting Federal Emergency Relief Administration funds to private agencies; soon government programs eclipsed nonprofit initiatives.[2] While nonprofit social service agencies would proliferate under the United Way following the New Deal, they would be dwarfed by governmental social welfare programs.

Second, the Social Security Act was structured in a manner that invited fragmentation. Social policy was fractured along several fault lines: contributory social insurance programs were differentiated from public assistance funded by general revenues; federal, state, and subordinate jurisdictions retained varying degrees of influence on social programs; later, cash benefits were complemented (or confounded) by in-kind benefits. With this complexity, it is no wonder that the "bible" of federal social programs—the 2004 *Background Material and Data on Programs Within the Jurisdiction of the Committee on Ways and Means* (mercifully known as "the Green Book") exceeded 1,500 pages.

Finally, any changes in public social programs were conditioned by activity in the private sector. "For much of the twentieth century, indeed, the development of U.S. social policy has followed an identifiable second track of intervention, one to which scholars of the welfare state, orthodox or revisionist, have paid only limited attention," noted Jacob Hacker. "The legislative milestones along this track have not been large and highly prominent social programs, but public policies of diverse form—tax breaks, regulations, credit subsidies, government insurance—designed to encourage and shape private responses to public social problems."[3] The implications of this are momentous. Once private-sector activities are calculated as part of the national welfare effort, the United States is similar in scale to European nations. Politically, any welfare state with competing public and private sectors can evolve separate solutions to citizens' needs, evident in liberal defense of Social Security contemporaneous with conservative preference for private alternatives, such as 401(k) plans.[4]

The fault lines running through the American welfare state leave social welfare fraught with contradiction, fragmentation, and duplication. Unlike the more unified arrangements of Europe, the American experience has been decidedly pluralist, affording room for nonprofit activity as well as commercial ventures. As a result, social policy in America is manifested by an extraordinarily diverse set of institutions; government departments, voluntary agencies, independent providers, and proprietary firms coexist and respond to segments of the social welfare market. Such varied activity invites metaphor; American social welfare is often likened to a swamp, though at times it more aptly resembles the La Brea Tar Pits.

STRUCTURAL INTERESTS

Despite its diversity and fragmentation, social welfare in America is organized into clusters of activity. Since the industrial era, it has become a large industry through which groups exert influence to achieve particular objectives. The characterization of social welfare, or its more recent iteration, human services, as an industry may seem counterintuitive given the altruism that is frequently invoked to describe its ambitions. Pieties notwithstanding, caring for individual and family needs has become big business, as evident in the franchises that now typify American health care, the use of commercial ventures by nonprofits to enhance their bottom line, and the popularization of private practice among human service professionals. Here, Wall Street parvenus and neo-Marxist scholars would agree: the service sector of capitalist post-industrial economies shows extensive "commodification," a clear shift of social activities away from non-profit and toward commercial auspices. Accordingly, self-interest has become the fulcrum of the post-industrial service sector. As interest groups outmaneuver competitors, they develop complex institutional networks that anchor them in the social structure. Eventually,

> the existence of a network of political, legal, and economic institutions which guarantees that certain dominant interests will be served comes to be taken for granted as legitimate, as the only possible way in which these . . . services can be provided. People come to accept as inevitable that which exists and even believe that it is a right. . . . Precisely because of this, the interests involved do not continuously have to organize or to defend their interests; other institutions do that for them.[5]

Groups that become embedded in the social structure are *structural interests.* As Robert Alford has proposed, structural interest theory stands pluralist theory on its head. While traditional interest group theory assumes that groups have to scramble for resources, structural interest theory states that, for the very reason that they are so embedded in social reality, their needs are met virtually automatically. Ultimately, altruism is subordinate to self-interest in addressing the common good. Yet, as Murray Edelman wrote in the early 1960s, "the most cherished forms of popular participation in government are largely symbolic, but also that many of the public programs universally taught and believed to benefit a mass public in fact benefit relatively small groups."[6] A modern affluent society has much to appreciate, but that does not obscure the fact that a compassionate morality and a democratic polity often conspire to guild the well-heeled while discarding the superfluous and confining the troublesome.

Structural interests can be classified into four categories according to their ability to develop the inter-institutional linkages that result in power and influence: (1) dominant, (2) challenging, (3) repressed, and (4) emerging. A *dominant structural interest* has consolidated an extensive organizational network of personnel and revenues that overshadows other structural interests. These manifestations of dominance are buttressed by an institutional ideology, "an official interpretation of the past that makes [other organizational arrangements] appear defective or just a step on the way to the present regime."[7] A *challenging structural interest* is cultivating a parallel network of organizations large enough to claim some of the resources controlled by a dominant structural interest. This goal can be achieved by demonstrating a superior method of service delivery, siphoning off desirable clients, maximizing efficiency through the introduction of information technology, or simply swaying public sentiment in favor of the challenging structural interest. A *repressed structural interest* previously enjoyed a dominant status but has been demoted by a challenging structural interest. Once a dominant structural interest becomes repressed, a reassertion of hegemony is unlikely; rather, other groups will bypass it as they seek to establish claims in the field. However, because of the remnants of the institutional network that repressed structural interests retain, demotion usually means a residual position in the industry and not outright extinction. An *emerging structural interest* is organizing a network that may challenge a dominant interest some time in the future. To attain emerging status, a structural interest must be organized sufficiently that survival is not a concern; instead, directing future growth is the primary issue. So configured, structural interest theory might be described most aptly as organizational Darwinism. A poignant issue in this context is the circumstance of *marginal interests* whose needs and aspirations remain outside of the power network created by structural interests.

In a Kuhnian sense, the ideology of structural interests provides a paradigm for its adherents, a set of preferred values that distinguish it from competitors and account for its viability. The institutionalization of values in the form of structural interests accounts for the endurance of member organizations, regardless of their performance. Moreover, the evolution of structural interests is a slow process that can consume decades and entire careers of professionals associated with a particular group. This may be contrary to conventional rhetoric that places high value on the virtues of self-sacrifice and elevating the common good, a shared theme for all parties of the social welfare industry; yet, it is evident that over time some value sets are more successful than others, accounting for the comparative advantage enjoyed by certain interests. In the United States, four structural interests comprise the welfare industry: (1) traditional providers (repressed); (2) welfare bureaucrats (dominant), (3) clinical entrepreneurs (emerging), and (4) human service executives (challenging).

Traditional Providers

Traditional providers seek to maintain and enhance traditional social relations, values, and activities in their communities through private, nonprofit agencies. Lay persons and committed professionals comprise the *heart* of this structural interest, a metaphor that is often invoked by its adherents.[8] Traditional providers hold an organismic conception of social welfare, seeing it tightly interwoven with other community institutions. According to traditional providers, voluntary nonprofit agencies offer the advantages of neighborliness, a reaffirmation of community values, a concern for community as opposed to personal gain, and freedom to alter programming so as to conform to changes in local priorities. To the cosmopolitan sophisticate, their sensibility would be decidedly nostalgic. The base of influence of traditional providers consists of the private, nonprofit agencies that have populated American communities since de Tocqueville celebrated them. Today, they are often referred to as the voluntary sector.

Much of the heritage of social welfare can be traced to this interest (e.g., Mary Richmond of the Charity Organization Society movement, and Jane Addams of the Settlement House movement). Charity Organization Societies and settlement houses were transformed by two influences: the need for scientifically based treatment techniques and the professionalization of charity.[9] Together, these factors functioned as an anchor for the social casework agencies in American industrial society. The agency provided the grist for scientific casework that was instrumental in the emergence of the social work profession. The new schools of social work, in turn, relied on casework agencies for internship training, a substantial portion of a professional's education. Once graduated, many professionals elected to work in the voluntary sector, ensuring agencies of a steady supply of personnel. As this sector has expanded, many universities have offered certificates in nonprofit management.

Voluntary agencies routinized philanthropic contributions by socializing charity. Beginning with Denver's Associated Charities in 1887, the concept of a community appeal spread so rapidly that by the 1920s more than 200 cities had community chests. The needs of workers for effective treatment techniques and the economic imperatives for organizational survival functioned together to standardize the social agency. Perhaps the best description of the casework agency is found in the Milford Conference Report of 1923, *Social Casework: Generic and Specific*, which comprehensively outlined the organization through which professional caseworkers delivered services.[10] By the 1940s, the social casework had become a predominant form of service delivery, characterizing agencies providing services ranging from public health, juvenile services, probation and parole, to family welfare.

During the 1960s, the expansion of nonprofit agencies paralleled that of government social programs. Reluctant to deploy its own services when the voluntary sector was available, governments engaged in "purchase of service agreements," effectively using nonprofits as sub-contractors in the provision of legislatively mandated activity. Ostensibly, this injected an element of competition into the nonprofit sector, though voluntary agencies were reluctant to bid amongst one another, such behavior being contrary to the organic values that typified the sector. Nonetheless, the War on Poverty effectively made nonprofit agencies partially dependent on government for operating funds, despite any awkwardness in the arrangement.

In the decades that followed, traditional providers faced a number of challenges. The openness of American culture invites groups of citizens to organize in order to address pressing community problems, and they did—in the thousands. Between 1977 and 1998, the number of nonprofit organizations increased from 1.12 million to 1.62 million, some 500,000.[11] Community initiatives were undertaken to address the needs of African Americans, Latinos, Asian Americans, Native Americans, gays, lesbians, and immigrants. As these groups became more established, they approached the local United Way of America for assistance, only to learn that most of the charitable revenues were likely to be funneled to established organizations, such as the YMCA, Big Brothers/Big Sisters, the Red Cross, and larger sectarian agencies. When United Way funding was not forthcoming or only dribbled in, some of the newer nonprofits elected to establish their own charitable giving campaign; after all, the United Way was a nonprofit that had been established to facilitate community generosity. When it became apparent that minority communities might threaten the status quo by establishing competing charitable giving campaigns, the United Way introduced "donor choice" through which it would divert contributions to non–United Way agencies.

At the same time, nonprofit reliance on government would prove to be a Faustian bargain. Throughout the 1980s, the voluntary sector struggled due to federal budget rescissions accompanied by the deepest recession since the Depression. During the Reagan and first Bush presidencies, federal support of nonprofit activities dropped each year, totaling $45 billion from 1982 to 1992. As the recession abated, individual contributions increased, despite the elimination of the tax deduction for non-itemizers instituted in 1986; yet, this failed to make up for the roll-back in federal funding. Between 1977 and 1997, governmental aid to voluntary agencies excluding health care decreased from 21.6 to 20.7 percent, while that to social and legal services dropped from 54.4 to 52.1 percent.[12] Static resources coupled with increasing demand contributed to the introduction of a corporate culture in charitable activities, with the expectation that a more business-oriented regime would increase efficiency and stretch scarce resources.

In order to enhance its stature, the United Way named William Aramony as its chief executive officer (CEO), concurring with his designs to institute a corporate culture in charitable activities. While the gambit would prove enormously successful financially, increasing contributions to United Way ventures, it proved a

moral disaster. During the early 1990s, bookkeeping irregularities and other improprieties were found at the United Way; Aramony resigned and was sent to
prison. Subsequently, United Way of America funding faltered; it would not be
until a decade later that it would resume an upward trajectory. By 2001, United
Way activities totaled $3.91 billion.[13]

These problems left local nonprofits struggling to reconcile reduced aid with
increasing demand for services. While private charitable giving remained at
slightly more than 2 percent of national income, as a percentage of nonprofit operating expenses, it fell from 48 percent in 1965 to 20.3 percent in 1995.[14] Many
found support from foundations; between 1975 and 1995, foundation grants increased from $1.94 billion to $12.26 billion.[15] Yet, much of foundation giving
failed to make up for governmental reductions in nonprofit activities that addressed social problems, which went instead to the arts, religion, and the environment; private contributions to health and human services remained essentially
constant.[16]

While government and foundation assistance for nonprofit social activities
continued to be inadequate, sectarian agencies were confronted with a revenue
crisis. During the early 1980s, revenues increased 10.1 percent, but plummeted to
2.7 percent a decade later.[17] Thus, the "faith-based" initiative mounted by George
W. Bush was well received even though the scale of the proposal was modest at
best. "Welfare policy will not solve the deepest problems of the spirit," Bush affirmed before the National Religious Broadcasters convention, "You don't fix the
crack on the wall until you fix the foundation."[18] Proposed at $5 billion over five
years, faith-based social services immediately enjoined a debate over the separa-
tion of church and state, then foundered on accusations that it would permit discrimination in hiring on the part of sectarian agencies. Although many liberal intellectuals were skeptical about the motivation of George W. Bush, recalling his
father's invocation of "a thousand points of light," faith-based organizations were,
in fact, more popular than conventional means for addressing social problems. In
2001, a survey conducted by the Pew Partnership for Civic Change ranked the
public's perception of problem-solving for various organizations. Generally, the
more distant the organization, the less favorable it was rated: 56 percent of respondents ranked sectarian agencies as important for "solving social problems in
their communities," compared to 53 percent for local nonprofits, 39 percent for
the United Way, 33 percent for state government, and only 28 percent for the federal government.[19]

The fortunes of the nonprofit sector received a boost as Americans turned out
their pockets to victims of the September 11 attacks. Charitable contributions in
the aftermath of September 11 swelled to $2.3 billion, the largest being the Liberty
Fund established by the American Red Cross.[20] Ultimately, the September 11 Victims Compensation Fund would dispense $7 billion to more than 5,000 fami-
lies.[21] But this outpouring of generosity would reverberate through the phil-

anthropic community; skeptics feared that September 11 contributions would dampen the support for traditional nonprofit activities. Furthermore, the outpouring of compassion raised awkward questions about such spontaneous expressions of good will: If the victims of terrorism that occurred on September 11 should receive substantial aid, why not those of the Oklahoma City bombing only a few years earlier?[22] These and other issues diminished public support for organized charity; one year after the attacks, a survey undertaken by Independent Sector, the Brookings Institution, and the Chronicle of Philanthropy reported that 42 percent of respondents had "less confidence in charities" after September 11.[23] Thus, while charitable giving received a boost from September 11, it subsequently dropped, reflecting the downward trajectory of the early 1990s that was attributed to improper practices of organized charities.[24]

Welfare Bureaucrats

Welfare bureaucrats are public functionaries who maintain the welfare state in much the same form in which it was conceived during the New Deal and amplified by the War on Poverty. "Their ideology stresses a rational, efficient, cost-conscious, coordinated . . .delivery system."[25] They view government intervention vis-à-vis social problems as legitimate and necessary, considering the apparent lack of concern by the private sector and local government. Moreover, they contend that government intervention is more effective because authority is centralized, guidelines are standardized, and benefits are allocated according to principles of equity and equality. For liberals, the governmental monopolies that are maintained by welfare bureaucrats are simply necessary for a humane society; for conservatives, they are nothing less than an American version of a Soviet five-year plan.

The influence of welfare bureaucrats grew as a result of the Social Security Act of 1935 and expanded significantly with the Great Society of the mid-1960s. To a limited extent, the larger community chests "exerted a pressure toward rationalization of the professional welfare machinery,"[26] but this did not diminish the effect of the federal welfare bureaucracy, which soon eclipsed the authority of traditional providers. An array of welfare legislation followed the Social Security Act, including the Housing Act of 1937, the G.I. Bill of 1944, the Community Mental Health Centers Act of 1963, the Civil Rights Act of 1964, the Food Stamp Act of 1964, the Economic Opportunity Act of 1964, the Elementary and Secondary Education Act of 1965, the Medicare and Medicaid Acts of 1965, Supplemental Security Income in 1974, Title XX of the Social Security Act of 1975, the Full Employment Act of 1978, and the Americans with Disabilities Act of 1990.

The flourishing of bureaucratic rationality concomitant with this legislative activity represented the institutionalization of liberal thought, which sought to control the caprice of the market, ensure a measure of equality among widely divergent economic classes, and establish the meritocracy that would maintain and perfect the welfare state. Confronted with a rapidly industrializing society lacking basic programs for ameliorating social and economic catastrophes, Progressives perceived the state as a vehicle for social reform, an application of philosophical pragmatism. Their solutions focused on "coordinating fragmented services, instituting planning, and extending public funding."[27] Implicit in the methods advocated by welfare bureaucrats is an expectation, if not an assumption, that the social welfare administration should be centralized, that eligibility for benefits should be universalized, and that social welfare should be firmly anchored in the institutional fabric of society.

The influence of welfare bureaucrats had been curtailed somewhat since the mid-1980s. The Reagan administration all but capped the growth of public social welfare, expenditures of which as a percentage of GDP hovered at 18.5 percent through the 1980s until increasing under the Clinton presidency to 21.8 percent in 1994.[28] For its part, the Clinton administration established the National Performance Review, an effort to make the federal government more efficient while saving $108 billion over five years.[29] Despite attempts by both political parties to reign in government, the number of public employees has continued to increase; from 16.2 million in 1980 to 20.9 million in 2000.[30] Between 1977 and 1997, government consumed 1.5 percent more of national income annually.[31] Yet these figures fail to depict the remarkable expansion of social program expenditures through the welfare state. Between 1990 and 2000, social programs virtually doubled, growing from $561 billion to $1,013 billion.[32] Protestations by Republican and Democratic presidents notwithstanding, the welfare state continued its relentless expansion.

Two developments reflect the dimming prospects of welfare bureaucrats: devolution and privatization. The work of David Osborne proves seminal to both. In *Laboratories of Democracy*, Osborne chronicled his travels among a handful of governors who were contending with fiscal crisis attributed to the Reagan administration, which reduced federal aid to the states during a period of escalating demand for social welfare benefits. To his surprise, Osborne found that the governors he followed were imaginative and innovative in addressing the problems of state governance.[33] That states would be vehicles for progress was counterintuitive to welfare bureaucrats who had perceived the federal government as the optimal source of social provision as well as liberals who had portrayed the states as bastions of repression, or worse. Yet, Osborne's observations reprised a theme that has been central to welfare in America, the prominent role of the states in child welfare, juvenile justice, corrections, and mental health. Welfare reform soon surfaced as a test of such apprehensions about devolution. Many liberals feared "a race toward the bottom," in which adjacent states continually underbid each other to make welfare less attractive to welfare recipients; eventually, they feared, welfare benefits in high-paying states would be driven down by lower-paying states. Yet, there was no evidence that this transpired; to the contrary many states, pioneered by Wisconsin, increased their welfare expenditures in order to move welfare recipients into the labor market. Their triumph in welfare reform led the second Bush administration to propose devolving other social welfare programs to the states, notably Medicaid and Head Start.[34]

Privatization reflects a more direct threat to welfare bureaucrats. Again, Osborne looms prescient, proposing in *Reinventing Government* that government establish the objectives of public policy, assigning the execution to the private sector.[35] And as before, Osborne tapped into a theme that had been integral to American social programs, reliance on the private sector to deliver the goods. Nowhere had this been more evident than in health care. When the social engineers of the War on Poverty crafted Medicare and Medicaid, they elected to reimburse private providers rather than deploy a government-owned healthcare system such as the Veterans Administration. The result, as we shall see momentarily, was the emergence of a for-profit industry in health care that was uniquely American. Indeed, when the Clinton administration presented its Health Security Act, it not only conceded the existence of commercial health providers but structured the plan to amplify their position in the market.

Devolution and privatization complicate the work of welfare bureaucrats. To the extent that devolution transfers the control of social programs from federal to state officials, the influence of welfare bureaucrats will be diminished; yet, their role will not disappear if only because the federal government will insist on some measure of accountability on how federal revenues are spent. In all likelihood, devolution promises to expand the network of relations that bind the federal government to the states. Privatization, however, has more ominous implications. Reliant on the private sector for provision of services, government has at best indirect control over the cost and quality of care for which it reimburses providers. A completely privatized system reduces welfare bureaucrats to bursars and regulators, roles that pale next to the noble aspirations attendant with the creation of the welfare state. Most significantly, privatization encourages welfare bureaucrats, lawmakers, and interest groups to form *industrial complexes* in order to manipulate social policy.

Clinical Entrepreneurs

Clinical entrepreneurs are professional service providers—chiefly physicians, psychologists, social workers, educators, and consultants—who work for themselves as opposed to being salaried employees within government or nonprofit agencies. Important to clinical entrepreneurs is the establishment of a professional monopoly, the evolution of which represents a concern on the part of practitioners that their occupational activity not be subject to political interference from government or the ignorance of the lay public. In the United States, the professions found that a market economy was conducive to occupational success. In the most fundamental sense, private practice reconciles the professionals' desire for autonomy with the imperatives of a market economy. The transition from entrepreneur to professional monopolist is a matter of obtaining legislation restricting practice to those duly licensed by the states, the jurisdiction responsible for licensing in the United States. Hence, "professionalism provides a way of preserving monopolistic control over services without the risks of competition."[36] As an extension of the entrepreneurial model of service delivery, professional monopoly offers privacy in practice, freedom to valuate one's worth through setting fees, and the security ensured by membership in the professional monopoly.

Prior to the rise of the service sector, professionals represented less than 5 percent of workers. The Progressive promise of the benefits of social engineering, complemented by the rapid expansion of American universities and their professional schools, contributed to the rapid expansion of the service sector; between 1968 and 1980, the percentage of service workers in the labor force increased by 40 percent.[37] Professionals, of course, enjoy the latitude of practicing under nonprofit or commercial auspices, but their preference for individual or group private practice has been striking. Between 1980 and 2000, the number of medical offices increased from 802,000 to 1.9 million, while the number of offices of non-medical professionals increased from 96,000 to 439,000.[38] For 1999, there were 234,000 partners in health care and social assistance, reporting gross receipts of $65.7 billion and a net income of $11.3 billion,[39] each clearing on average $48,290, after taxes.

The income from clinical entrepreneurs may appear modest, but much of the appeal of private practice is due to the negative perception of practicing under other auspices: government and nonprofit agencies. The inferiority of nonprofit and public sectors as a setting for human service practitioners is one of the dirty little secrets in American social policy. After more than a decade of frustration in trying to upgrade services to vulnerable children in the United States, the Annie E. Casey Foundation commissioned a seminal study of the 3 million employees that constitute the human service workforce. In addition to explaining the entropy that characterized human services, the report was not sanguine about the future of public and nonprofit agencies whose employees served as subjects for the study.

> Human service delivery is reaching a state of crisis. Frontline jobs are becoming more and more complex while the responsibility placed on workers remains severely out of line with their preparation and baseline abilities. Many are leaving the field while a new generation of college graduates shows

little interest in entering the human services sector. Millions of taxpayer dollars are being poured into a compromised system that not only achieves little in the way of real results, but its interventions often do more harm than good.[40]

While the report helps explain the overt failure of public services that are sustained by *networks of negligence*, it also accounts for the popularization of private practice, the preferred context of clinical entrepreneurs. After earning a postgraduate degree, having attained state licensure, and perhaps securing independent professional certification, how many human service professionals would aspire to work in a setting characterized by low pay, high caseloads, inept supervision, and poor public confidence? Although many newly graduated professionals do elect to work in such settings, once full licensure is obtained, they often exercise the exit option, usually in favor of private practice.

The rise of clinical entrepreneurs has been abetted by the feminization of the labor force. Between 1980 and 2000, women's employment as a percentage of the population increased 21 percent, while that of mothers increased twice that, 42 percent. Despite the feminization of the labor market, employers have been slow to adjust to the requirements that women, especially professional mothers, bring to the labor market. In 2001, only 27.4 percent of the 43.5 million working women in America had flexible work schedules. Paradoxically, women working in professional and technical fields were actually slightly less likely to have flexible work schedules.[41] By allowing the freedom to establish their own working hours, independent of the standard work week, private practice is more congruent with the needs of working women, particularly mothers, than governmental and voluntary agencies.

Social work provides a case study in the enthusiasm of human service professionals for private practice. Not officially recognized until 1964, the private practice of social work not only became a primary modality within the profession, but it also allowed social workers to claim that they were the largest provider of professional mental health services, eclipsing psychiatry and psychology. In 1975, the National Association of Social Workers estimated that from 10,000 to 20,000 social workers were engaged in private practice. By 1983, Robert Barker, author of *Social Work in Private Practice*, speculated that about 30,000 social workers, or 32 percent of all social workers, engaged in private practice on a full- or part-time basis.[42] By 1985, a large portion of psychotherapy was being done by social workers, and the *New York Times* noted that "growing numbers of social workers are treating more affluent, private clients, thus moving into the traditional preserve of the elite psychiatrists and clinical psychologists."[43] Between 1988 and 1995, the percentage of social workers in government fell from 40.4 to 33.7 percent, and the number employed by nonprofits decreased from 39.8 to 38.4 percent, while those working under for-profit auspices increased from 19.8 to 27.9 percent.[44] Accordingly, social workers' race to practice under commercial auspices continued unabated: in 2003, for the first time the percentage of social workers practicing in the private for-profit sector (36 percent) eclipsed those working for nonprofit agencies (35 percent) or government (26 percent).[45]

Clinical entrepreneurs are an emerging structural interest in social welfare, though as of late, one whose health is in doubt. Despite its rapid evolution, the future of clinical entrepreneurs has been circumscribed by a group of competitors, managed care companies, which have exploited the weaknesses inherent in private practice. All states license physicians, psychologists, and social workers, and a significant number also recognize smaller human service professions. Accordingly, a primary objective of the state human service professional associations has been the expansion of their professional monopoly and its aggrandizement through lobbying for vendorship privileges that allow more regular income through insurance held by clients. Through this strategy, clinical entrepreneurs would have been well positioned to become a more influential interest in American social welfare had it not been for the incursion of managed care, the attempt by human-service corporations to diminish the influence of clinical entrepreneurs. Capitalizing on the Kaiser-Permanente prevention model in health care, the Health Maintenance Act of 1973 spawned an industry of Health Maintenance Organizations (HMOs). The result was a competitive scramble for patients that first favored HMOs then Individual Practice Associations (IPAs) as clinical entrepreneurs organized in defense of their traditional prerogatives. During the 1980s and early 1990s, HMOs controlled the patient market, but IPAs have commanded more patients since 1995; subsequently, mixed plans have grown in popularity.[46] Thus, the days of the solo private practitioner appear to be numbered.

It is not difficult to extrapolate the impact of managed care on clinical entrepreneurs: had the 79.5 million members of 541 HMO plans in 2001[47] received care from private practitioners instead, clinical entrepreneurs would be in a more influential position with respect to the other structural interests that comprise the social welfare industry. Having lost momentum, their strategy has been a rearguard action. In addition to affiliating with a competitive network of IPAs, clinical entrepreneurs have fought to hold managed care companies accountable for their occasionally shoddy performance by insisting on professional standards of care. For example, by 2002 the National Committee for Quality Assurance boasted that it had accredited 466 managed care plans serving 51 million people.[48] But this has been an attempt to alter an industry that has already established its supremacy. Too late, clinical entrepreneurs have been eclipsed by the structural interest that has attenuated their prerogatives, human service executives. Having lost their autonomy, the best that clinical entrepreneurs can hope for is making accommodations with human service corporations that allow them at least a measure of independence.

Human Service Executives

Human service executives share an important characteristic with clinical entrepreneurs: both represent ways of organizing service delivery in the context of the market. However, in some important ways they differ. Unlike clinical entrepreneurs, human service executives are salaried employees of proprietary firms and, as such, have less autonomy. Yet, because human service executives command corporations that function across state lines, they can appeal to a larger group of subscribers than has been the case for clinical entrepreneurs who have practiced locally. Equally important, they can appeal to investors who capitalize corporate ventures. As managed care firms have prospered, the salaries and bonuses of human service executives have approximated those of other American CEOs. As administrators or CEOs of large corporations, human service executives advance market strategies for promoting social welfare. Welfare bureaucrats emphasize the planning and regulatory functions of the state, whereas human service executives favor the rationality of the marketplace in allocating resources and evaluating programs. In the present circumstances, human service executives advocate market reform of the welfare state—the domain of welfare bureaucrats—and thus are in a position to challenge this dominant interest. Because the prospects of human service executives were initially predicated on reimbursements from the state through Medicaid and Medicare, they were dependent on government; however, the expansion of the private-service sector has provided access to revenues from private sources, particularly consumers or their third-party fiduciaries. This independence from government revenue is the primary reason why human service executives can challenge welfare bureaucrats for dominance in American social welfare. As Americans look less to government and more toward the private sector for security, the prospects of human service executives soar.

For-profit firms became prominent in American social welfare during the 1960s, when Medicaid and Medicare funds were paid to proprietary nursing homes and hospitals.[49] Since then, human service executives have been rapidly creating independent, for-profit human service corporations that provide an extensive range of nationwide services. Human service corporations have established prominent, if not dominant, positions in several human service markets, including nursing home care, hospital management, health maintenance, child care, home care, corrections, and welfare. In 1981, 34 human service corporations reported annual revenues above $10 million; by 1985, the number of firms had increased to 66; by 2000, the number had risen to 268. Of these, sixteen corporations reported revenues higher than the total annual contributions to all of the United Ways of America! If the largest human service corporations boasted revenues that overshadowed the nonprofit sector, they also boasted work forces that rivaled those of welfare bureaucrats. During the mid-1990s, hospital management firm Columbia/HCA claimed more than 131,000 employees, while nursing home franchise Beverly Enterprises reported 82,000.[50]

Corporate mismanagement on such a scale invariably becomes headline news. The improprieties of human service executives sometimes match the size of the companies they manage. In 2003, Columbia/HCA agreed to reimburse the federal government $631 million for fraudulent Medicare billings; coupled with other fines, HCA paid a total of $1.7 billion in penalties for fraudulent practices.[51] In the spring of 2003, the largest mental health corporation, Magellan, filed for bankruptcy when it was unable to cover $1 billion in debt, leaving in suspension the 67.4 million people for whom it was contracted to pay for services as well as the 2,300 therapists with whom it had contracts.[52] In 2003, the Securities and Exchange Commission charged HealthSouth's CEO, Richard Scrushy, with overstating earnings by $1.4 billion since 1999, leading to his ouster.[53] A Birmingham, Alabama, philanthropist, Scrushy had played prominent roles with numerous voluntary agencies, which subsequently distanced themselves from the generosity of HealthSouth.[54]

If self-aggrandizement on the part of human service corporations makes them the object of derision—indeed, the Left enjoys it as blood sport—their position within American social welfare has been firmly established. Much of this can be attributed to the nation's political economy, democratic capitalism, in which markets have been used to allocate goods and, with increasing frequency, services. Any nascent capitalist suspecting that a public utility could be converted to a social market is free to try; this explains the emergence of corporations in activities that, only a generation ago, would have been understood as common goods: health care, child care, corrections, and welfare. Short of legal and market restraints, investors are free to explore such opportunities. As corporations have attained a commanding presence in the service sector, most Americans have come to take their presence for granted. From banking to entertainment to communications, corporations have become a fixture in post-industrial America, so it should not be surprising that they essentially control health care (Columbia/HCA, Tenet Healthcare, Humana) and nursing home care (Beverly Enterprises), have established beach heads in corrections (Corrections Corporation of America) and welfare (Maximus), and are making incursions into education (several consulting firms). Much as extractive and manufacturing corporations shaped the American economy during the industrial era, human service corporations are defining the service sector of post-industrial society.

THE DYNAMICS OF STRUCTURAL INTERESTS

The structural interests just described can be located in relation to two variables: span of influence and type of economy. As Figure 2-1 indicates, power shifts as a result of significant social influences: privatization and bureaucratization.

Scully told a House Democratic aide who had requested the memo, "I'll fire him so fast his head will spin."[70] Foster, a career civil servant, stuck to his story, accusing the White House of having full knowledge of his projections, but favoring lower estimates generated by other agencies.[71] A subsequent House inquiry failed to clarify the matter, in large part because the Republican leadership was unwilling to grant subpoena power to the committee, making testimony voluntary. When the House committee asked Scully to testify about the suppression of Foster's projection, he said he was "unable to appear" because he was traveling.[72]

Lacking a majority in the House, Democrats were unable to get a full hearing on the scandal. No longer a fed, Scully had been employed by a firm that would benefit from exploiting provisions of the legislation he had facilitated. In the same week that the Scully scandal broke, trustees of Social Security and Medicare announced projections on the solvency of Medicare's Hospital Insurance, stating that the fund would be exhausted in 2019, seven years earlier than had been anticipated, in part because of the impact of the just-passed Medicare reforms.[73]

The emergence of a medical-industrial complex was suggested by C. Wright Mills who inveighed against the military-industrial complex after World War II, a concern echoed by President Eisenhower. Writing critically of the second Bush White House's adventures in Iraq, Russell Baker targeted "a small conservative foreign policy clique based in the Pentagon," which "is now such a vast power structure that it is something of a government within a government, and like a separate government it now has its own foreign policy."[74] Theodore Lowi, in Article VII of his facetious "constitution of the Second Republic," prophesied that "actual policy making will not come from voter preferences or congressional enactments but from a process of tripartite bargaining between the specialized administrators, relevant members of Congress, and the representatives of self-selected organized interests."[75] More recently, Alice O'Connor identified the pivotal role of the "analytic subculture, or 'subgovernment'" in poverty research:

> An expanding and interlocking institutional network of think tanks, university institutes, and both non- and for-profit research corporations devoted to analytic social research. These institutions and the analysts who circulated easily in and between them, nurtured a distinctive subculture in public policy and government, held together by a shared language if not always a consensual understanding of social problems, and by a shared appreciation for the possibilities of scientifically controlled social experimentation, econometric modeling, and outcomes evaluation as tools—and, more and more, as requirements—of the policy trade.[76]

In its military, health, and research manifestations, the fundamental problem of industrial complexes is holding them accountable to the public. In those sectors where the stakes are high, especially with respect to public revenues, the continued emergence of industrial complexes can be expected. The implications of this for a broad spectrum of Americans who receive health and human service benefits are great.

NETWORKS OF NEGLIGENCE

The conceptual parallel to an industrial complex is evident further down the social stratification in the form of a network of negligence where linkages between private agencies, trade associations, university professional schools, and public officials sustain inferior programs. In areas where poverty is endemic, the result is second-class services provided to second-class citizens, justified by second-class knowledge, all under the guise of public service. In decrying the inability of public education to assure basic security to inner-city students, Colbert King editorialized about the

> habitual indifference . . . reflected in the quality of services we provide children. Millions of dollars have been squandered by second-rate officials in school central administration on a second-rate security program run by second-rate managers. Because we have come to think so little of our children, we saddle them with teachers and mid- and low-level administrators who zealously cling to jobs they couldn't get anywhere else because, truth be told, they wouldn't qualify.[77]

This, of course, is contrary to the portrait presented to the public, one that features altruistic professionals, helping motivated clients, overseen by efficient administrators who, in turn, are appreciative of the resources provided by beneficent government agencies or noble foundations. The myth of social service delivery systems is exposed when riveting headlines of injury and death depict agencies populated by poorly trained and overworked staff, resentful or recalcitrant clients, absent administrators who are struggling to reconcile inadequate government funding with erratic foundation support. When networks are compromised, staff turnover subverts continuity of care, clients get lost in the bureaucratic labyrinth, and managers are not held accountable for inferior performance, leaving government overseers and foundation officers shaking their heads in exasperation. When the print and electronic media feature graphic illustrations of systemic failure, mayors and governors announce commissions of inquiry and new program administrators are appointed, staff qualifications are upgraded, and focus groups may be conducted with clients, leaving government agencies and private foundations reassured about future performance—until the next exposé.

A paradox of the American welfare state is the persistence of need, despite the multiplicity of structural interests and the extensive resources they control. Social policy in America is populated by numerous groups that have been neglected by social programs, populations that struggle at the margins of social policy. Often more vocal representatives of these groups can be found clamoring at the gates of the welfare state, demanding access to its benefits; yet, extant structural interests find ways of diverting, if not denying, their claims. In reaffirming local values and priorities, voluntary agencies frequently disavow responsibility for the strangers in their midst, especially when they violate local norms, as in the cases of undocumented workers, the mentally aberrant, and the chronically homeless; instead of mounting outreach initiatives, agencies often contrive ways to deny or ration services to such groups. Welfare bureaucrats have a more direct rationale for avoiding marginalized populations: unless such groups conform to legislative dictates of categorical programs, they are simply ineligible for benefits. Clinical entrepreneurs and human service executives are circumscribed by another consideration: the bottom line. While commercial providers may elect, or be required in some cases, to provide charity care, it represents negative revenue flow and is avoided. Thus, despite the proliferation of organizations committed to enhancing the common good, providers that sometimes compete for clients within the same community, many Americans are not able to access benefits that most of their compatriots take for granted.

Multiple factors contribute to networks of negligence. The vestiges of discrimination continue to adversely affect inner-city minorities, Latinos in the Southwest, and Native Americans, impeding not only their individual mobility but the prosperity of their communities as well. Deinstitutionalization and the demise of the community mental health movement consigned thousands of mental patients to homelessness.[78] The termination of the amnesty provisions of the 1986 Immigration Reform and Control Act has contributed to more than seven million undocumented workers in the United States.[79] The failure to deploy rehabilitation and reentry programs for 2 million people incarcerated in the United States pose a threat to the stability of the communities to which most will be released.[80] As these examples illustrate, entire populations have born the brunt of systematic marginalization.

Addressing marginalization is often confounded by ideological polemic, with liberals arguing for collectivist strategies through which government assures greater security for vulnerable groups, while conservatives advocate individualistic virtues that encourage self-sufficiency. These tropes are recited with regularity. Liberals cite economic disparities in income and wealth, the millions of American without health insurance, and families struggling to reconcile static incomes with increasing housing costs—all true. Conservatives, for their part, have wondered why continuing expansion of government social programs has not been associated with *diminishing* claims on the part of the disadvantaged. Of particular objection by conservatives has been the plethora of categorical programs targeted at the poor, the inefficiencies of which are such that they seem intended to assure employment opportunities for liberal professionals rather than provide any substantive assistance to the troubled poor. Conservatives are fond of arguing that the welfare state is not under-funded, as liberals claim: divide the number of poor by the cost of social programs and everyone is instantly raised above the poverty level—also true. Social problems are more likely to be addressed when competing political parties move toward the center and replace ideological posturing with authentic dialogue. The increasing ideological polarization in American politics militates against finding common ground on compelling social issues, in effect affirming the *status quo ante* of marginalization.

Paradoxically, professional education contributes to marginalization. Claims of public service notwithstanding, professional schools often give short shrift to public service. While this is not so surprising given the inducements toward private practice considered in the discussion of clinical entrepreneurs earlier, it does not excuse the professions from honoring the public service promise that is explicit in obtaining from the state a professional monopoly.[81] Social work, the profession most directly associated with the welfare state, not only fails to assure that professional education includes exposure to those areas traditionally associated with the profession—public welfare, child welfare, and the mentally disabled— but its accreditation authority does not insist on the rudiments of a sound professional education. Social work is a profession that prides itself on its cultural diversity yet fails to require proficiency in a language other than English; that boasts about its ability to generate knowledge yet fails to require a research thesis for a graduate degree; and promotes professional values yet fails to require completion of a course in ethics during the course of education.[82] Nor can the public have much confidence in those social workers who do elect public service. In 2002, the Educational Testing Service published Graduate Record Examination scores for 44 graduate disciplines; at the top was public policy studies with a combined score of 1664; one notch from the bottom was social work with a combined score of 1380.[83] Such factors increase the likelihood that social workers will not have the necessary foundation to work effectively with marginal populations. Rather than assume leadership roles in evolving policies and services for the marginalized, professionally trained social workers are more likely to ration care congruent with the dictates of the status quo.

The interaction of these factors—historical marginalization, ideological wrangling, and weak professional preparation—can be mutually reinforcing, subverting the best intentions of public policy. The collapse of social infrastructure came to the attention of representatives of the Fourth Estate in the 1990s when journalists began to inquire about the damage attributed to social programs. In 1990, Margie Lundstrom and Rochelle Sharpe won a Pulitzer Prize for "Getting Away with Murder," an exposé of child fatalities in the United States.[84] Stories such as this would become standard fare for metropolitan dailies. In 2002, Clifford Levy of the *New York Times* reported 946 deaths of mentally ill adults in community-care facilities in New York City during the 1990s, of which 126 were under age 50. Levy's series described a squalor that rivaled the infamous public warehouses that had made state psychiatric hospitals notorious in the 1960s: "The analysis shows that some residents died roasting in their rooms during heat waves. Others threw themselves from roof tops, making up some of at least 14 suicides in that seven-year period. Still more, lacking the most basic care, succumbed to routinely treatable ailments, from burst appendixes to seizures."[85]

Although the state health department was responsible for investigating unnatural deaths, it had files on only three of the almost 1,000 deaths; and the city medical examiner was unable identify a single autopsy conducted on a mentally ill adult who had died of unnatural causes.[86]

In 2004, David Fallis of the *Washington Post* chronicled the substandard care of state-licensed assisted living homes in Virginia.

> In 51 deaths over the past eight years, records raise questions about the quality of care or show that the homes bore some responsibility for the death. In more than 135 other cases, residents suffered sexual assaults, physical abuse or serious injuries, including head wounds, broken bones, burns and life-threatening medication errors. About 4,400 residents have been victims of abuse, neglect or exploitation since 1995, records show.[87]

One facility operator admitted resident injuries, citing their frequency to justify her failure to notify state officials: "If I called them every time I had an incident, I'd never get off the phone."[88] For its part, the state had incentives for propping up a substandard patchwork of care. Many assisted living residents might have warranted care in a state mental hospital where per diem costs were $460 per patient, compared to the state payment to a group home of $28 per day. Despite rumors of inferior care, the Virginia Department of Social Services was unable to identify patterns of negligence due to an inadequate information system: "Its system of collecting information about the homes is so fragmented that officials cannot say how many people have died or been seriously injured because of abuse or negligence."[89]

In the worst instances, multiple failures overlap, creating the conditions for a perfect storm of negligence. The public services of Washington, D.C., provide a graphic illustration of infrastructure failure. In 1999, Katherine Boo won a Pulitzer Prize for "Invisible Deaths," a chronicle of mistreatment of retarded adults in community-care facilities in the District of Columbia. Prompted by an initial discovery of 350 incidents of abuse, neglect, molestation, and theft that had not been officially investigated, Boo uncovered a more sinister omission: between 1993 and 1999, 114 retarded adults had died as a result of maltreatment, not one of which had been investigated as required by law.[90] An exasperated mayor immediately fired five administrators and said he admitted that he wanted to "blow up" the city agency that served the retarded.[91] After Boo identified the most egregious instances in which the District failed to protect its most defenseless citizens, the series generated a series of legal suits on behalf of victims' families. Perversely, when judgments were levied in favor of claimants, the District attempted to reclaim some of the settlement "by threatening to file (and in some cases, filing) liens for the living and medical expenses" that the District had failed to provide, thus contributing to the deaths of the retarded whom it was mandated to protect![92]

In 2001, Sari Horwitz, Scott Higham, and Sarah Cohen won a Pulitzer Prize for their documentation of 229 children who died between 1993 and 2001 in the District of Columbia, vivid evidence of the failure of child protection in the nation's capital.[93] In 2004, the District's United Planning Authority (UPO), which oversaw a budget of $36 million to fight poverty, came under the scrutiny of journalists who discovered that the recently fired agency director had been assigned two Lincoln Town cars for personal use as well as a credit card that had $221,000 in charges, of which only some could be validated. For 2003, UPO had spent $2.9 million for consultant services; one contract for at least $500,000 went to an official who had been fired for previous contractual improprieties.[94] Also in 2004, the former head of the United Way of the National Capital Area, who had held the position for 27 years, was sentenced to prison for defrauding the agency of $500,000.[95] The same day that the United Way CEO was sentenced, an accord was reached placing the District's Youth Services agency under the control of an overseer because juveniles "were exposed to many of the same problems they encountered on the streets from sexual violence to rodent infestation."[96]

Aside from illustrating networks of negligence, the institutional implosion of Washington, D.C., is notable for two reasons. First, each of these incidents occurred after the publication of Fred Siegel's *The Future Once Happened Here*, in which he attributed much of the corruption of the nation's capital to its former mayor, Marion Barry. By the mid-1990s, liberal columnist Richard Cohen satirized the District's appeal to statehood, noting that "it's become a republic, a banana one at that."[97] Siegel contended that the mismanagement that he chronicled in Washington, D.C., New York, and Los Angeles was finally grinding to a halt: "Today the make-work-social-service economy is being questioned as never before. It is increasingly derided as 'Poverty, Inc.,' a lucrative business for those who directly benefit by peddling pathology to a willing buyer in the federal government but death for the cities and neighborhoods that encourage it."[98] Siegel would be chagrined to discover that the problems of Washington, D.C., have continued well after Marion Berry left office, effectively sustained by networks of negligence. Second, recurrent debacles in social welfare have not gone unnoticed by conservatives who came to control Congress after the Republican "revolution" of 1994. Although opinion data are not available on the perceptions of members of

Congress about the District, it is likely that the imbroglios did not go unnoticed. The *Washington Post* is the paper of record for the District, and, despite its liberal reputation, it has assiduously covered human service fiascos. In addition to the scandals mentioned earlier, the paper chronicled public mismanagement so extensive that entire agencies—including child welfare, housing, and mental health—had been placed under court supervision. Thus, Republican members of Congress had to look no further than their front stoop in the morning to have their prejudices about social welfare validated: The welfare state had become an intractable mess.

Alford explains how networks of negligence could occur within a society of abundance, attributing the problem to politics in social welfare: "Politics serves simultaneously to provide tangible benefits to various elites and symbolic benefits to mass publics, quieting potential unrest, deflecting potential demands, and blurring the true allocation of rewards."[99] In the name of social policy, in other words, the public is offered symbolic reassurance that essential help is provided to the needy while structural interests receive tangible benefits in terms of employment, income, status, and authority. Although systematic negligence is most often associated with marginal groups, it is also congruent with the minimal benefits provided through more established programs. Social Security benefits, for example, are inadequate to support a retiree; Medicaid services are contingent on locating a participating provider; behavioral health services are increasingly attenuated by managed-care companies. Thus, while absence of benefits is typical of marginal groups, inferior benefits are often provided to beneficiaries of even more successful programs.

By the end of the twentieth century, the trans-Atlantic welfare state accord had unraveled, a victim of over-confident liberalism as well as a cynically opportunistic conservatism. Post–World War II economic prosperity subsidized the bureaucratic vision of welfare liberals, extending program benefits to needy Americans who had been left out of the New Deal. Yet, the proliferation of the welfare state would prove problematic. As more groups became dependent on social programs, their demands began to appear more self-serving than related to the prosperity of the nation as a whole. Special-interest liberalism thrived as the structural interests that comprised the welfare state prospered. However, their proliferation was contradicted by a series of exposés that questioned the validity of the welfare state project. In various ways, the public came to question welfare liberalism as the basis of social policy. Social programs consumed greater volumes of revenues, yet large numbers of Americans remained vulnerable to misfortune. Despite the spread of governmental authority, social welfare evidenced increasing fragmentation; instead of assuring adequate care for the needy, services often inflicted injury and death on the unfortunate. Despite its commanding presence, the liberal welfare state was ripe for an overhaul.

3

CONTROLLING THE MEANS OF ANALYSIS

There are two kinds of lineage in the world: some who trace and derive their ancestry from princes and monarchs, which time has gradually undone, and in the end they finish in a point, like a pyramid turned upside down; others have their origin in lowborn people, and they rise by degrees until they become great lords. Which means that the difference between them is that some were and no longer are, and others are what they once were not.

DON QUIXOTE

The political economy of the United States is democratic capitalism, an arrangement that has undergone profound technological and social changes over time. Ted Halstead and Michael Lind provide a serviceable chronology beginning with the creation of a "decentralized agrarian republic," followed by the early stages of the Industrial Revolution driven by steam power, concomitant with the Civil War and Reconstruction, the sequel being a mature industrial economy, dominated by electricity and fossil fuels, which generated the economic surpluses that made the welfare state a reality.[1] These eras have had a pronounced effect on social policy. The first affirmed representative government through the Constitution, in the process, articulating the federal legislative process. The second introduced manufacturing and attendant immigration, which prompted the Progressive movement. The third inaugurated the American welfare state. Accordingly, social theorists have identified the primary issues that have accompanied modernism. Karl Marx proposed the central question as, "Who controls the means of production?" As a corrective to rampant capitalism, the expansion of government led Max Weber to ponder, "Who controls the means of administration?" A rapidly articulating information age poses a new question in social affairs, "Who controls the means of analysis?" As will become evident, by deploying a network of think tanks to counter the liberal bias of American universities, conservatives have organized social intelligence toward their ideological ends.[2] The consequences of this are evident in the dissipation of the liberal momentum that propelled the expansion of social programs from the New Deal through the War on Poverty. In organizing think tanks to shift public philosophy to the Right, conservative intellectuals stole a page from Progressives who used universities for this purpose; in effect, the Right hijacked pragmatism.

THE POLICY PROCESS

For all its elegance as political template, the Constitution was a product of agrarian America, an era since eclipsed not only by industrialization but by the information age as well. As a result, the public policy process has been profoundly altered to meet the requirements of contemporary society. The primary distortions in American social policy can be attributed to socioeconomic stratification, the rise of vested interests, and the proliferation of policy institutes.

Social Stratification

A variety of schemes have been presented to differentiate groups with influence from those lacking it. The most simple of these consists of a dual stratification: for instance, capitalists and the proletariat, which Marx used. A three-part stratification is common to Americans: an upper class, a middle class, and a lower class. Placement of individuals in the appropriate class is usually made on the basis of income, education, and occupational status. This three-part stratification is limited in its capacity to explain very much about American social welfare, however. If asked, most Americans identify themselves as middle class, even if by objective criteria they belong to another social station. Furthermore, the designation *lower class* is not particularly informative about the social conditions of a portion of the population that is pivotal to social policy.[3]

A more informative stratification was developed by social psychologist Dexter Dunphy who identified six social groups, which he differentiated according to wealth, internal solidarity, and control over the environment (Table 3-1).[4]

This stratification illustrates several peculiarities with respect to social policy. Ironically, the groups at the top (the wealthy) and the bottom (the underclass) have less direct involvement in social programs than might be expected, though for quite different reasons. The wealthy shape high culture by subsidizing the symphony, ballet, museums, and the like; their influence in social welfare is through charitable philanthropy. In 1999, the top corporate foundations made

TABLE 3-1.

Social Stratification of the Population into Six Groups

NAME OF GROUP	EXAMPLES	CHARACTERISTICS
Wealthy	Upper elites, independently wealthy, large stockholders	Ownership of resources is the main source of power; control over goals is very high, but control over means is through executives
Executives	Top administrators in business, nonprofits, government (executive, legislative, judicial, and military)	Organizational solidarity facilitates effective policy implementation; some control over goals and a high degree of control over means
Professionals	Middle-level managers, technical experts, private practitioners, community leaders	Limited solidarity; control over means is high, and goal setting can be influenced if collective action is undertaken
Organized workers	Semiskilled workers, civic and political clubs, social action organizations	Environment encourages solidarity; groups have some control over the means by which goals are realized
Working/welfare poor	Temporary and part-time workers earning minimum wage and who use welfare as a wage supplement	Subjugated position with no control over the environment; frustration is shared and irrational; explosive behavior results
Underclass	Unemployables and illiterates; substance abusers; itinerants, drifters, migrant workers	Subjugated position with no control over the environment; a sense of failure coupled with mobility reduces social interaction and leads to retreatism

Source: Dexter C. Dunphy, *The Primary Group: A Handbook for Analysis and Field Research,* 1972, pp. 42–44.

substantial charitable contributions, so much so that many had become household names (Table 3-2).[5]

Despite such largesse, the wealthy tend not to be involved in the pedestrian activities of the foundations they establish, preferring to delegate decision-making to subordinate executives. The underclass has little to do with social policy primarily because its members are so psychologically and sociologically disorganized that they have difficulty maintaining program eligibility—providing they even become eligible for benefits. It is for this reason that the most troubled among the underclass—the homeless, street addicts, HIV+ substance abusers—are the sub-

TABLE 3-2.
Top Corporate Foundations Making Charitable Contributions

COMPANY	YEAR ESTABLISHED	ASSETS ($/BILLIONS)	GRANTS ($/MILLIONS)
Gates Foundation	1994	17.1	500
Packard Foundation	1964	13.0	440
Ford Foundation	1936	11.4	550
Lilly Endowment	1937	11.1	500
R. W. Johnson Foundation	1936	8.1	440
Kellogg Foundation	1930	6.2	221
Pew Charitable Trusts	1948	4.8	230
MacArthur Foundation	1978	4.2	168
Mellon Foundation	1969	3.5	153
Rockefeller Foundation	1913	3.5	175

Source: Sam Verhovek, "Elder Bill Gates Takes on the Role of Philanthropist,"
New York Times (September 12, 1999), p. 22.

ject for aggressive outreach efforts. Their behaviors are so individually destructive and socially costly that programs are designed to get them into treatment, sometimes through methods that are quasi-coercive.

Another oddity is related to social distance. The policy process is dominated by executives who make decisions affecting people at least two social stations below them. Not surprisingly, the decisions formulated by legislators—who are likely to be affluent, Anglo, male attorneys—have little correspondence to the circumstances of the uneducated minority poor. A classic example is Child Support Enforcement (CSE). Conceived more than two decades ago with the best of bourgeois intentions, CSE has proven a mixed bag: For more stable male workers, CSE has generated increased support payments for their children; but for mothers on welfare, CSE has operated at a net loss with program expenditures exceeding increased child support payments. The initial reaction on the part of policy-makers to the failure of fathers to support their children on welfare has been punitive, frequently denying them licenses to engage in specific activities, such as being a skilled tradesperson or having a drivers license. Idaho went so far as denying sportsmen's licenses—hunting and fishing—to deadbeat dads. Later, it became evident that low-wage men were probably in the same boat as their low-income ex-wives and children, many unable to comply with child support orders because of poor work history or the erratic availability of employment. Yet, supportive efforts to increase child support proved disappointing. An evaluation of Parents' Fair Share, a program designed to increase the child support of men whose dependents were on welfare, actually resulted in reduced child support payments despite the multiple interventions incorporated in the program.[6]

A poignant problem related to social distance is the difficult position of human service workers. Situated between the bourgeois values implicit in policies enacted by affluent law makers and recipients who scramble to maintain a hand-to-mouth existence, staff operating public social programs find themselves in an organizational purgatory. Legislators perceive public welfare workers as "bleeding-heart do-gooders" who bend program guidelines to address the circumstances of "irresponsible" clients, while the clients view the program staff as heartless automatons who have little real appreciation for their struggles. Many welfare recipients who have had to deal with fragmented programs, indifferent staff, and the surreal requirements to secure benefits eventually develop a vocal contempt for "welfare" as they have experienced it, a defiant response that alienates them from decision-makers and welfare staff alike.

Within the policy arena, opposing ideological camps have come to appreciate stratification differently. Liberals have used income and wealth distribution to argue for more progressive social programs; conservatives have cited mobility as a natural process that typifies the social economy. A staple of the liberal case in favor of social programs has been the nation's skewed income distribution. Kevin Philips, a conservative, noted the remarkable shift in income during the last two decades of the twentieth century: between 1979 and 1997 the income of the lowest quintile of Americans dropped 1 percent while that of the top quintile increased 53 percent (that of the top 1 percent skyrocketed 175 percent).[7] The 1990s witnessed a significant upward redistribution of income from the poorest to wealthiest families (Table 3-3).[8]

More recently, economists have noted the inadequacy of income as an indicator of economic justice and focused on wealth distribution.[9] If income distribution is skewed in favor of the affluent, assets are even more so (Tables 3-4, 3-5).

TABLE 3-3.
Average Family Cash Income, 1989–1998

INCOME QUINTILE	1989 ($)	1998 ($)	PERCENTAGE CHANGE (%)
Highest	102,163	120,037	17.5
Fourth	53,075	54,912	3.5
Middle	33,947	34,007	0.2
Second	19,860	19,844	−0.1
Lowest	7,711	7,247	−6.0
Total	43,351	47,209	8.9

Source: *Overview of Entitlement Programs* (Washington, D.C.: USGPO, 2000), p. 1312.

TABLE 3-4.
Changes in the Distribution of Wealth, 1962–1998*

WEALTH CLASS	Percentage Share of Wealth				Percentage-Point Change
	1962	1983	1992	1998	1962–1998
Top 1%	33.4	33.8	37.2	38.1	4.7
Top quintile	81.0	81.3	83.8	83.4	2.4
Fourth quintile	13.4	12.6	11.5	11.9	−1.5
Middle quintile	5.4	5.2	4.4	4.5	−0.9
Second quintile	1.0	1.2	0.9	0.8	−0.2
Lowest quintile	−0.7	−0.3	−0.5	−0.6	0.1

*Wealth is defined as net worth (household assets minus debts)

Source: Lawrence Mishel, Jared Bernstein, and Heather Boushey, *The State of Working America* (Washington, D.C.: Economic Policy Institute, 2003), p. 281.

Notably, the bottom quintile is chronically in debt, its obligations exceeding its assets. Moreover, African Americans report significantly less wealth than whites; in 1998, the median wealth of whites was $81,700, while that of blacks was $10,000.[10] That assets are consistently negative for the lowest quintile reflects the difficulty of poorer families to buffer themselves from economic shocks. Thus, asset poverty, the wealth needed to survive for three months at the poverty level, exceeds income-based poverty. In 1999, the official poverty level was 11.8 percent, while the asset poverty rate was 27.9 percent; however, the asset poverty rate for minorities was much higher—for blacks 57.6 percent and Hispanics 52.3 per-

TABLE 3-5.
Change in Average Wealth, 1962–1998*

WEALTH CLASS	(Thousands of 1998 dollars)				Annualized Growth %
	1962	1983	1992	1998	1962–1998
Top 1 %	$4,851.8	7,175.1	8,796.4	10,203.7	3.1
Top quintile	587.4	864.5	991.9	1,126.7	2.5
Fourth quintile	97.2	133.6	135.7	161.3	1.8
Middle quintile	39.4	55.5	51.9	61.0	1.6
Second quintile	6.9	12.5	10.5	11.1	1.7
Lowest quintile	−5.3	−3.2	−6.0	−8.9	−1.9

*Wealth is defined as net worth (household assets minus debts)

Source: Lawrence Mishel, Jared Bernstein, and Heather Boushey, *The State of Working America* (Washington, D.C.: Economic Policy Institute, 2003), p. 281.

cent.[11] In 2000, the asset poverty rate was 25.5 percent, twice the conventional poverty level, 12.7 percent.[12] The consequences of the tax cuts engineered during the second Bush presidency would be expected to exacerbate the chasm between rich and poor.

The conservative rebuttal to income and wealth maldistribution has been to cite the upward mobility that Americans exhibit over time. Being poor with respect to income and assets may be an adverse experience, but it is far from permanent. W. Michael Cox and Richard Alm noted the consequences for the poor:

> Only 5 percent of those in the bottom fifth in 1975 were still there in 1991. Where did they end up? A majority made it to the top three fifths of the income distribution—middle class or better. Most amazing of all, almost 3 out of 10 of the low-income earners from 1975 had risen to the uppermost 20 percent by 1991. More than three-quarters found their way into the two highest tiers of income earners for at least one year by 1991.[13]

Significantly, even liberal researchers have validated upward mobility. Bradley Schiller, the author of a widely used text, *The Economics of Poverty and Discrimination*,[14] identified significant earnings improvements among low-wage workers. "The available perceptions of minimum-wage youth seem to dispel the notion that minimum-wage jobs offer low wages and nothing more," he found in one study of young workers.

> Over 85 percent of the minimum-wage entrants stated that they liked their jobs, and over 60 percent felt that they were learning skills that would be valuable in attaining better jobs. Only one of eight minimum-wage youth perceived a total lack of on-the-job training—a condition compatible with he notion of "dead-end" jobs. Over half (56 percent) of the minimum-wage workers perceived opportunities for promotion with the same employer.[15]

"The longitudinal experiences of minimum-wage youth . . . refute the notion of a 'minimum-wage trap,'" concluded Schiller. "Youth who started at the minimum wage in 1980 recorded impressive wage gains over the subsequent seven years both in absolute and relative terms."[16] Subsequently, Schiller evaluated the employment success of teens aged 16–19 and youths aged 20–24 over the first 10 to 15 years in the labor market. "Relative mobility is pervasive among younger workers," he found. "Less than one-fourth of either cohort stayed in the same or adjacent rank of the earnings distribution."[17]

Summarizing the research on wage gains over time, Daniel McMurer and Isabel Sawhill of the Urban Institute concluded that

> mobility in the United States is substantial, according to the evidence. Large portions of the population move into a new income quintile with estimates

ranging from about 25 to 40 percent in a single year. As one would expect, the mobility rate is even higher over longer periods—about 45 percent over a 5-year period and about 60 percent over both 9-year and 17-year periods."[18]

Of course, there is much more to mobility than just income distribution, including education, occupation, and place of residence. While available data with respect to income supports conservative contentions that stratification is quite fluid, data on wealth clearly favor the Left.

Vested Interests and Advocacy Organizations

If stratification has a general effect on policy by virtue of the social stations that different groups occupy, the specific outcomes are registered by the actions of vested interests. Traditionally, vested, or as they are sometimes called "special," interests were classified according to the nature of their activities: prior to elections, interest groups influenced the composition of legislatures by establishing Political Action Committees (PACs); in between elections, interests exerted pressure strategically through lobbying around specific legislative proposals. Such conventional efforts have been augmented by novel ways to influence public policy.

As special interests learned to skirt federal campaign regulations, increasing amounts of "soft money"—non-PAC funds—influenced election activity.[19] As Table 3-6 indicates, substantial funds have been funneled through PACs, lobbying,

TABLE 3-6.
Contributions to Federal Candidates, 1999–2000

PAC SECTOR	NUMBER OF PACS	TOTAL CONTRIBUTIONS
Labor	203	$25,499,562
Finance, insurance, and real estate	434	20,240,275
Health	186	9,798,568
Miscellaneous business	309	8,889,215
Energy and natural resources	268	8,370,040
Transportation	147	8,352,784
Communications/electronics	130	7,589,715
Agribusiness	243	7,576,433
Lawyers and lobbyists	147	5,589,421
Construction	101	4,101,135
Defense	47	3,656,200

Source: "15-Month Fundraising Figures of Major Parties Detailed," (Washington, D.C.: Federal Election Commission, June 5, 2000), p.1.

and "soft money" in order to influence elections for the purpose of shaping public policy. An examination of campaign finance might leave a cynic to conclude that American democracy produces the best politics that money can buy. In 2000, successful Senate candidates spent on average $7 million, while their House counterparts expended over $840,000.[20] For all the monies lavished on election campaigns, the result was strikingly static. In 2002, 98 percent of House incumbents and 86 percent of Senate incumbents were reelected.[21]

Significantly, individual contributions continued to represent the bulk of Party revenues. Typically, between 70 and 80 percent of political contributions were made by individuals.[22] These contributions notwithstanding, strategically targeted gifts from organized groups have disproportionate impact—hence the concern about PACs, "soft money," and lobbyists. The Center for Responsive Politics has ranked the major PACs by sectors. If PAC contributions have favored conservatives, once combined with other sources of campaign funds, the influence is even more pronounced: while business outspent labor PACs by a factor of three, once all other sources are included the factor increases to sixteen.[23]

"Soft money," funds that are not restricted by federal campaign law, have increased substantially in recent years. For example, "soft money" contributions to the major political parties have more than quadrupled from $79.1 million in 1991–1992, to $220.7 million in 1997–1998[24] to $450 million in 2000.[25] According to Common Cause, in 1999, "soft money" contributions by business eclipsed those of labor by a factor of ten.[26] For the 2000 election year, the Democratic Party received $206.6 million in "soft money," an amount eclipsed by the Republicans, who received $242.5 million.[27] Other patterns in the origins of "soft money" have been discernable. While contributions on the part of individuals are evenly split between the political parties, corporations, and trade associations heavily favor Republicans over Democrats almost two to one. The largest "soft money" corporate and trade association contributors for 2000 are shown in Table 3-7.

Organized labor attempts to compensate for corporate "soft money" by diverting its resources to liberals. Accordingly, 99 percent of labor contributions have been directed to the Democratic Party. The largest labor union contributors are listed in Table 3-8.

While the "soft money" issue commanded the headlines of the nation's dailies, the real money was in lobbying; the lobbying activity of many industries swamped PAC contributions in total. Unlike campaign contributions, which are regulated, lobbyists can shift major amounts of cash depending on their particular needs. As Table 3-9 attests, vested interests expended significant amounts to influence germane issues; in 2001, Congress deliberated the future of Medicare and considered adding a drug benefit, reviewed telecommunications deregulation, debated tort reform, and considered increasing fuel mileage requirements for passenger cars, each of which generated lobbying activity.

In national politics, the key to influence is choreographing the resources of

TABLE 3-7.

Major Corporate Campaign Contributions, 1999

CORPORATIONS		TRADE ASSOCIATIONS	
AT&T	$3,626,230	Blue Cross & Blue Shield	$1,130,890
Bank of America	2,676,023	Assoc. of Trial Lawyers	981,050
Freddie Mac	2,398,250	Natl. Assoc. Chain Drugstores	621,415
Philip Morris	2,322,291	Public Securities Assoc.	585,000
SBC Communications	1,822,738	National Assoc. of Realtors	520,934
Microsoft	1,660,331	Amer. Council of Life Insurance	520,430
Pfizer	1,545,660	Cellular Telecom Ind. Assoc.	518,100
Bristol-Myers Squibb	1,486,749	National Assoc. Homebuilders	506,950
Verizon	1,464,461	Edison Electric Institute	505,265
Federal Express	1,327,100	American Gas Assoc.	482,575

Source: "Overall Campaign Finance Statistics" (Washington, D.C.: Common Cause (June 11, 1999).

PACs, "soft money," and lobbyists to attain party objectives. By way of illustration, having won control of Congress as a result of the 1994 midterm elections, Republicans moved swiftly to reverse the revenue flow of PAC contributors away from the Democratic Party. Leading the effort was Representative Dick Armey, House Majority Leader, who, in April 1995, sent a letter to Fortune 500 CEOs complaining that their contributions to such "liberal" charities as the American Cancer Society were contrary to Republican intentions in political reform. In order to

TABLE 3-8.

Major Labor Campaign Contributions

LABOR UNIONS	
American Federation of State, County, and Municipal Employees	$5,914,000
Service Employees International Union	3,912,696
United Brotherhood of Carpenters & Joiners	2,921,250
Communications Workers of America	2,355,000
United Food & Commercial Workers Intl. Union	2,146,450
Intl. Brotherhood of Electrical Workers	1,731,000
American Federation of Teachers	1,536,000
Sheet Metal Workers Intl. Assoc.	1,255,854
National Education Association	946,300
Intl. Brotherhood of Painters & Allied Trades Union	945,000

Source: "The Power of Soft Money," *Washington Post* (February 13, 2002), p. A25.

TABLE 3-9.
Lobbying, 2002

	EXPENDITURES ($/MILLIONS)
Industry	
Health care	$264.00
Communications, technology	221.48
Finance, insurance	220.93
Energy, natural resources	159.42
Transportation	147.08
Business-retail, services	140.85
Miscellaneous	134.55
Manufacturing	76.23
Agriculture	67.94
Single-issue groups	65.85
Interest Group	
U.S. Chamber Inst. for Legal Reform	$22.30
U.S. Chamber of Commerce	19.26
American Medical Association	14.84
PhRMA	14.26
Philip Morris	14.04
General Electric	13.02
National Association of Realtors	12.92
Edison Electric Institute	12.05
Business Roundtable	11.88
Northrup Grumman	11.77

Source: "Top Lobbyists," *Washington Post* (June 24, 2003), p. A19.

clarify his intentions, Armey's staff let PAC contributors know that contributions to Republican ventures were expected and that those to Democrats would also be tallied. Accordingly, vested interests seeking access to the new Republican leadership should be zeroing out their contributions to Democrats. In the annals of special-interest politics, Armey's brazen tactics ploughed new ground: "By imposing an ideological test on givers they have introduced a new level of coercion," observed journalist Ken Auletta.[28] Yet, Armey's strategy broke no laws, and the money rolled in. In the first eight months of 1995, the Republican Party received $60 million in contributions compared to just $36 million in 1993.[29]

During the second Bush presidency, Armey teamed-up with Grover Norquist, president of Americans for Tax Reform, to launch the K Street Project. Frustrated that lobbyists were frequently wedded to liberal social programs and the interests that sustained them, Norquist proposed routinizing Armey's vetting strategy: If the lobbying industry expected access to Capitol Hill, it needed to hire Republicans. In short order, K Street complied: virtually all new hires by lobbying firms were card-carrying Republicans. In effect, the K Street Project cemented the relationship between conservative interests and Congress.

> Now the Republican Party is using its sway over both K Street and the wider business community to build a private-sector equivalent to Roosevelt's machine. It hands out government contracts to businesses that fill its coffers: look at the way the pharmaceutical industry should gain from the new prescription-drug benefit in Medicare. It provides its most loyal footsoldiers, from congressional aides to congressmen, with a pot of gold on K Street when they retire.[30]

The massive amounts of soft money that flooded into campaign coffers, beyond oversight of the Federal Election Commission, prompted calls for campaign reform. Pulled from the brink of legislative oblivion on more than one occasion, the McCain-Feingold Campaign Finance Reform Act was signed into law in 2002. As if to defy its provisions, President Bush promptly hosted a fund-raising dinner that generated an eye-popping $33 million.[31] Although the McCain-Feingold act withstood a Supreme Court challenge, many skeptics anticipated that the 2004 campaign would only generate more imaginative ways to skirt campaign finance regulations. They were not disappointed. With contributions limited to $25,000, the Bush reelection campaign began acknowledging those who had bundled contributions: Pioneers raised $100,000, Rangers $200,000, and Super Rangers $300,000. Six months before the 2004 election, the Bush reelection campaign had raised a record-breaking $296.3 million through this strategy.[32] Following suit, Democrats designated those who raised $100,000 as Patriots, and Trustees for contributions of $250,000.[33]

In order to evade campaign finance reform, Democratic and to a lesser extent Republican operatives quickly employed Section 527 of the Internal Revenue Service code to establish committees that could receive unrestricted funds as long as they operated independently of specific campaigns, avoided endorsing specific candidates, and honored the prohibition of airing messages 30 days prior to a primary and 60 days prior to a general election.[34] By the summer of 2002, "527 committees" were actively soliciting contributions, the largest associated with liberal constituencies. Since June 2000, the AFSCME Special Account reported $16.5 million; an abortion rights group funded by Jane Fonda, Pro-Choice Vote, claimed $12.7 million; and Emily's List raised $6.2 million. 527s associated with the major parties were, for a change, behind the curve. The New Democrat Network raised $3.6 million, and the Republican ARMPAC reported $400,000.[35] By summer

2004, liberal 527s had already spent $50 million of an anticipated $300 million to unseat Bush, while Republicans had only just established their primary tax-exempt issue organization, Progress for America.[36] Six months before the election, Democrats had bested Republicans in 527 fundraising by a factor of three; but Republicans still enjoyed a significant advantage in total campaign contributions, out-raising Democrats $557.6 million to $393.6 million.[37]

Compared to business, labor, and lobbyists, advocacy groups tend to bring fewer assets to bear on the political process. Limited by meager resources, advocates usually rely on a small cadre of lobbyists, which they sometimes share, or volunteer lobbyists. Within social policy, several advocacy groups have been instrumental in advancing legislation to assist vulnerable populations—among them, the American Public Human Services Association, the Child Welfare League of America, the National Association for the Advancement of Colored People, the National Urban League, and the National Organization for Women. Of these only one, the American Association of Retired Persons (an organization so influential that it changed its name to its acronym: AARP), ranked seventieth of the top 100 lobbyists on Capitol Hill. Despite the number of advocacy organizations and their successful record in evolving more comprehensive social legislation, changes in the policy process are making their work more difficult. Increases in the number of governmental agencies as well as in their staffs make it difficult to track policy developments and changes in administrative procedures. More significantly, the escalating cost of influencing social policy, evident in the number of paid lobbyists and the contributions lavished by PACs, is simply beyond the means of most advocacy organizations. As one Democratic candidate for the Senate lamented, "Only the well-heeled have PACs—not the poor, the unemployed, the minorities or even most consumers."[38]

This is not to say that proponents of social justice have been ineffectual. Despite their disadvantaged status, advocacy groups were able to mobilize grassroots support to beat back some of the more regressive proposals of the Reagan administration. In the early 1980s, for example, scholars from the conservative CATO Institute and the Heritage Foundation proposed cutting the Social Security program. They were trounced by an effective lobbying campaign mounted by the AARP under the leadership of the late octogenarian congressman Claude Pepper. Other social welfare programs did not fare as well; at the very time that Social Security was spared, social programs for the poor were reduced by significant margins. During the Summer of 2003, the pharmaceutical industry was brought up short, when, over its vociferous objections, legislation was passed allowing the importation of drugs from Canada, but then triumphed when Medicare reform was passed only months later.

Among the newer advocacy organizations, the Children's Defense Fund (CDF) initially benefited significantly from the election of Bill Clinton because First Lady Hillary Rodham Clinton had been a former chair of its board of directors and

Clinton's Health and Human Services (HHS) Secretary, Donna Shalala, had succeeded Rodham Clinton at CDF. Although CDF claimed a substantial victory with incorporation of the Children's Initiative in the Clinton 1993 economic package, children's advocates were distraught when Clinton signed a 1996 welfare reform plan that they thought was injurious to poor children. If being dismissed by Clinton on welfare reform was dismaying, CDF then had to contend with outright theft by George W. Bush. In search of a banner for his education reform initiative, the Bush White House brazenly lifted the "Leave No Child Behind" initiative of CDF, shuffling the words to "No Child Left Behind." Subsequently, Bush's education reform was used to illustrate "compassionate conservatism," an initiative later complemented by faith-based social services, funding to combat AIDS in Africa, and Medicare reform.

Compared to the resources commanded by PACs and lobbyists, advocacy organizations are paupers. With few exceptions such as AARP, advocates lack the money to sponsor junkets for members of Congress and their staffs, the professional capacity to mount initiatives on a national scale, and sufficient weight to leverage any given legislation. Symbolically, they provide an important counterpoint to the moneyed interests and politicians that pull the legislative strings behind the stage. If the apparatchiks in charge of PACs and lobbies are the captains of vested interests, the staff of advocacy organizations are the guerrillas fighting an insurgency. However valiant their skirmishing, their tactics tend to be rearguard. Usually, they lose.

Think Tanks

Of all the factors that distort the ideal of a representative legislative process, policy institutes, or think tanks, are the least well known, failing to register on the radar screen of most Americans. Structurally, think tanks are private institutions and, as such, can secret their affairs from public scrutiny. Functionally, they endeavor to predefine the options that law makers consider and then shape the contours to better conform to their ideological preferences; as a result their work is sometimes so esoteric as to leave the layperson yawning. Geographically, they are located in Washington, D.C., the nation's largest cities, and sometimes in the capitals of the biggest states; as a result, citizens living elsewhere would be ignorant of their existence. Thus, while many citizens would know that vested interests lobby Congress and that high-rollers leverage campaigns, they would be unable to identify a think tank, the purveyors of ideas that form the grist of the legislative mill, much less a network of them assembling ideas in order to transform public philosophy. "I am sure that the power of vested interests is vastly exaggerated compared to the gradual encroachment of ideas," stated John Maynard Keynes presciently in 1947. It is ideas, not vested interests, which are dangerous for good or evil."[39] Despite their low visibility, policy institutes have not only become central to the policy process, but, as will be seen shortly, have been the source of an unprecedented transformation, the replacement of liberalism with conservatism as the nation's public philosophy.

Prior to the nineteenth century, it would have been accurate to state that policy formulation began with the legislative phase. Clearly, this was intended by the framers of the Constitution, but theirs was a largely agrarian society with comparatively little institutional specialization. With industrialization, many complexities were injected into the society and, in time, special institutions emerged to assist the legislature in evaluating social conditions and preparing policy options. Eventually, even constitutionally established bodies, such as Congress, lapsed into a reactive role, largely responsive to other entities that preformulated policy options.[40] Initially, institutions of higher education provided this technical intelligence to assist the legislative branch, and some still do. For example, Harvard's Kennedy School of Government and the University of Wisconsin Institute for Research on Poverty provide analyses on important social policies.[41]

That legislators at the federal level, as well as those in the larger states, would rely on experts to assess social conditions and develop policy is not surprising given the rise of the professional intelligentsia beginning with the Progressive Era. Just as important are the quotidian demands placed on any member of Congress (and the larger state legislatures for that matter). The fact that each legislator must attend to multiple committee and subcommittee assignments requiring expertise in particular matters, while at the same time contending with the general concerns of a large constituency and keeping an eye on the next reelection campaign, makes for a daunting schedule. A typical day in the life of a legislator has been reconstructed by Charles Peters, a longtime Washington observer:

> The most striking feature of a congressman's life is its hectic jumble of votes, meetings, appointments, and visits from folks from back home who just drop by. From an 8 A.M. breakfast conference with a group of union leaders, a typical morning will take him to his office around 9, where the waiting room will be filled with people who want to see him. From 9 until 10:30 or so, he will try to give the impression that he is devoting his entire attention to a businessman from his state with a tax problem; to a delegation protesting their town's loss of air or rail service; to a constituent and his three children, who are in town for the day and want to say hello; and to a couple of staff members whose morale will collapse if they don't have five minutes alone to go over essential business with him. As he strives to project one-on-one sincerity to all these people, he is fielding phone calls at the rate of one every five minutes and checking a press release that has to get out in time to make the afternoon papers in his district. He leaves this madhouse to go to a committee meeting, accompanied by his legislative aide, who tries to brief

him on the business before the committee meeting begins. The meeting started at 10, so he struggles to catch the thread of questioning, while a committee staff member whispers in his ear. And so the day continues. The typical day . . . usually ends around 11:30 P.M., as the congressman leaves an embassy party, at which he has been hustling as if it were a key precinct on election eve. He is too tired to talk about any but the most trivial matters, too tired usually to do anything but fall into bed and go to sleep.[42]

Thus, the typical member of Congress struggles constantly to reconcile finite time and resources with an avalanche of information, the mass of which has grown exponentially over time. "The steady evolution of Big Government, starting with the New Deal, grounded in new public responsibilities, and propagating new federal agencies, helped to generate a flood of information," observed David Ricci. "This the legislators tried to handle by acquiring more staff to analyze data and by parceling out the legislature's expanding workload to a growing number of specialized subcommittees."[43] Even with the assistance of legislative staff, information overload means that law makers are unable to devote sufficient time to legislation to be proactive. The demands of re-election, of course, further compromise an elected official's efficacy. Because reelection is a primary concern for legislators, their staffs are frequently assigned to solve the relatively minor problems presented by constituents. In fact, placating unhappy constituents has become so prominent a concern that one legislative observer notes that constituency services—called *casework* by elected officials—have become "more important than issues" for representatives.[44] The typical member of Congress will have a handful of staff to assist in the committee work that is essential for constituents in the home district, hardly sufficient resources to deal effectively with major legislative initiatives. As a result, public policy tends to get short shrift.

Under these circumstances, law makers are appreciative when policy institutes offer guidance not only in critically assessing the value of given legislation but also providing options for considerations. During the past four decades, institutions have proliferated, specializing in the provision of social intelligence necessary for policy formulation. These policy institutes now wield substantial influence in the social policy process, not only vetting policy options for their ideological correctness, but also inundating members of Congress with monographs on preferred bills. Since the 1980s, conservative think tanks have distinguished themselves from their liberal predecessors by using the media to disseminate their ideas to the public. Not unlike prestigious colleges, think tanks maintain multidisciplinary staffs of scholars who prepare position papers on a range of social issues. With multimillion-dollar budgets and connections with national and state capitals, think tanks are well positioned to shape social policy. Generally, financial support is derived from wealthy individuals and corporations with a particular ideological inclination, a fact evidenced by the types of think

Institute for Policy Studies	Urban Institute	Brookings Institution	American Enterprise Institute	Heritage Foundation	CATO Institute

Liberal   Conservative
(Left)   (Right)

FIGURE 3-1.
Ideological Orientation of Select Policy Institutes

tanks they support. Several prominent policy institutes are located along the ideological continuum shown in Figure 3-1. Within policy institutes, prominent scholars, usually identified as senior fellows, hold endowed chairs, having often served in cabinet-level positions within the executive branch. When Republican administrations came into power, large numbers of senior fellows from conservative policy institutes assumed cabinet appointments, while their Democratic counterparts returned to liberal institutes, where senior chairs awaited them. For junior staff, an appointment in a think tank can provide invaluable experience in how the governmental policy process actually works. Despite their influence in public policy, it is important to recognize that think tanks are private, non-governmental institutions, by virtue of having obtained tax-exempt status from the Internal Revenue Service because they serve an important service: public education.

Through much of the twentieth century, a first generation of largely liberal policy institutes, led by the Brookings Institution and later the Urban Institute, contributed to the formulation of governmental social policy and therewith the creation of the American welfare state. Their role continued the trajectory of the Progressive Era by providing technical expertise to legislators and governmental agencies upon request. Guided by the social engineers of the New Deal and the Great Society, liberal think tanks evolved a style that was distinctly academic, generating quantitative analyses across a range of program activities. Sophisticated technical analysis of social policy did not go unnoticed, to be sure. C. Wright Mills questioned the dominance of "abstracted empiricism," the reliance on formulas and data that were decipherable only by the academic priesthood. "This model of research is largely an epistemological construction; within the social sciences, its most decisive result has been a sort of methodological inhibition," Mills wrote. "By this I mean that the kinds of problems that will be taken up and the way in which they are formulated are quite severely limited by The Scientific Method."[45]

The complexity of research that piqued Mills paled in comparison to the elaborate designs that emerged a generation later. As Alice O'Connor recounted in her history of poverty studies, research became a subsector of the welfare state, replete with its own lexicon:

The technical jargon of recent decades has taken poverty knowledge to a level of abstraction and exclusivity that it had not known before. It is a language laced with acronyms that themselves speak of particular data sets, policies and analytic techniques (PSID, NLSY, TRIM, FAP, PBJI, EITC, and, albeit without a detectable sense of irony, Five Year Plans and a model known as the KGB). It also speaks of a self-contained system of reasoning that is largely devoid of political or historical context.[46]

The influence of abstracted empiricism in social policy was sustained by the interaction of elite university social science departments that prepared researchers and liberal policy institutes, which in turn provided the setting for the application of their analyses. Annual conferences held by professional organizations such as the Association for a Public Policy Analysis and Management featured young researchers displaying their virtuosity in command of mathematics and logic.

For all its scientific elegance, abstracted empiricism in social policy would founder on the shoals of its own formulas. That the work of abstracted empiricists was characterized as apolitical was something of a conceit since it was predicated on the existence and incremental expansion of the welfare state; hence its political assumptions were decidedly liberal. Beyond an implicit liberalism, policy research was obtuse, virtually indecipherable to officials who were making and interpreting public policy. One of the great ironies of the conservative triumph in social policy is that it was largely executed by simple descriptive statistics seasoned with a good dose of traditional social values. Liberal policy research typified what Kuhn had described as "normal puzzle-solving activity," work that was designed to fine-tune a welfare state that was on auto-pilot.[47] Within this context, the capacity to conceive of bold alternatives to existing social programs atrophied for the simple reason that the province of such speculation lay well beyond the data.

By the mid-1970s, a second generation of policy institutes emerged, notably the American Enterprise Institute and the Heritage Foundation, and moved aggressively to shape public philosophy so that it was more congruent with conservative values. The elections of Ronald Reagan and George H. W. Bush did much to further the influence of these organizations, and the works of scholars from these policy institutes became important to the implementation and continuation of the "Reagan revolution."[48] As counterpoint, a somewhat specialized group of liberal policy institutes emerged. The Children's Defense Fund and the Center on Budget and Policy Priorities endeavored to reassert the needs of the disadvantaged in social policy.[49] Subsequently, the election of Bill Clinton to the presidency in 1992 brought to the forefront the Progressive Policy Institute, a think tank responsible for much of the policy research he used during his campaign, and later in establishing domestic policy during his presidency. Most recently, George W. Bush pushed social policy hard to the Right, promoting the restructuring of Medicare and privatization of Social Security. These were themes that had been trumpeted by the CATO Institute, a libertarian think tank, and its fortunes soared accordingly. By century's end, conservative policy institutes had not only displaced liberal think tanks in shaping social policy, but those from the far Right of the ideological continuum were increasingly influential, replacing those at the center.

In little more than two decades, conservative think tanks had maneuvered public philosophy to the Right. "Heritage and CATO have become so proficient in generating and promoting ideas that the liberal movement has had to create its own think tanks to compete," noted columnist David Broder. "With generous corporate and foundation support and thousands of grassroots contributors, Heritage boasts a staff of 185 and a budget of $28 million; CATO, 98 staff and $16 million."[50] Significantly, none of the new liberal policy institutes has anywhere near the resources of Heritage, CATO, or the American Enterprise Institute, save the staid Brookings Institution. While the liberal think tanks remained reflective with respect to social policy, responding to requests by law makers and studying program impacts, policy institutes from the Right adopted a more aggressive, entrepreneurial stance through which they promoted those options congruent with conservatism. After three decades on the defensive, liberals finally launched their own think tank in the fall of 2003, the Center for American Progress, with $10 million, under the leadership of John Podesta, former chief of staff in the Clinton White House.[51]

TRANSFORMING PUBLIC PHILOSOPHY

That public philosophy would be up for grabs toward the end of the twentieth century would go unnoticed by most Americans, even those who had become ensconced within the welfare state by virtue of positions they held within social programs, the academy, and policy institutes. Insofar as welfare liberalism, the Democratic sequel to Progressivism, had laid the foundation of the welfare state—an enormous edifice that consumed hundreds of billions of dollars, provided services and income to millions of beneficiaries, and employed thousands of professionals who labored to enhance the public good—this is not too surprising. The American welfare state was so well established that it had not only weathered the intermittent turbulence of conservative presidents, but continued to expand despite them. Spawned by philosophical pragmatism and buoyed by a burgeoning economy, welfare liberalism had become the American public philosophy, commanding domestic policy for most of the twentieth century.

Upon close scrutiny, the American welfare state might appear embarrassingly inadequate compared to its European counterpart, and American scholars would qualify U.S. social programs as the "semi-welfare state"[52] or the "reluctant welfare state,"[53] but why quibble with incremental success? No one could seriously question the accomplishments of the pragmatically designed welfare state. In protecting vulnerable Americans against the predations of poverty, illness, and ignorance, it had generated the largest middle-class ever known. Anchored to institutions that enjoyed wide popularity, such as universities, labor unions, and the liberal wing of both political parties, it had become a self-sustaining enterprise, enlisting the fealty of tens of millions of Americans. Its signal social insurance programs—Social Security, Medicare, Unemployment Compensation—were so inviolate that they became known as the "third-rail of American politics"; any elected official challenging them faced instant death. Even the less popular public assistance programs (i.e., Medicaid, Food Stamps, and Supplemental Security Income) cultivated strong vested interests—healthcare providers, agriculture and food distributors, and the disabled, respectively—which defended them through lobbying on Capitol Hill. Compared to its European counterparts, the American welfare state might have appeared haphazard and laggardly, but it had become an enduring feature of the national culture nonetheless.

The unprecedented prosperity attributed to welfare liberalism was not universally acclaimed, however. By the late 1970s, conservatives were voicing reservations about the apparent infinite expansion of federal social programs. The conservative critique of the welfare state was multifaceted: social entitlement programs consumed half of the federal budget, crowding out discretionary funding for defense, research, education, transportation, and space exploration, among other vital governmental functions. Governmental obligations to beneficiaries were of such a magnitude that they diverted capital away from the private sector, impeding economic growth. Social benefits subverted individual initiative and self-sufficiency, fostering long-term dependency instead. At worst, social programs actually inflicted damage, as evident in rising rates of teen pregnancy, broken homes, and juvenile delinquency often among the very beneficiaries of social programs.

At the heart of the critique was an indictment of the professionals who had perpetrated a calamity masquerading as public policy, conservatives contended. The professionalization of the civil service under the guise of altruism served to elevate a "new class" of do-gooders: "the vast educational system, the therapeutic "helping" complex, sizeable portions of government bureaucracy," observed sociologists Brigitte and Peter Berger.

> What these all have in common is that bodies of symbolic knowledge (as distinct from the knowledge of the physical scientist or the marketing expert) are to be applied to indoctrinate ("educate"), inspire ("help"), and plan for other people. This group, certainly numbered in the millions in America today, fulfills the category of "class" in a number of specifics: It has a particular relation to the economic system (one important aspect of this relation is that a large portion of this group is either on the public payroll or is publicly

subsidized), has particular collective interests (the most important being
the maintenance and, if possible, expansion of the welfare state), and also
has a particular subculture that is more than a direct expression of its vested
interests.[54]

Professionals, of course, are operatives of social programs that employ them, and,
as such they tend to reflect the received wisdom. "Big Government is massively involved in education, social welfare, defense, and environmental protection, [so] it
is always possible that those authorities who make up the state will act more to
advance their own preferences than to serve others held by fellow citizens," observed David Ricci. As a result, policy decisions "often reflect the needs of government agencies rather than the society at large."[55]

Despite a comprehensive critique of social policy, the Right faced a daunting
task: as a testament to the pragmatist faith that every social problem warranted
analysis, a dutifully crafted program, staffed by properly certified professionals,
and subsidized at public expense, the welfare state was so well incorporated into
the national culture that it resisted radical downsizing. Chafing at the perceived
cultural excesses of the anti-war/student movement, *neo*conservatives questioned
the relaxation of social norms; and in response to the War on Poverty, they challenged the rapid expansion of unconditional, open-ended entitlements for the
poor. Initial forays into social programs during the first term of the Reagan presidency, however, proved unsuccessful, despite David Stockman's creative bookkeeping. Having failed to reverse the continued escalation of public expenditures
for social programs, conservatives later readjusted their sights and began to contrive organizational and programmatic alternatives to the welfare state. The key to
the conservative triumph in social policy was strategy, identifying those instances
where welfare liberalism was vulnerable, trumpeting the failures of established
social programs, and boldly proposing alternatives. In the mold of classic pragmatism, the Right began to identify problems with respect to social policy, broadcast doubts about existing programs, and propose alternatives, reprising the formula that Progressives had used with such success decades earlier. Bringing the
conservative critique of the welfare state to scale, however, presented a major lo-
gistical problem.

The Right soon discovered that the conventional means through which the intelligentsia debated social issues, the university, was closed off to them, having
largely become the employer of liberals and leftists. Blocked from participation in
mainstream intellectual institutions—social science departments of elite universities and liberal policy institutes—conservatives opted for a novel solution to the
problem. "If you wish to make a productive investment in the intellectual and
educational worlds," Irving Kristol admonished corporate executives, "you find
competent intellectuals and scholars—'dissident' members, as it were, of the 'new
class'—to offer guidance."[56] In short order, a parallel network of think tanks,

nonprofit organizations dedicated to educating the public about conservative designs in social affairs, was envisioned. Corporate executives and conservative foundations channeled tens of millions of dollars to refurbish the American Enterprise Institute (AEI) and establish the Heritage Foundation. By the early 1980s, the institutional scions of liberalism—the Brookings Institution and the Urban Institute—found their positions on social policy challenged by a cabal of conservative policy institutes—AEI, Heritage, the Hoover Institution, the Manhattan Institute, the Hudson Institute, and the CATO Institute. From the mid-1970s through the mid-1980s, conservative think tanks would claim a breathtaking accomplishment: Within two decades—a sliver of time by institutional standards—they had transformed American public philosophy. This represented an ideological reversal, both in direction and magnitude, according to Terry Eagleton: "Traditionally, it had been the political left which thought in universal terms, and the conservative right which preferred to be modestly piecemeal. Now, these roles have been reversed with a vengeance."[57]

Liberal intellectuals missed the flanking maneuver altogether. After all, they had essentially attained command of the means of social administration. The expansion of governmental social programs had spawned a veritable industry in program evaluation. Stung by the abuses of the executive branch during Watergate and the Vietnam War, Congress established additional oversight agencies to review federal programs.[58] As a result, multiple units within the executive and legislative branches of government had the evaluation of programs as their primary mission, not unlike the empiricists who populated university social science departments and liberal think tanks. At the federal level, the most important of these included the Government Accountability Office (GAO), the Office of Management and Budget (OMB), the Congressional Budget Office (CBO), and the Congressional Research Service (CRS). When the need for program evaluation outstripped agency capacity, state and federal government contracted with outside organizations. As a result, many universities, such as the University of Wisconsin's Institute for Research on Poverty, provided essential research services to government. More recently, private consulting firms such as the Manpower Demonstration Research Corporation, Abt Associates, Maximus, and Mathematica have entered the field, often hiring former government officials and capitalizing on their connections in order to secure research contracts.

Smug in their assumption of continued elaboration of the welfare state, many human service providers, program administrators, and policy analysts busied themselves with incremental adjustments in the dominant paradigm, the liberally inspired social programs. To some extent, liberal myopia about the conservative insurgency could be attributed to the size of Big Government; with 24,000 legislative staff members needed to keep tabs on the proliferation of social programs, the prospect that the welfare state project would be subverted was unimaginable.[59] Ditto for liberal intellectuals inhabiting policy institutes where work fo-

cused on esoteric evaluations of social programs. Scholars in the liberal think
tanks often originated from, or had dual appointments with, prestigious universities, and their analyses were uniformly state-of-the-art. Yet, the mountains of data
that liberal analysts generated were oddly devoid of life. Conforming to epistemological standards, they had been cleansed of any value orientation; despite being
concerned with social problems, they studiously avoided moral pronouncements.
The social sciences had developed a fetish about the neutral fact, as C. Wright
Mills characterized it: "The details are piled up with insufficient attention to
form; indeed, often there is no form except that provided by typesetters and
bookbinders." In his criticism of disembodied social science, Mills anticipated
how conservatives would address this problem by putting data toward ideological
ends. Social science "is not based on any new conception of the nature of society
or of man or upon any particular facts about them."[60] To be sure, increasingly sophisticated methodologies and statistical techniques were useful for purposes of
securing tenure and marking one's territory in relation to researchers at other
prestigious universities; whether this served any greater public purpose was another question. "Unfortunately, the technical jargon that scholars tend to use, and
the fact that they often publish their findings in out-of-the-way journals, make
many of their discoveries inaccessible to most policymakers."[61] Communicating
with each other, liberal researchers lost touch with the larger, public purpose of
their work. Meanwhile, the Reagan administration elected to avoid being encum-
bered by social science: "Reagan officials turned instead to a privately funded network of conservative think tanks that specialized in producing clear, uncompli-
cated, overtly ideological policy advice," noted Alice O'Connor.[62]

The stance of liberal researchers reflected their conceit about social policy. Liberals assumed that since the major structural impediments had been scaled, the
ideological problems overcome, and connections to allied institutions established,
the only thing that remained of the welfare state project was extending benefits to
larger segments of the population. Thus, the Progressive/liberal meritocracy that
administered the welfare state was confident about its continued expansion following the northern European model. Blithely unconcerned about the ideological
maelstrom swirling around them, welfare liberals failed to notice a wolf at their
door.

In seeking to reverse liberal momentum in social affairs, conservatives were
clear about their ambitions. Shortly after the inauguration of Ronald Reagan,
AEI's then-president William Baroody, Jr., summarized the Institute's objective:

The public philosophy that has guided American policy for decades is un-
dergoing change. For more than four decades, the philosophy of Franklin
Delano Roosevelt's New Deal prevailed, in essence calling upon government
to do whatever individual men and women could not do for themselves.
Today we see growing signs of a new public philosophy, one that still seeks to

meet fundamental human needs, but to meet them through a better balance between the public and private sectors of society. The American Enterprise Institute has been at the forefront of this change. Many of today's policy initiatives are building on intellectual foundations partly laid down by the Institute.[63]

By the time the 1980 presidential campaign was heating up, AEI had 30 scholars and fellows in residence (earning $30,000 to $50,000 per year), 77 adjunct scholars, and 250 professors associated with the Institute nationwide. AEI's senior staff and board members represented a *Who's Who* of the nation's conservative and political elite.

In domestic affairs, AEI focused its considerable resources and talent on two projects in its mission of reforming the welfare state. The "mediating structures project" enlisted the services of sociologist Peter Berger and theologian Richard John Neuhaus. In the major publication of the project, *To Empower People*, Berger and Neuhaus stated that the fundamental problems of our times was the growth of megastructures, such as big government, big business, big labor, and professional bureaucracies, and a corresponding decline in the importance of individuals. The route to empowerment of people, then, was to revitalize "mediating structures": the neighborhood, family, church, and voluntary association.[64] *To Empower People* was a readable and lucid work that served AEI well. The apparent impartiality of the mediating structures project, however was little more than veneer—Peter Berger's hostility toward liberals would surface in later works.[65] The project's implicit critique of government programs was clearly evident in a modest study of the Meals on Wheels program by AEI's Michael Balzano. In *Federalizing Meals on Wheels*, Balzano argued that the Older Americans Act diminished the voluntary impulses of church and community groups (mediating structures) by subsidizing nutrition programs for the elderly. "In most cases, common sense and the desire to help one's neighbor are all that are necessary," Balzano concluded. "One does not need a masters degree in social work or gerontology to dish out chow at a nutrition center."[66]

Following the mediating structures project, the project on democratic capitalism endeavored to elevate the role of the corporation in public life. This necessitated a bit of theoretical hanky-panky since the mediating structures project had portrayed big business as a megastructure and, therefore, inimical to the vitality of mediating structures. The problem was disposed of deftly by Michael Novak, a theologian and director of the project. In *Toward a Theology of the Corporation*, Novak used no more than a footnote to transfer big business from its designation as megastructure to that of a mediating structure, leaving big government and its allies—big labor and professional associations—as an institution of cultural and economic oppression against a corporate sector that had been the genius behind the American experience.[67] Thus, in what is arguably the most consequential

footnote in contemporary social policy, Novak manipulated the mediating structures project so that it indicted specifically the primary institutions of American
liberalism: government, labor, and the professions, in the process associating
business with the mediating structures that were essential to a robust society.

Under the direction of Novak, the project on democratic capitalism intended
to transform public philosophy by portraying the corporation as a promoter of
cultural enlightenment, as opposed to a perpetrator of vulgar capitalism. "The social instrument invented by democratic capitalism to achieve social goals is the
private corporation," he proselytized. "The corporation . . . is not merely an
economic institution. It is also a moral and a political institution. It depends on
and generates certain moral-cultural virtues; it depends upon and generates new
political forms . . . Beyond its economic effects, the corporation changes the
ethos and the cultural forms of society."[68] At the same time, Novak took careful
aim at the public sector: "I advise intelligent, ambitious, and morally serious
young Christians and Jews to awaken to the growing dangers of statism. They will
better serve their souls and serve the Kingdom of God all around the world by
restoring liberty and power of the private sector than by working for the state."[69]

The methods of the conservative policy institutes were decidedly entrepreneurial, a marked contrast with the more reserved liberal think tanks. A student
of policy institutes, James Smith, noted the differing styles: "[Conservative think
tanks] were argumentative, more certain about their policy convictions. Their
publications were shorter, more likely to take the form of a briefing paper, and always more quickly produced and disseminated. Their reports seemed to resonate
with the press and within wider political constituencies." Meanwhile, "at Brookings and other mainstream institutions, we still thought in terms of scholarly
books, hoping and praying that a few journalists might attend our occasional
press conferences; we still conceived of an audience that was limited mostly to
Washington policymakers and university-based policy scholars."[70] The audience
of the liberal policy institutes consisted largely of the meritocracy that had managed social legislation since the New Deal, a group that the conservatives maneuvered around by crafting a populist message and dispatching it persistently
through the media. "[Conservatives] built new institutional bastions; recruited,
trained and equipped their intellectual warriors; forged new weapons as cable
television, the Internet, and other communications technologies evolved; and
threw their full resources into policy and political battles."[71]

The result was a rout. Conservatives commanded the print and electronic
media, saturating a public whose appetite for social affairs had been ignored by
liberal intellectuals who were comfortably ensconced in university ivory towers
and the citadels of policy institutes. In an ebullient moment during the Reagan
presidency, Heritage's Burton Pines acknowledged the pivotal role that think
tanks had played in the rapid evolution of conservatism in the United States. Including the Hoover Institution of Stanford in the campaign, Pines likened their

work to a crusade: "Together, Hoover, AEI and Heritage can today deploy formidable armies of the battlefield of ideas—forces which traditionalist movements previously lacked."[72] Two decades later, a military metaphor was still apropos: "AEI softens up the liberal establishment with long-range bombing, Heritage then sends in the ground troops to capture territory and convert it into a conservative fief."[73]

Indeed, it was almost two *decades* after conservatives laid the foundation to their intellectual infrastructure that liberals became aware of the Right's strategy. "Conservative think tanks outspend liberal organizations (loosely defined) by at least four to one," observed Karen Paget. On many of the most important measures backed by conservative funders, left-liberal organizations simply aren't in the game. Meanwhile, over the past ten years the conservative right has excelled in changing the rules of the game by devising big, bold initiatives that tilt the system to their advantage.[74] Reflecting mastery of the means of analysis, Paget noted that "conservative funders pay meticulous attention to the entire 'knowledge production' process. They think of it in terms of 'a conveyer belt' that stretches from academic research to marketing and mobilization, from scholars to activists." The outcome? "We've largely won the battle of ideas," boasted Kate O'Beirne, formerly of the Heritage Foundation, "We are in the implementation stage now."[75]

The conservative critique of the welfare state, elaborated and revised at AEI, Heritage, and Hoover, spread throughout the intellectual world of the ideological Right. William Schambra, formerly of AEI, cycled through the Department of Health and Human Services as a speech writer during the first Bush presidency and assumed a position with the Bradley Foundation in Milwaukee, headed by Michael Joyce. In collaboration with Joyce, Schambra redefined "citizenship" to refer to the civic activities of individuals in neighborhoods and communities, the efforts of which were often thwarted by the liberal social programs that had been justified out of the mistaken notion that the nation was one giant community. Rather than bind a group of diverse nationalities, the national community assumption that underpinned the welfare state actually robbed localities of their capacity for self-sufficiency. What was worse, Schambra and Joyce complained, the liberal's national community model was elitist, suggesting that only policy experts in Washington, D.C., had the wisdom to determine matters of domestic concern; local residents were, by implication, ignorant rubes. Community-based problem solving would be much more effective, *not* with the assistance of the federal government, but *only* if Washington got out of the way.[76]

The conservative indictment of social policy thus contained not only a powerful critique of federal programs, but also a direct appeal to local control. By characterizing the liberal control of social programs as elitist, conservative populism not only isolated "San Francisco liberals" from the mainstream, but also fueled Right-wing populism. Liberalism "was alien to the blue-collar Democratic rank and file," noted Barbara Ehrenreich. "The New Class alliance with the poor and minority groups left an obvious strategic alliance for the Republicans—with the working class."[77] What differentiated this conservative populism from earlier forms was its accompaniment by the technology that rapidly disseminated it to the hinterlands. Control of the means of analysis allowed conservatives to script an antiliberal tract on social programs at the same time it cultivated a constituency outside of Washington, D.C., which would eventually elect representatives to reverse the social damage attributed to elaboration of the welfare state. Conservative policy institutes were key to the shift in public philosophy: "The think tanks are becoming America's shadow government," observed two British observers, serving "as a general command center for the intellectual Right."[78]

Marketing ideas differentiated the conservative think tanks from their liberal competitors. Congruent with the corporate support that financed their activities, intellectuals on the Right believed in "the commercial concept of a product" whatever its composition. "I make no bones about marketing," explained AEI's Baroody. "We pay as much attention to dissemination of the product as to the content. We're probably the first major think tank to get into the electronic media. We hire ghost writers for scholars to produce op-ed articles that are sent to one hundred and one cooperating newspapers—three pieces every two weeks. And we have a press luncheon monthly."[79]

Not to be outdone, the Heritage Foundation pioneered innovative ways to spread the conservative message. One of its earliest products was *The Backgrounder*, a concise policy monograph scripted for such brevity that it could be read during the cab ride from Reagan/National Airport to Capitol Hill. Later, Heritage introduced its Center for Data Analysis (CDA), which trained journalists in use of federal data. Integrating the largest federal data sets for the first time gave Heritage unprecedented firepower in the battle of ideas. For example, CDA's analysis of Bush's 2003 Economic Growth Package, which continued the tax cuts of 2001, employed a macroeconomic model developed by a Nobel laureate and employed a dynamic scoring model, concluding that over nine years the proposal would increase gross domestic product $69 billion, generate 844,000 jobs, and add $121 billion in disposable personal income, while reducing federal tax revenues only $274 billion, "far less than the U.S. Treasury's static estimate of $638 billion."[80]

Economic modeling has allowed the Right to minimize the impact of tax cuts that had become central to its attempts to deconstruct the welfare state. Instrumental in this gambit was Grover Norquist, the president of Americans for Tax Reform, known for advocating a tax cut for every year of the second Bush presidency.[81] Norquist's ambition was to make tax cuts the vehicle for permanent conservative control of public policy, a "realignment of American politics" that "would make the Republicans the natural party of government in the same way the Democrats once were."[82] The end game of the strategy was to reduce government "down to the size where we can drown it in the bathtub," Norquist admitted.

"One of the steps for getting there is a permanent Republican government, in the sense of fifty-five Republican senators, and a thirty-vote margin in the House and a Republican President for twenty years in a row. That's when you can do to the left what the left did to us in the thirties and the forties."[83] Insofar as the policy debate in an information society had become data-driven, CDA became essential to the Right's designs on the welfare state. Bob Moffit, Heritage's then-Vice President for Domestic Policy, put it boldly, claiming that CDA made Heritage "the Vatican of numbers."

By the end of the 1990s, the conservative media strategy was paying off. Conservative think tanks eclipsed liberal policy institutes in the number of citations in major newspapers, although liberal think tanks were more frequently interviewed by the electronic media.[84] Through AEI, Hoover, and Heritage, among other think tanks of the Right, conservative intellectuals controlled the means of analysis in order to promulgate a persuasive critique of federal social programs at the same time they aggressively hustled alternatives to the public. The welfare state was hazardous for several reasons, they maintained: First, social programs were funded through revenue derived from taxes that, if they were not so diverted, could be used for further capitalization of the private sector. Through tax cuts, money could be restored to private parties, in the process denying the Treasury of essential funds for future social programs. Second, social programs invariably granted the state the right to intrude into areas that should be held private, such as the family. By limiting the authority of human service professionals and establishing tax credits that allowed individuals to bypass the welfare bureaucracy, conservative legislation contained the authority of professionals while addressing the human service needs of taxpayers. Third, social programs were administered through a meritocracy that administered an unresponsive and expensive public bureaucracy. A sure way to make the welfare state more cost-effective was through assigning its responsibilities to the private sector (i.e., privatization) or, short of that, by eliminating unnecessary red tape (i.e., deregulation); but, the best way was simply circumventing social programs altogether, allowing people to "keep their money" (i.e., tax cuts).

THE CONSERVATIVE IMPRIMATUR

In retrospect, two decades of conservative investment in ideas and technology generated legislative returns that were handsome, indeed. Liberals watched with increasing apprehension as the Right chalked up a series of victories: With the 1981 Omnibus Budget Reconciliation Act, welfare was cut significantly, a preliminary shot across the bow of the welfare state that would be amplified through the 1988 Family Support Act and the more draconian 1996 Personal Responsibility and Work Opportunity Reconciliation Act. 1989 marked the repeal of Catastrophic Health Insurance, the first repeal of a social insurance program in the history of the American welfare state. During the 1980s, Housing and Urban Development programs were savaged: not only were federal funds cut significantly, but the conceptual rationale for urban aid changed from unconditional grants to urban enterprise zones. At every opportunity, conservatives reformed social programs by converting unconditional, open-ended entitlements to discretional programs that were devolved to the states as block grants, as was done with mental health and substance abuse programs. Any liberal aspirations about social policy were dowsed with the defeat of the Health Security Act of 1993.

The grand prize in the conservative foray into social welfare was, of course, Social Security. Accordingly, intellectuals from the Right looked at the 2000 presidential election as tacit permission to privatize the ultimate social insurance program, the bedrock of the American welfare state. Unlike Reagan, who had tried a frontal assault on social insurance programs, the second Bush administration was more indirect. Noting the wide popularity of Social Security and Medicare, but knowing that both programs would crumble under the weight of retiring baby boomers without additional revenues, conservatives used tax cuts as a preemptive strike. The two massive tax cuts during the first term of George W. Bush's administration not only absorbed the Social Security surplus but left "$25 *trillion* in total unfinanced liabilities" for Social Security and Medicare.[85] The CATO Institute's Michael Tanner has projected that, according to intermediate assumptions, the payroll tax would have to rise to 18 percent to cover Social Security and 28 percent if Medicare were included; however, according to the worst-case scenario, the payroll tax could reach 40 percent to maintain both programs as currently structured.[86]

These accomplishments served to reverse welfare liberalism that had placed the welfare state front and center of domestic policy. While scholars might parse the consequences of conservative policy initiatives as temporary or partial—admonishing Cassandras that, with the exception of family welfare, all the entitlement programs remained intact—the damage was profound and extensive. "Whatever is happening to the welfare state is not the result of the particular politics of any one country," concluded Alan Wolfe.

> Across all of Europe and North America, the social democratic century has come to an end. Solidarity, social citizenship, the gift relationship, and the difference principle—all of them representing formulations of the idea that all who live in a society are obligated to insure the welfare of everyone else— are terms bandied about in academic circles, but they no longer make much of an appearance in real politics.[87]

The triumph of conservatism in social policy was due primarily to the network of think tanks and the provocative proposals they advanced. "Over the past 20 years, virtually every big Republican idea and many small ones—school choice, welfare reform, enterprise zones, Social Security privatization—have originated in think tanks, rather than on Capitol Hill," recalled a journalist. "Think tanks have sponsored some of the most important conservative books and published some of the best conservative magazines."[88] Ironically, their objective was reform; like the Progressives who preceded them, conservatives based their proposals on empirical data. In the Progressive tradition, they advocated for changes in social policy through established political institutions. Yet, the conservatism advanced late in the twentieth century was qualitatively different from the reformist strategy perfected by Progressives a century earlier; the think tanks on the Right developed an unprecedented capacity to massage data, incorporate it in alternative policy scenarios, and market these to law makers and the public. In this manner they controlled the means of analysis and used their new skill to up-end the Progressively inspired welfare state.

That conservatives would reverse liberal momentum in social policy is suffused with irony. Essentially, conservative think tanks employed pragmatism toward their own ends, accomplishing objectives completely at odds with the philosophy's adherents a century earlier. Relying on the sponsorship of corporate donors, conservatives evolved a populist antigovernment social theory that eroded political and economic support for the welfare state. For Progressives, the result was as galling as it was astonishing; not only had the Right assumed control of public philosophy, but it did so by cultivating broad public support. With the advent of the new millennium, the Progressive pragmatism originating in nineteenth century was eclipsed by a regressive pragmatism that ushered in the information age.

Paradoxically, liberal intellectuals missed the Right's maneuver altogether. Lamenting the demise of "public intellectuals" in social discourse, Russell Jacoby correctly noted the drift of liberal intellectuals to the academy: "The academization of a left-wing intelligentsia was not simply imposed, it was desired. For the leftists, appointment to state or academic bureaucracies constituted small steps on the path to power—or so they fantasized. Careerism and revolution converged."[89] A captive of the very intellectual community that he faulted, Jacoby failed to note the revolution in public philosophy that had sped past. To be sure, Jacoby chronicled the sniping of individual conservative intellectuals as they scored points for the more preposterous postmodern claims of the Left; but revolutions are not accomplished by snipers. Endeavoring more than the random assault, the Right was organizing its intelligence through think tanks that were not only producing work of comparable, if not superior, quality to the university-based Left, but also systematically marketing its ideas to receptive law makers and a discriminating public, audiences that the Left often disparaged.

In examining the relationship between "private interest and public action," Albert O. Hirschman also elided the focal role of policy institutes. According to Hirschman, public endorsement of governmental institutions is a fundamental problem for industrialized capitalist societies, which emphasize individual competitiveness while generating social and economic dislocations that require collective action. "Western societies," Hirschman observes, "appear to be condemned to long periods of privatization during which they live through an impoverished 'atrophy of public meanings,' followed by spasmodic outbursts of 'publicness' that are hardly likely to be constructive."[90] Disenchantment with governmental solutions to social problems makes public welfare programs vulnerable to their critics, leading to reductions in staff and fiscal support, often followed by an escalation in the social problem for which the social program was initially designed. Thus, the episodic nature of public support for programs designed to alleviate social problems further impedes effective implementation. Once again, the sense of events is correct, yet the catalyst is omitted; Hirschman paints with historical sweep, failing to recognize that the events had been choreographed by specific institutions—in this case, conservative policy institutes.

Preoccupied with quintessentially liberal institutions, the university and the welfare state, progressive intellectuals became victims of their own conceit. Recognizing that these were controlled by the Left, the Right went about constructing a parallel infrastructure. "It is amazing both how organized conservatives have been and how focused on the importance of ideas," noted British observers. "Conservatives laboriously built a counterestablishment of think tanks, pressure groups and media that was initially intended to counterbalance the liberal establishment but has now turned into an establishment in its own right—and one with a much harder edge than its rival."[91] By the time liberal intellectuals attempted to counter the Right's control of public policy by establishing the Center for American Progress, it was too late; conservatives were already engineering social policy toward their ends.

MARGINALIZATION

It will come as no surprise to anyone who has studied public affairs that the social policy process is not representative. Groups in the upper levels of the social stratification populate the institutions through which policy is made; those at the lowest registers bear the burden of their decisions. The primary players in the social policy game are executives and professionals. The wealthy usually opt out, leaving their social obligations in the hands of executives who manage their foundations. As one goes down the social stratification, the remaining groups have less and less influence on public policy. The issues of groups at the center of the stratification are advanced by vested interests; generally, vested interests representing business outflank those of labor. The interests of the working/welfare poor and the underclass are left in the hands of maverick professionals who work through advocacy organizations, although occasional unrest on the part of working/welfare poor can result in important concessions. Thus, the lack of influence on the part of lower socioeconomic groups in the social policy process is virtually built into governmental decision-making. Political scientists have coined the term "nondecision-making" to describe this phenomenon—the capacity to keep the interests of some groups off the decision-making agenda.[92] Nondecision-making has a long history in the United States; generations of African Americans and women were legally excluded from decision making prior to emancipation and suffrage. Since formal exclusion of such groups has been ruled unconstitutional, a more apropos term denoting the lack of influence experienced by certain groups would be "marginalization." Today, large groups remain excluded from decision-making, most importantly immigrants and children. The interaction of social stratification and stages of the policy process are depicted in Figure 3-2.

Attempts to increase the influence of disadvantaged groups in decision-making have been problematic at best. A classic illustration of an effort to broaden democratization occurred during the War on Poverty when poor people were to be guaranteed "maximum feasible participation" in the Community Action Program (CAP). Even though this was interpreted to mean that a third of the members of CAP boards of directors must be poor people—a seemingly reasonable expectation—the militancy of poor people in some cities led to utter chaos in many CAPs. As a result of pressure from mayors and other officials, this requirement was rescinded in order to make CAPs more compliant.[93] Since then, the representation of lower socioeconomic groups in decision-making has been limited, for all practical purposes, to an advisory capacity.

Exclusion from the policy process is also reflected in the inferior position many lower strata groups experience with respect to social programs, reinforcing *networks of negligence*. Thus, if marginalization connotes lack of influence in the construction of social programs, it often means a humiliating experience vis-a-vis obtaining benefits. "Workers on the front lines of the welfare state find themselves in a corrupted world of service," wrote Michael Lipsky in his award-winning *Street Level Bureaucracy*. According to Lipsky, "Workers find that the best way to keep demand within manageable proportions is to deliver a consistently inaccessible or inferior product."[94] In response to the irrelevance often characteristic of governmental welfare policies, personnel in public welfare offices consequently deny benefits to people who are eligible for them, a process Lipsky labeled "bureaucratic disentitlement."[95] It should come as no surprise, then, that public welfare programs mandated by governmental policy have acquired an undesirable reputation within the professional community. The executive director of the California chapter of social workers candidly stated that "public social services are being abandoned by M.S.W. social workers. It seems to be employment of last resort."[96] Another veteran observer was even more graphic: "To work in a public agency today is to work in a bureaucratic hell."[97] Within the context of public welfare, it is not surprising to find that burnout has become pervasive among welfare professionals.

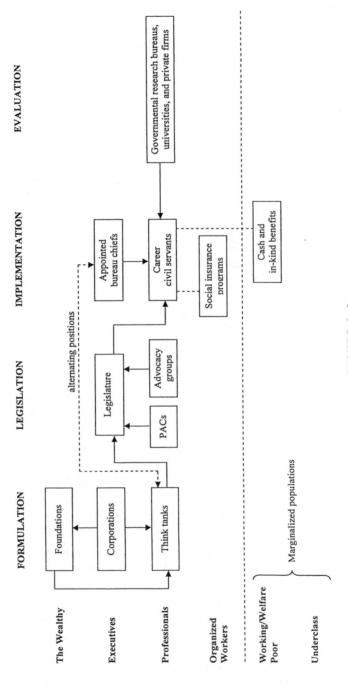

FIGURE 3-2.
Stratification and the Public Policy Process

Not all welfare programs are perceived in such a negative light, of course. Generally, programs that benefit persons solidly in the working class fare better. The social insurance programs, such as Social Security, Unemployment Compensation, and Medicare, are usually regarded more highly by beneficiaries. Of course, the insurance programs require people to first pay into the program in order to claim benefits later, so they are designed to be different from the means-tested programs intended for the poor. Precisely because the social insurances enjoy such popular support and consume such a large volume of revenues, the Right has begun to target them for reform.

Making the social policy process more representative is a primary concern of liberal advocates of the marginalized. Since the Civil Rights movement, African Americans and the poor have recognized the power of the ballot, and voter registration has become an important strategy for advancing the influence of these groups. The registration of Hispanic Americans in the Southwest has been the mission of the Southwest Voter Research Institute, founded by the late Willie Velasquez. Under the visionary leadership of Velasquez, Latino voter registration grew steadily, reflected in an increase in the number of elected officials who are Chicano. Fifteen years of voter registration campaigning by the institute contributed to a doubling of the number of Hispanic elected officials in the Southwest.[98] The most visible example of the political empowerment of people usually excluded from the decision-making process was Jesse Jackson's 1988 campaign to be the presidential nominee of the Democratic Party. Expanding on the grassroots political base built during his 1984 bid for the nomination, Jackson's 1988 Rainbow Coalition demonstrated the support he commanded from a wide spectrum of disenfranchised Americans. Thus, mobilization of the working and welfare poor, as Velasquez and Jackson have shown, can make the policy process more representative.

Yet, pandemic voter apathy makes the prospect of re-engaging marginalized Americans in the political process an uphill struggle. In national elections, only about half of American voters exercise the franchise, the lowest turnout among industrialized nations. A survey conducted by the Pew Research Center for the People and the Press revealed that substantial majorities of respondents agreed with such statements as "government is inefficient and wasteful," "politicians lose touch pretty quickly," and "government controls too much of daily life."[99] Apathy, however, is less evident among the affluent. "The privileged participate more than others and are increasingly well organized to press their demands on government," concluded a task force of the American Political Science Association. "Public officials, in turn, are much more responsive to the privileged than to average citizens and the least affluent."[100] Within the voting population, more affluent voters are more than twice as likely to exercise their franchise compared to those who are poor: In 1996, 65.7 percent of voters with incomes above $50,000 voted in the presidential election versus only 28.6 percent of those with incomes less than

$10,000.[101] Some 30 million prospective voters are inactive, a group made up disproportionately of minorities and the poor.[102] Increasing the involvement of apathetic voters would not only make inroads against *marginalization,* but would also make public social programs more responsive to their circumstances.

The virtue of an open culture is that it allows groups the opportunity to organize around mutual concerns and bring them to bear on the policy process; the reality of democratic capitalism is that the political economy erects substantial barriers to full participation. Marginalization of so many Americans reflects a pattern of dominance within the social policy process that favors the upper strata over the lower, a contortion of the democratic ideal that has enormous ramifications for social policy. Nonetheless, it is important to recognize that for much of the twentieth century, liberals who sought to include the marginalized in public life not only dominated public policy, but in the process erected one of the prevailing institutions of the modern era, the American welfare state. It is just as striking to acknowledge their plummeting fortunes, especially as those of the Right have risen. "In theory, liberals have more than enough brain and brawn to match conservative America," observed writers of *The Economist.* "The great liberal universities and foundations have infinitely more resources than the American Enterprise Institute and its allies. But the conservatives have always been more dogged. The Ford Foundation is as liberal as Heritage is conservative, but there is no doubt which is more ruthless in its cause."[103]

This is not to suggest that the Right is monolithic. Conservatives fracture along basic fault lines—Wall Street investors favoring support from the Federal Reserve Bank; libertarians advocating minimal government; traditionalists promoting prayer in school, restrictions on reproductive freedom, and prohibitions of same-sex marriage—and these can be as divisive as the internal squabbling that has characterized liberal Democrats. By way of illustration, during the 1980s, conservative investors established the Club for Growth, advocating massive tax cuts in order to rebate money to taxpayers while cutting funding for social programs. When some Republican members of Congress strayed from the Club's party line, it promised to fund opponents to run against them in primary elections, infuriating Karl Rove, the chief strategist for George W. Bush.[104] Yet, the Right has maintained a relatively coherent vision of domestic policy at the same time it has insisted on party discipline within Congress.

What has often been unstated has been disarray among those at the other end of the ideological continuum. "The New Right took far better care of its intellectuals than the left or liberals ever had: recruiting them in college, financing campus newspapers for them, grooming them in conferences and special retreats, housing them (between other forms of employment) in its rich, Washington-centered bureaucracy," noted Barbara Ehrenreich at the end of the Reagan presidency. "It is possible for a conservative intellectual to enjoy the life-long munificence of the corporate 'milch-cow' so successfully harnessed by the New Right,

from his youth as a right wing campus activist to his declining years in a gra-
ciously appointed right-wing think tank."[105] Essentially, the Right contrived
cradle-to-grave care for its intellectuals.

> A conservative thinker can now spend his or her entire life in the move-
> ment's warm embrace, starting as a student working on a campus newspaper
> funded by one of the foundations, becoming a young intern at Heritage and
> ending up as a senior fellow at AEI, with diversions to the University of
> Chicago, a regional think tank and a spell in a Republican administration on
> the way.[106]

While the aptitude of conservatives to nurture their offspring has been notewor-
thy, it does not explain the implosion of welfare liberalism.

Given its control of American higher education and its command of the welfare state, the wonder is that the liberal Left was so ineffectual when the engineers
of the conservative juggernaut wrested the levers of public policy from them. Instead of putting up a noisy and effective counterattack, the response was a muf-
fled silence. One factor in welfare liberalism's demise was its overinvestment in esoteric methods of policy analysis, a style of inquiry that may have suited the
university well but was incapable of developing options for social policy that were
superior to those advanced by the Right. The other factor has been given less consideration, except for conservative pundits who have had a field day lampooning
it: Many liberal intellectuals had begun an infatuation with postmodern philosophy that was not only outright critical of the Western intellectual tradition, but
skeptical of the welfare state itself. Rather than challenge the Right using the quite
ample resources they had inherited since the Progressive era, the liberal Left
walked away from the confrontation. They had defected from the welfare state
and joined the Liberati.

4

THE LIBERATI

Your grace, come back, Senor Don Quixote, I swear to God you're charging sheep! Come back, by the wretched father who sired me! What madness is this? Look and see that there are no giants or knights, no cats or armor or shields either parted or whole, no blue vairs or bedeviled ones, either. Poor sinner that I am in the sight of God, what are you doing?

SANCHO PANZO

Routed by the Right, liberals scrambled for purchase on a continually eroding policy terrain. Presuming a continuation of the welfare state, liberals reflexively defended existing social program arrangements. But, while the meritocracy continued to manage the welfare state as if it were on autopilot, Leftist intellectuals in the academy abandoned the field, running pell-mell after postmodernism. A philosophical tangent of Romanticism, postmodernism was "the contemporary movement of thought which rejects totalities, universal values, grand historical narratives, solid foundations to human existence and the possibility of objective knowledge," wrote Terry Eagleton. "Postmodernism is skeptical of truth, unity and progress, opposes what it sees as elitism in culture, tends towards cultural relativism, and celebrates pluralism, discontinuity and heterogeneity."[1] A product of an enchantment with French philosophy, postmodernism quickly enlisted American professors of the humanities who might otherwise have sustained the Progressive project. This, combined with the complacency of professionals staffing the welfare state, split liberalism right down the middle; subsequently, the meritocracy and the university diverged on separate, uncoordinated vectors. Decades earlier, Progressive pragmatism had integrated knowledge and application, but this convergence disintegrated in the final decades of the twentieth century. While the meritocracy nudged the welfare state forward according to precepts established during the industrial age, academics entertained themselves with obscure and exotic explorations of social reality. In a development that would baffle many liberal intellectuals, postmodernists actually turned against the university, subverting a role that liberalism had so assiduously crafted early in the modern era as the engine of knowledge and social advancement. "The traditional core values underlying the academic mission are themselves under unprecedented assault from postmodernists and others whose epistemological and moral subjectivism now permeates entire disciplines," concluded a former professor and current board member of two prominent universities.[2] As a result of the break-up of the Progressive consensus on social policy, the Right would encounter a divided field in advancing its designs on public policy; by the end of the century, conservatism would dominate American public philosophy.

The university was a desirable locus for Leftist intellectuals for several reasons: Unlike the social movements that had to strive for public recognition, American higher education was an established institution, one highly regarded by the public; unlike social movements where organizers strove for converts, universities introduced large numbers of fresh, eager faces with each matriculating class, automatically generating a new cadre of prospective recruits; unlike social movements where the avatars of social justice bounced from organizing job to organizing job in a seemingly endless struggle to mobilize the masses, the academy offered permanent employment once tenure was achieved; unlike traditional employment where ridicule of the status quo might lead to dismissal, the tradition of academic freedom in higher education not only permitted but encouraged criticism of established institutional practices. Subsequently, Leftist academics settled contentedly into higher education, scripting the scholarly articles necessary for the security of tenure and lifetime employment. Reviewing the Left's infusion into higher education, Russell Jacoby concluded with subtle understatement, "radical intellectuals were not inherent opponents of institutional power, and when the possibility emerged to enter, perhaps to utilize, these institutions, they did so."[3] With ample intelligence and a surfeit of time, the "tenured radicals" turned their backs on the more immediate questions of public affairs that had animated earlier debates about social policy and began skirmishing over arcane criticism of the Western canon through articles in refereed journals. In the latter decades of the twentieth century, American academics were avoiding matters of public import and becoming preoccupied with intradisciplinary trivia. Battened in the university, tenured Leftists indulged in debating the nuances of the latest philosophical fashions, all derivative of postmodernism.

FLIRTING WITH PHILOSOPHY

At issue in the American infatuation with postmodernism was a philosophical dispute that pit Europe against the United States. Between the Civil War and World War II, American philosophers had crafted pragmatism to evolve the welfare state as a means to modulate the excesses of industrialization. The legislative infrastructure that emerged also served to update the legal basis of government, the Constitution, which was the product of an agrarian society. The meritocracy that oversaw the welfare bureaucracy and the intellectuals who populated universities and policy institutes organized the best intelligence available to address pressing social problems. Certainly, American pragmatism had its detractors—adherents of Freud preferred a psychodynamic model of behavior, whereas proponents of Marx advanced class conflict as a vehicle for economic development—yet, these formulations were discredited by cognitive psychologists who required experimental explanations of behavior and economists who developed multivariable models of the economy, both instances illustrating pragmatism's intellectual power. In the expansion of the welfare state, there remained obvious concerns, such as poverty and health care; but few doubted that a judicious application of pragmatism could subdue these much as it had retirement security.

Pragmatism's faith in the beneficial application of organized intelligence was challenged by postmodernism's criticism that this was an assumption at best naive and at worse malevolent. Significantly, the postmodern critique of pragmatism struck at the vulnerable underbelly of American philosophy—its provincialism. By European standards, American philosophy was mediocre, so intellectually unchallenging as to border on the anti-intellectual. Pragmatism played well among the American masses, justifying almost anything that received broad public support, but it was a philosophy of Babbits. As such, the vast majority of Americans may have reveled in their prosperity, yet they were unable to comprehend the philosophical precepts upon which it was based, let alone its flaws. For American intellectuals insecure about their status vis-à-vis their European counterparts, Freudianism and Marxism represented an escape from the bland thinking that furthered the status quo. The product of conflating the primary themes of these European thinkers was bourgeois repression, a superficial celebration of the good life while denying the more sinister forces lurking beneath. Discontent with mass consumption, the organization man, and jingoism, American intellectuals sought more profound explanations for a moribund culture. Thus, it is not surprising that, when French philosophers of the 1960s—Jacques Lacan, Jacques Derrida, Michel Foucault—developed a critical theory of contemporary society that focused on disassembling it, American intellectuals were receptive.[4]

Postmodernism merged the Marxian notion that history is the product of conflict among divergent strata with the Freudian presumption that much of behavior, individual as well as collective, is subconscious. The integration of these posed a powerful critique of the status quo as well as the welfare state as it had evolved in the United States. Instead of being the institutional manifestation of collective compassion, social programs were the product of an elite that used the welfare state to manage the oppressed, the process necessitating an intentionally obfuscating language of intervention that authorized professional control of the disorganized poor while reassuring an apprehensive public. Rather than being the means for alleviating human suffering, the professions were implicated in its emergence and directly invested in its continuation. Early European iterations of postmodernism, structuralism and post-structuralism had no direct application to social problems; however, they resonated with intellectuals who inhabited American higher education where it soon flourished.

Rejecting the pragmatic use of empirically based data, postmodernism based its formulations on "Theory." In culture studies that emerged under various sects of postmodernism, theory provided the method for detailed dissection of texts which, once parsed in sufficient detail, revealed the subliminal mechanics by which the power of corporate and governmental elites was exercised. Postmodern critiques, thus, attained a notoriety for their complex hermeneutics, exposing the subtle evidence of influence by representatives of capital, the patriarchy, and the media. For postmodernists, society showed patterns of power relations that were of considerable nuance, but also so extensive that they were evident throughout the Western canon. Domestically, the professions were the handmaidens that did the bidding of a hegemonic plutocracy. Accordingly, empiricism was just another ideology, a sophisticated methodology that the professions used to muffle the authentic voice of the oppressed. Internationally, the network of power was sustained by the electronic media, which broadcast Western values worldwide, converting Third World economies into neocolonial regimes.

Launched in France, the postmodern trajectory accelerated in the United States to become a global intellectual movement. Compared to the empirical methods of science and the comparative methods of the humanities, postmodernism was presented as bold and exciting. Even if its methods tended to be arcane, its refutation of Truth gave postmodernism an irreverence to established institutions and social conformity that was attractive to young, aspiring intellectuals. Eschewing established methods of inquiry, postmodernism created its own, in the process abbreviating the length of academic apprenticeship. Postmodernism characterized the Western canon as an imperial project that obliterated countervailing interpretations of reality held by oppressed groups. Only by rejecting colonialism and its methods could a genuine portrait of subjected peoples emerge. "In the long run, and on a wider stage," reflected David Lodge, "Theory won, inasmuch as it established itself by the early Nineties as a new orthodoxy in university humanities departments around the world, existing alongside the traditional practices of empirical historical scholarship and textual editing in a kind of uneasy détente, but definitely the dominant party."[5]

During the 1990s, conservatives had a field day with postmodernism. "Every special interest—women's studies, black studies, gay studies, and the like—and every modish interpretive gambit—deconstruction, post-structuralism, new historicism, and other postmodernist varieties," lamented Roger Kimball, "has found a welcome roost in the academy, while the traditional curriculum and modes of intellectual inquiry are excoriated as sexist, racist, or just plain reactionary."[6] Gradually, the postmodern denigration of truth, skepticism of history, and disregard for standards migrated from the humanities to the professions, and liberal academics voiced alarm. In his best-selling novel, Stephen Carter characterized his law students at a prestigious American university:

> I return to my dreary classroom, populated, it often seems, by undereducated but deeply committed Phi Beta Kappa ideologues—leftists who believe in class warfare but have never opened *Das Kapital* and certainly have never perused Werner Sombart, hard-line capitalists who accept the inerrancy of the invisible hand but have never studied Adam Smith, third-generation feminists who know that sex roles are a trap but have never read Betty Friedan, social Darwinists who propose leaving the poor to sink or swim but have never heard of Herbert Spencer or William Sumners's essay on *The Challenge of Facts*, black separatists who mutter bleakly about institutional racism but are unaware of the work of Carmichael or Hamilton, who invented the term—all of them our students, all of them hopelessly young and hopelessly smart, and thus hopelessly sure they alone are right . . . [7]

In *The Human Stain*, Philip Roth made the same point. "In my parents' day and well into yours and mine, it used to be the person who fell short," a small town African American school teacher tells Professor Zuckerman. "Now it's the discipline. Reading the classics is too difficult, therefore it's the classics that are to blame. Today the student asserts his incapacity as a privilege. I can't learn it, so there is something wrong with it. And there is something wrong with the bad teacher who wants to teach it. There are no more criteria, Mr. Zuckerman, only opinions."[8]

Postmodernism evolved as a reaction to the grand and increasingly unsatisfactory explanations of the human condition that had dominated nineteenth- and twentieth-century philosophy: "the Enlightenment's ideal of a rationally ordered society, and the Romantic notion of the Promethean self-transformation of man."[9] Reality, as postmodernists saw and experienced it, was typified by rampant commercialism, corrupt politics, and superficial culture that was transformed at warp speed by turbo-capitalism. The result was a transient reality, increasingly global in scope, that defied the possibility of any coherent understanding. Rejecting unitary philosophy, postmodern philosophers contended that "there [wa]s no final narrative to which everything [wa]s reducible, but a variety of perspectives on the world, none of which can be privileged."[10] Conventional means for understanding reality were inherited from an industrial context that was rapidly dissipating; indeed, one philosopher contended that postmodernism was "a post-cultural condition."[11] "The postmodern condition," noted Steven Connor,

> manifests itself in the multiplication of centres of power and activity and the dissolution of every kind of totalizing narrative which claims to govern the whole complex field of social activity and representation. The waning of the cultural authority of the West and its political and intellectual traditions, along with the opening up of the world political scene to cultural and ethnic differences, is another symptom of the modulation of hierarchy into heterarchy, or differences organized into a unified pattern of domination and subordination, as opposed to differences existing alongside each other but without any principle of commonality of order.[12]

The target of the postmodern critic was an industrial society that, regardless of its achievements, was instantly suspect and profoundly unsatisfactory. The critique of modernism was concisely summarized by Bruno Latour in, suitably, nonlinear form:

the modern world
secularization
rationalization
anonymity
disenchantment
mercantilism
optimization
dehumanization
mechanization
westernization
capitalism
industrialization
postindustrialization
technicalization
intellectualization
sterilization
objectivization
Americanization
scientization
consumer society
one-dimensional society
soulless society
modern madness
modern times
progress.[13]

It would be difficult to image a more graphic description of modern society and the philosophical paradigm that propelled it—pragmatism.

The Western canon, alleged postmodernists, maintained educated elites in institutions of power all at the expense of indigenous populations. The hegemony of academicians was predicated on an empirical understanding of Truth, evident not only in the esoteric journals that chronicled their scholarship, but in the very offices, classrooms, and laboratories through which they did their work. The postmodern critique held that Enlightenment philosophy and its sequel, the social sciences, generated theory and methods that were oppressive of the populations that were the subject of academic scrutiny. Accordingly, the way to liberation was the abandonment of the entire repertoire of the social sciences: knowledge became multifaceted; theory was deconstructed; methods were devalued; ethics became subjective; standards were degraded.

Inspired by the arts and humanities, postmodernism approached reality from the opposite direction taken by modernists, in the process creating a new vocabulary for analysis. "The Center is the engine of the Empire, the motor of Power," observed the poet and National Public Radio commentator Andrei Codrescu. "It is important to capitalize this triumvirate because it represents the main antihuman force operating in the world today. The media Center empowers the status quo of the new World Empire (McLuhan's Global Village) to marginalize human beings until they are no more than producers of fuel for the new god Techne."[14] While such an analysis would resonate with those for whom the primary features of reality were fragmentation and ennui, the problem of locating and identifying the Center remained.

Subsequently, markets and knowledge became central to postmodern thought. Frederic Jameson targeted the globalization of capital as the independent variable in postmodernism: "the new forms of economic production and organization thrown up by the modification of capitalism—the new global division of labor—in recent years."[15] And globalization was nothing less than metastatic, Jameson suggested. "American postmodern culture is the internal and superstructural expression of a new wave of American military and economic domination throughout the world: In this sense, as throughout class history, the underside of culture is blood, torture, death, and terror."[16] The internationalization of capital was led by economic elites that controlled finance and industry, but the media as well, crafting print and electronic narratives to further their hegemony. Under these circumstances, a radical analysis cuts to the core of such messages, deconstructing them in order to identify covert motives, expose internal contradictions, and posit more humane alternatives.

Postmodernists understood that the currency of a postindustrial age was information, viewing this as a primary means by which elites maintained control. Jean-Francois Lyotard contrasted postindustrial from industrial information: "The transmission of knowledge is no longer designed to train an elite capable of guiding the nation towards its emancipation, but to supply the system with players capable of acceptably fulfilling their roles at the pragmatic posts required by its institutions."[17] The meritocracy assured its reproduction through the creation of professions that assumed command of social institutions, and the welfare state served as a primary base of activities related to domestic policy. Thus, the modern professions emerged for purposes of assuring elites social control: "The human sciences have established certain norms and these are reproduced and legitimized through the practices of teachers, social workers, doctors, judges, policemen, and administrators. The human sciences have made man a subject of study and a subject of the state," concluded Madan Sarup. "There has been an unrelenting expansion of rationalized systems of administration and social control."[18] Postmodernism identified the professions as the means by which elites managed the marginalized. Within the context of the American welfare state, the obvious candidate for postmodern vilification was social work, a profession that was not only inseparable from public policy, but had embraced empiricism as well.

POSTMODERNISM IN SOCIAL WELFARE

A primary occupation that evolved parallel to the American welfare state was social work; indeed, the profession's strategic sense of altruism was evident in social workers attaining leadership in the emergence of the New Deal and later the War on Poverty. The social programs that represented the first and second phases of the American welfare state bore the clear imprint of social work's preference for professional services available universally to needy populations. However incomplete the social welfare project, American social workers claimed a prominent role in its institutionalization; its heroes and heroines including Harry Hopkins, Frances Perkins, the Abbot sisters, Wilbur Cohen, and Whitney Young, Jr., among many others. What modernists would take for granted as incremental advancement toward a just social order, postmodernists would view with suspicion, alleging that social work controlled the poor and disadvantaged through its institutional affiliation. Suddenly, social work was not part of the solution; social work was part of the problem.

The clearest indictment of social work as an instrument of oppression was Leslie Margolin's *Under Cover of Kindness*. After 17 years of social work experience as an M.S.W., Margolin became an "academic sociologist."[19] Employing a Foucauldian analysis, Margolin contended that social work's principle function was social control of the poor. Since this contradicts social work's professed expression of altruism, Margolin focused on how social workers and their clients colluded in maintaining the power of elites at the expense of the underprivileged. This occured through the narrative that social workers have spun, attesting to their good works, when, to the contrary, social workers were insinuating themselves in the privacy of their clients' homes and using their subtle influence to make the poor conform to extant social norms: "Prior to social work, political surveillance was more or less restricted to public domains—streets, businesses, schools. With social work, however, it became possible to keep track of marginal and common people in their homes as they pursued the most personal activities."[20] Unable to exert significant countervailing influence, clients essentially validated social work's power by participating in deceptive interactions through which they struggled, however ineffectually, to resist professional domination. In the end, social workers ratified elite command of the social structure by serving as its unwitting henchmen, all the while cloaking their role as agents of social control in the mantel of compassion.

Postmodernism's infiltration of social work might have been confined to a cabal of intellectuals steeped in the fashions of the humanities, but that was not to be the case. Postmodernism dovetailed nicely with political correctness that had come to dominate professional social work. Lacking empirical substantiation for its activities, social work situated the cause of social problems with environmental influences, a rationale that was simplified as the "-isms": capitalism, racism, sexism, and ageism. Essentially, social work adopted what Steven Pinker called "the Myth of the Noble Savage," the assumption that all clients are inherently capable, sincere, and motivated; except that a conspiracy of environmental circumstances subverted their autonomy.[21] Accordingly, social problems should not be attributed to individual behavior, but traced back to social influences. The true source of dysfunction had to be, perforce, environmental. Since the welfare state was a primary feature of the environment, its activities could be implicated in the problems of its beneficiaries. Appended to the welfare state, the motives of social workers were immediately suspect. If social work was the professional means by which elites controlled the poor, social programs provided the means through which this was systematized. Rather than providing needed services and benefits, the welfare state was an edifice of oppression.

As postmodernism provided a vehicle for challenging the validity of the welfare state, it served to subvert the validity of social services, since both reflected the Western canon. Dorothy Van Soest chastised social work for its traditional embrace of a " 'white' or 'European' norm" that had excluded marginal groups. "[Social work] education will be enriched by the inclusion of different experiences, perspectives, and truths," she contended. "Those reflecting a European perspective are neither universal nor the only standard."[22] Social work, according to Van Soest, was left wanting not only for its exclusionary practices (ignoring marginal groups), but also for its endorsement of European structures (formal education) and means (empiricism). Ultimately, social work's construction of truth was suspect, a derivation of social privilege that was foisted upon vulnerable populations who were once again exploited by a neo-colonial welfare state. In refutation of its origins as a force of social change during the Progressive era, social work had gradually become an instrument of oppression by a professional elite.

Postmodernism would reach its institutional apogee in American social work with Stanley Witkin's assumption to the editorship of the profession's flagship journal, *Social Work*. Immediately, Witkin steered *Social Work* away from empiricism and toward postmodernism. Citing the dichotomy between literary versus scientific depictions of reality, Witkin stated a preference for the former. Invoking "alternative forms of writing or nonpositivist forms of knowledge," Witkin employed postmodernism to challenge "Western enlightenment thinking. Previously unassailable notions such as progress, objectivity, and rationality have all been subject to critique—unpacked and reassembled as historical expressions."[23]

> An alternative view, informed by developments in literary theory and cultural studies, is that what is taken as the true meaning of a text depends on whose interpretation is privileged. For example, in universities, instructors' interpretations are privileged; in practice settings privileged interpretations are associated with various experts—for example, social workers, supervisors, judges, psychiatrists. True meaning becomes synonymous with authoritative interpretations, and authoritative interpretations are based on conferred power within particular contexts. Uniformity, associated with efficiency and the reproduction of relations of authority, rather than multiplicity, becomes rewarded. Thus, teaching social work students "correct" interpretations is a way to socialize them into the social work community while restraining the relationship between teacher and student. They learn to read in a manner that accepts certain literary conventions and beliefs—for example, the relationship between authority and citations or the privileging of experts' opinions about others over others' opinions of themselves.[24]

Having established social workers in higher education and agency practice as "privileged," Witkin advocated literary theory for political ends: "dislodging" authority.[25]

The practical implications of postmodernism were explored by Ann Weick, who championed a female "first voice" as authentic for a social work that had largely succumbed to a dominant culture typified by a rational, male "second voice." Late in her career, Weick discovered that "I perfected, as most women do, my second voice—the voice of dominant culture—framed in logic, rationality, and rules, where right and might are more important than care and comfort and where winning eclipses warmth and worry."[26] Weick located her experience within the larger social work project, embracing a prescientific *practice wisdom* as superior to scientific sources of knowledge that the profession had since embraced.

> In the ensuing years the profession has moved more vigorously to authenticate its approach to practice by aligning with the dominant voice epitomized by the scientific enterprise. In contrast to the ordinary concerns of human

relationships, social improvement, and community well-being, the methodology of scientific research requires parsing and dissecting discrete elements.
Emotions are replaced with studied disinterest; complexity is resolved by
narrowing the point of study; mystery evaporates in the face of calibrated instruments and precise numbers. Nowhere to be found are the living tissues
of human drama and human triumph. In choosing this dominant voice as
the official voice of the profession, social work has let slip through its fingers
the language that fills its veins with the fullest expression of human experience and that most essentially gives social work its distinctive character as a
profession.[27]

The implications of Weick's "first voice" for American social work reversed the
profession's historical allegiance with science. It "will require us to move away
from our naive enchantment with theories that emanate from the more distant
voice of the scientific and social scientific disciplines."[28]

Postmodernism would prove problematic for social work. At the conceptual
level, it rejected conventional epistemology, substituting "theory" with "text" as
well as units of analysis, such as "class" and "income" with "the center" and "the
other." This led one postmodernist to suspect that incongruence between social
welfare and postmodernism would hamstring the movement until its concepts
"appear as *operational* and *utilizable*."[29] Just as troubling was the question of
gathering evidence. For postmodernists, the emergence of social science and the
human service professions was but another example of an industrial-era dualism
that allowed certain groups to dominate social affairs. Thus, positivism in sociology was nothing less than ideology masquerading as social science: "Attempts
to apply the model of natural science inquiry in the social sciences are rejected
because post-modernists consider such methods to be part of the larger techno-
scientific corrupting cultural imperative, originating in the West but spreading
out to encompass the planet."[30] In practice, the social and applied social sciences
behaved as a "reality police,"[31] dampening and diminishing human interaction.

The implications of postmodernism left American social workers who were in-
fatuated with the new philosophy in something of a quandary. Like sociology, social work had emerged during the industrial era and had adopted empiricism as
the means for elevating its status among the human service professions. In suggesting that professions were instruments of oppressive institutions and employed means that diminished the authenticity of clients, postmodernism required social work to reject much of its industrial-era legacy. The result was an
exploration of postmodern methods that emphasized the natural capabilities of
marginal populations. Central to this was the "strengths perspective," an intervention that focused on clients' assets rather than deficits. Emerging in reaction to
the negative labeling associated with the *Diagnostic and Statistical Manual of
Mental Disorders,* the strengths perspective posed an alternative to "disease and

disorder"—the deficit model—that had become associated with American psychiatry.[32] "The strengths perspective is a dramatic departure from conventional social work practice," claimed Dennis Saleeby, "helping to discover and embellish, explore and exploit clients' strengths and resources in the service of assisting them to achieve their goals, realize their dreams, and shed the irons of their own inhibitions and misgivings."[33] In citing the virtues of his approach, Saleeby waxed Romantic: "It is an approach honoring the innate wisdom of the human spirit, the inherent capacity for transformation of even the most humbled and abused. When you adopt the strengths approach to practice, you can expect exciting changes in the character of your work and in the tenor of your relationships with your clients."[34] Enthusiasm for clients' assets notwithstanding, when strengths-based case management was subjected to rigorous review, researchers found that evaluating the method was difficult given the ambiguity of its terminology. That aside, after scrutinizing available studies on the strengths perspective, researchers concluded that "there is little support for it as a distinct and uniquely effective practice model."[35]

A postmodern complement to the strengths perspective was "empowerment practice." Loosely defined as "a process of increasingly personal, interpersonal, or political power so that individuals can take action to improve their life situation," empowerment also highlighted clients' strengths:

> Clients are treated as subjects rather than objects, the focus is on clients' strengths rather than pathology, clients actively participate throughout the helping process, resources are seen as the total community rather than just formal services, emphasis is placed on the rejuvenation or creation of informal social networks, and monitoring, evaluation, and advocacy are done in a collaborative fashion.[36]

Research on empowerment practice has been limited. Reflective of postmodernism's refutation of empiricism, most studies have been qualitative. Quantitative researchers bold enough to test the shifting shoals of postmodernism have often uncovered the obvious: Capable and concerned professionals can help motivated clients given adequate resources and effective supervision. A study of 30 social workers in Israel concluded that "administrators need to create an environment that encourages achievement and self-direction while also embracing universalism. Additionally, administrators need to adopt agency policy that supports workers' continuing education based on learning material values and those spiritual values that were found to correlate to workers' self-empowerment."[37] A survey of 95 mental health consumers that focused on a cohesive environment, collaboration with professionals, a strengths-based assessment, and an educational focus revealed that these features were generally agreeable.[38] Like the strengths perspective, empowerment practice has yet to demonstrate its efficacy through randomized clinical trials, the standard for outcome research adopted by other health and human service professions.

At issue here was not social work's intentions nor its promise, but its perform-ance. By failing to engage in the difficult work of establishing categories of activity and subjecting them to the highest standards of evaluation, social work essentially dismissed the empirical project. While related disciplines—nursing, public health, and psychology—exploited the hierarchy of knowledge of which the sci-entific method represented the apogee, social work pursued inferior methods. Logically, the ultimate method for evaluating interventions is the randomized controlled trial (RCT), used extensively in medical and pharmaceutical research. When that is implausible, multivariate survey methods are employed. Case stud-ies are of less value, the anecdote even less so. That social work rarely mounted RCTs, occasionally used multivariate analysis, but preferred anecdotal methods— most evident in "single subject designs"—reflected its aversion to developing knowledge in accord with standard empirical methods. Instead of embracing sci-ence, social work sought justification through formulations that were impression-istic, intuitive, and ideological—drive-by research. If the intellectual movements about which social work enthused gave short shrift to empiricism, that was ra-tionalized by postmodernism, which viewed science as an instrument of oppres-sion. In rejecting science, social work thus allied itself with victimized popula-tions, albeit figuratively, portraying itself as being subjugated by the same forces that diminished the oppressed.

This would prove a Faustian bargain. Postmodernism allowed social work to establish a symbolic identification with victims of social injustice, but doing so meant rejecting the very methods that would empower the profession. It also meant forfeiting opportunities to comprehend accurately the circumstances of the vulnerable poor and act effectively on their behalf. Postmodernism may have afforded social workers the illusion of being closer to their clients, but it sacrificed an objective understanding of their plight in the process. Essentially, social work discarded one of the most important tools that a profession can wield: truth. Terry Eagleton would have admonished postmodern social workers that "it be-longs to our dignity as moderately rational creatures to know the truth. And that includes knowing the truth about truth. It is best not to be deceived if we can pos-sibly help it."[39]

The consequence of postmodernism for the viability of the American welfare state would be significant. Metaphorically, beneficiaries are the miners' canaries of the welfare state; when social programs generate unintended and perverse out-comes on clients, it is professionals who are expected to identify the neglect and harm that ensues. In a post-industrial society in which information technology is central, the means for professional effectiveness are decidedly empirical. By em-bracing postmodernism, social work, the profession best positioned to compre-hend the problems of social programs that conservatives would later exploit, willfully elected *not* to conduct serious research and generate the data necessary to guide social policy. By embracing postmodernism, social work endorsed a series of fads—opposing trans-racial adoption, supporting recovered memories—which would later be debunked by research. Ultimately, the idea of a postmodern profession was an oxymoron. "The creature who emerges from postmodern thought is centreless, hedonistic, self-inventing, ceaselessly adaptive," observed Eagleton acidly. "He thus fares splendidly in the disco or supermarket, though not quite so well in the school, courtroom, or chapel"[40]—or, one might add, the social service agency.

In the early 2000s, the blowback from postmodernism was prompting a small number of academics to reconsider social work's disregard of empiricism. Many scholars became concerned that what was passing as professional knowledge was at best conventional wisdom, at worst ideological tract. As a corrective, some advocated "evidence-based practice," a method that had evolved to evaluate the effectiveness of healthcare interventions.[41] But, this would be a tardy correction; social work's infatuation with postmodernism and its rejection of empiricism meant that it sacrificed at least a generation of sound research.

While social work experimented with novel applications of postmodernism, it grew more tangential to the institutions and methods that were increasingly vital to the service sector of a post-industrial environment. Having disparaged not only primary social institutions, including those of the welfare state as well as the university, but also the empirical processes by which scholars, scientists, and administrators had learned to interpret their domains, social workers who were enthralled with postmodernism became less competent in an increasingly competitive environment. The handy postmodern response to the willful marginalization of social work was a critical approach to structure and method, which, if nothing else, offered a reassuring sanctimony. Empowerment notwithstanding, such piety reflected the increasing irrelevance of social work. Ultimately, it would be but a short step from criticism to indictment. As postmodernism ratcheted up the critique, social institutions became imbued with intentional malevolence, depicted as instruments of oppression as experienced by entire classes of marginalized groups. The implications were as sweeping as the indictment: rather than vehicles of benevolence, social welfare programs were characterized as instruments of domination; rather than benign instruments for understanding reality and managing social programs, empiricism became part of the means of oppression. "To postmodernists there is no objectivity[;] to believe in science means you support an oppressive existing social order that seeks to deny equality to oppressed citizens," observed Harris Chaiklin.[42]

The refusal to explicate systematically how theory related to practice left postmodernism adrift, subject to the whims that wafted through the humanities and the dogma that defined social studies. Without delineating the connection between theory and practice—the epistemic correlation—postmodernism tended to degrade into ideology. The ultimate concern became not demonstrating efficacy, but seizing power. Given the multicultural refrain suffused throughout postmodernism, this invited further diffusion; if the postmodern gambit entailed a power grab, its beneficiaries would be the disparate groups comprising the marginalized.

The basis for such a power shift could not be predicated on rationalism, per se, since this would be inconsistent with the postmodern rejection of empiricism. (In this sense, the postmodern project was profoundly and proudly irrational.) The end game of postmodernism thus became a reality in which marginalized groups would be central in a milieu that more resembled Brownian motion than the rigid demarcations associated with modernism. Yet, the seduction of this vision was troublesome, if only because it jettisoned any formal means for judging differences. "If all competing claims to knowledge and values are viewed as equally valid, then there is no moral basis for supporting nondiscrimination, humanitarianism, and social justice as superior values, nor for opposing oppression, victimization, and discrimination," observed Charles Atherton and Kathleen Bolland. "All moral values are reduced to politics."[43]

All things being equal, postmodernism failed to justify the primacy of certain values, and therewith the status of specific groups over others. At best, the result would be paradoxical; at worst, perverse. If various cultural perspectives were equally valid, then those of minority conservatives could claim automatic credibility. Angela Dillard, for example, found that minority conservatives objected to "a powerful civil rights establishment that had determined who is allowed to speak in the name of African Americans, Latinos, Asian Americans, women and homosexuals, as well as how they are permitted to do so." As the minority Right saw it, the obstacle to social justice was not a capitalist patriarchy, but a civil rights establishment.

> Hence, conservatives say, more reasonable voices (their own) are suppressed in favor of hurling charges of racism, sexism, homophobia, and rampant discrimination. That tactic, they insist, is the hallmark of a profitable industry that serves neither the poor nor the disenfranchised, but rather the leadership of the civil-rights establishment itself—to the detriment of the very groups those advocates claim to represent and of society as a whole. Said to be located at the nexus of a diverse array of groups, including the NAACP, La Raza, ACTUP, as well as the remnants of the old New Deal coalition, the civil rights establishment stands accused of perpetuating a dangerous brand of liberalism that perverts the American political system.[44]

Conservatism was not welcome in many institutions of higher education, leading some prominent scholars to complain about discrimination. Summarizing the prevalence of the problem, Princeton's Robert George invoked language that might have been apropos of the Civil Rights movement: "We need to send our best soldiers into battle, even though we're going to lose a few . . . I hate to tell kids they shouldn't take risks, they shouldn't go for their [conservative] dreams."[45] Intolerance of conservatism in higher education led David Horowitz to propose an Academic Bill of Rights, in order to assure that colleges and universities represented "a plurality of methodologies and perspectives."[46] Stealing a page from the very postmodernism that the Academic Bill of Rights was intended to refute, Horowitz justified it on the grounds of diversity.[47]

Ultimately, postmodernism failed to establish criteria from which to establish the validity of claims advanced by different groups. While there was general agreement among postmodernists that an Anglo, male, capitalist patriarchy dominated social institutions globally, and their defense of victimized populations was a guiding virtue, the status of other groups was not as clear. Given the relativism that pervaded Theory, suspect groups—Arian supremacists, homophobes, homeschoolers—could just as legitimately claim their oppression on the very forces that postmodernism vilified. In one breath, the well-read neo-Nazi might employ the Constitution to defend his right of free speech and, in another, cite postmodernism to validate his group's ideology. Unless it could be demonstrated otherwise, bigotry enjoyed the same validity as justice; ignorance was an alternative way of knowing, on equal footing with learning; hate was just another form of expression, parallel to compassion. "The postmodern prejudice against norms, unities, and consensus is a politically catastrophic one," concluded Eagleton. "It is also remarkably dimwitted."[48]

Eventually, liberal scholars began to express misgivings about postmodernism. "Twenty-first-century feminists need to become a force for literate, civil democracies," wrote Phyllis Chesler and Donna Hughes. "They must oppose dictatorships and totalitarian movements that crush the liberty and rights of people, especially women and girls. They would be wise to abandon multicultural relativism and instead uphold a universal standard of human rights."[49] Even the Left had misgivings about postmodernism as it was manifested in identity politics. "Unfortunately, the political assertion of identities, particularly national and ethnic identifies, too readily devolves into a narrow, insular politics," observed Richard Noble. "Internecine conflicts around issues of race, class, and gender also complicate the Left's effort to present itself to a wider public that isn't sure what to make of these claims."[50]

TILL EULENSPIEGEL

If American baby boomers were asked to identify Richard Strauss, most would think of him as the composer to the soundtrack of Stanley Kubrick's movie *2001*; few would know that the opening bars were actually from *Also sprach Zarathustra*, Strauss's Romantic tone poem about a Persian religious philosopher, which premiered in 1896. A year after the first performance of *Don Quixote* in 1898, Strauss turned his attention to a picaresque figure of country lore, Till Eulenspiegel, whose merry pranks strained the patience of a superstitious town folk until they had simply had enough; Till was unceremoniously marched to the gallows and hung.[51] In all this, Strauss's Romanticism was evident in his selection of figures that did not fare well when subjected to the pedantic predisposition of the ignorant. When life approximates a charade, few of those in power brook the irreverence of the unfaithful.

During the 1990s, empirically minded scholars suspected that there was little substance to postmodernism; instead of representing a vanguard in the development of knowledge, Theory was, upon closer scrutiny, vacuous. Two events highlighted faults in the postmodern foundation. In 1996, *Social Text* published "Transgressing the Boundaries: Toward a Transformative Hermeneutics of Quantum Gravity," a parody by Alan Sokal, a physicist who suspected that postmodern editors would publish "an article liberally salted with nonsense if it (a) sounded good and (b) flattered the editors' ideological preconceptions."[52] Sokal's announcement of the hoax in *Lingua Franca* attracted wide media attention nationally and internationally.

Less well known, but better constructed, was William Epstein's exposé of editorial practices of social work journals. Like Sokal, Epstein hypothesized that journal editors would reject impartial standards of manuscript evaluation and look favorably upon submissions that affirmed, as opposed to negated, professional interventions. From previous experience, Epstein had found that reviewers often lacked the basic knowledge necessary to the task before them.

> Some of the reviewers' comments which I received showed clear misunderstandings of statistical methodology and hypothesis testing. Many were intemperate. Reviewers were particularly upset by articles that suggested the inefficacy of social work interventions, and often chose, confronted with evidence to that effect, to comment upon ideological and rhetorical, rather than substantive, points. Given reviewers with such priorities, the possibility that articles were being judged by how they reflected on current professional orthodoxy rather than on "scientific" grounds seemed worth investigating.[53]

Using an experimental method, Epstein constructed two fictive studies then randomly distributed the positive version to 74 journals, the negative manuscript to 72. Epstein confirmed his hypothesis: editors' preference for the positive article demonstrated confirmational bias that was statistically significant. After announcing his findings, Epstein was roundly excoriated by editors who suddenly found themselves in the embarrassing position of having been the subjects of an experiment. Subsequently, the National Association of Social Workers conducted a disciplinary hearing and recommended that Epstein apologize or be censured.[54] Epstein won on appeal, putting an end to the debate, but not dissuading him from further research on social work editors.

A decade later, Epstein constructed two fictive interventions—family preservation and pregnancy prevention—and randomly distributed these to social work journals. The purpose of the study was not only to determine if confirmational bias continued as an editorial practice, but also to assess the quality of manuscript reviews. With regard to confirmational bias, only the family preservation manuscript reached statistical significance. With respect to the quality of reviews, Epstein's independent raters of reviewers' comments determined that 73.5 percent "were assessed to be inadequate."[55] Epstein concluded that "the publication decisions of social work journals are biased to accept confirming papers and routinely rely on the uninformed enthusiasms of referee reviewers."[56] Orthodoxy continued to trump science in social work journals.

That social work journal editors would consistently select for publication research that reinforces the conventional wisdom is, of course, counter to empirical evaluative standards as established by the scientific community. The failure to rigorously assess new knowledge leaves a discipline susceptible to fads and exposes its clients to risk. Equally problematic, the public's allegiance to social policy is likely to erode as it is asked to underwrite program failures. The public relies on a professional community to uphold optimal standards of performance; when that is compromised, the public's trust fades. Because the public lacks the knowledge of the inner workings of any profession, it cannot be expected to register its ambivalence clearly; rather, the penalty evolves gradually in the form of deteriorating credibility and status, which can take decades to repair. Metaphorically, social workers may be the sentinels of the welfare state; but their romance with postmodernism has left them nodding off on the watch.

DEAD END

Postmodernism's obtuse syntax and convoluted logic might be dismissed as academic sophistry except that it was associated with professional practices that were not simply wrong but damaged people as well. As will be elaborated in subsequent chapters, with respect to poverty policy, adherents of the "feminization of poverty" insisted that conservative welfare reform was a plot by the Right to further oppress poor minority women, despite evidence that welfare mothers themselves endorsed conservative precepts of welfare reform. In avoiding the miserable treatment they had received in public welfare offices, to say nothing of eroding benefit values, many welfare mothers were already working, a fact that welfare liberals might have put to good use had they conducted research on the matter and not insisted that public welfare was instead an instrument of oppression. As a result, a generation of welfare mothers was consigned to dependence on public assistance when welfare liberals could have crafted ways to encourage welfare recipients to work and augment their wages by cashing out benefits. With respect to child welfare, the damage was more conspicuous. Opposition to trans-racial adoption meant that thousands of minority children were maintained in foster care or in institutions, even though white parents could have adopted them. Enthusiasm for repressed memories and satanic abuse resulted in modern-day witch hunts, eventually leading to the incarceration of innocent people. Yet, all of this occurred within the auspices of publicly subsidized social programs of the American welfare state.

The postmodern preference for ambiguity over certainty, the denigration of the status quo as a manifestation of patriarchal imperialism, and its rebuke of the West in favor of the Third World came to a crashing halt on September 11, 2001. As the nation contended with the first attack against sovereign ground in recent memory, a profound cultural reassessment took place. Suddenly, Americans appreciated their democratic heritage, their political freedom, their mastery of technology, and their stature in the world. Absolutes mattered. "For a while, we did without history. We were at the end of history, our circumstance novel beyond compare. Modernity was triumphant, and it would bring democracy everywhere and a Dow without limit," David Remnick reflected a year after the attack. "But an attack on an iconic center of modernity on September 11, 2001, and then a war in an ancient place, along the Tigris and Euphrates, brought back history with a rush."[57]

A signal event, September 11 ended intellectual infatuation with postmodernism. "The public response to the attacks was spontaneously and unequivocally patriotic, suggesting that the divisions animating the so-called 'culture wars' ran less deep than the cultural warriors supposed, and partly because the cultural pluralism that had once seemed threatening became, overnight, an all but official attribute of national identity," reflected Louis Menand. "Inclusiveness turned out to be a flag around which Americans could rally. It was what most distinguished *us* from *them*."[58] The national unity catalyzed by September 11 did not solve the social and political divisions that beset the nation, anymore than it would provide justification for war with Iraq; however, it indelibly underscored the finality of fact, instantly consigning relativism to the salons of European dilettantes. Curiously, while many American intellectuals were still imbued with French sophistry, "the younger generation of French thinkers were pondering civil society, human rights, and the implications of cognitive science,"[59] all traditionally American themes.

If Americans were jolted into a renewed respect for international affairs by September 11, their confidence in social programs was disassembling. The philosophical consensus that had undergirded the American welfare state was dissolving. Researchers in liberal policy institutes behaved as if the American welfare state remained the regnant paradigm, just as conservatives maneuvered influential think tanks and their control over the three branches of the federal government to further its deconstruction. Meanwhile, the Liberati's infatuation with postmodernism impaired the ability of human service professionals to address two compelling social policy issues: family welfare and children's services.

POOR POLICY

At that moment they caught sight of two great water-mills in the middle of the river, and no sooner did Don Quixote view them than he exclaimed to Sancho in a loud voice: "Do you see? There, my friend stands the city, castle, or fortress. In it must lie the persecuted knight, or the Queen or Princess in distress, for whose succour I have been brought here."

"What the devil does your worship mean by city, or fortress, or castle?" asked Sancho. "Can't you see that those buildings in the river are water-mills, where they grind corn?"

"Hush, Sancho!" said Don Quixote. "They may seem to be water-mills, but they are not. I have already told you that spells transform all things and change them from their natural shapes. I do not mean that they actually change them, but they appear to, as we learnt by experience in the transformation of Dulcinea, sole refuge of my hopes."

DON QUIXOTE

By the 1990s, conservatives had exploited a policy process that already favored the affluent and influential by deploying a network of think tanks to reverse the liberal trajectory in social policy and reform the welfare state. To be sure, their track record on restructuring social programs was uneven. Previous forays into social policy reform that had targeted social insurance had been aborted when Social Security and Medicare were found to be unexpectedly popular; yet, the Right came to appreciate the poignant vulnerability of public assistance programs, especially family welfare—Aid to Families with Dependent Children (AFDC). An earlier attempt to reform AFDC through the Family Support Act (FSA) of 1988 could hardly be claimed as an unqualified success. Although FSA mandated work requirements for AFDC recipients and included "transitional benefits" through which beneficiaries could receive Medicaid, Food Stamps, and a transportation allowance for a year after finding work, the job participation rates fell far short of what had been expected. Regardless, conservatives learned much from the disappointments of FSA; subsequently, their learning curve spiked sharply upward. Analysts in conservative policy institutes calculated that a more rigorous welfare reform, such as that proposed by Newt Gingrich in the 1994 "Contract with America," could yield multiple benefits. Eventually, the family welfare entitlement would be ended, and AFDC would be converted to a work program. Moreover, the devolution of family welfare to the states as a block grant might presage similar reforms of Food Stamps, Medicaid, and Head Start. Ultimately, these ventures would prove valuable for the end game of the strategy: Social Security and Medicare. In this respect, welfare reform served as a shot across the bow of the welfare state, one that conservatives would find spectacularly successful.

The tale of welfare reform would be littered with paradoxes. Eventually, Republican governors would find themselves affirming a principle that feminists had advocated since the beginning of the women's movement: the ticket to female independence was not reliance on a male breadwinner, but getting a job. Subsequently, conservative governors basked in photo opportunities where they embraced poor African American welfare mothers who were caught beaming back at them. Gnashing their teeth, liberals avowed that welfare reform was a diabolical plot by the Right to oppress minority mothers, and they began to organize a non-violent resistance to the scheme. Liberal academics forecast a "race to the bottom" in which more generous states cut benefits in order to keep benefits in line with stingier neighboring states. Leftist feminists found themselves defending a program that insisted that mothers stay home to care for their children, metaphorically wedded to a welfare bureaucracy for which welfare mothers felt little but contempt. Progressives projected increases in family violence, and rising rates of child abuse, with more children placed in foster care. Senator Edward Kennedy labeled the Welfare Reform Act as "legislative child abuse." Peter Edelman, one of three senior appointees who resigned in protest, projected that "there will be suffering. Some of the damage will be obvious—more homelessness, for example, with more demand on already strapped shelters and soup kitchens," he said. "There will be more malnutrition and more crime, increased infant mortality, and increased drug and alcohol abuse."[1] Penultimately, what liberals would describe as the most punitive welfare legislation ever would be signed by a Democratic president. But the greatest paradox would be this: Despite their dogged persistence in joining the labor force, the vast majority of welfare mothers would remain in poverty, welfare reform having offered them a way out of the ranks of the welfare poor only to join those of the working poor. "About a year after welfare reform, more than half of the sample members avoided poverty and a similar percentage avoided economic hardship," concluded a study of welfare reform in Wisconsin, one of the most progressive in the nation. "But only about one-fourth achieved 'independence.' Moreover, in a broader list of means-tested benefits, fewer than one in ten received no benefits."[2]

THE OLD MATERNALISM

Fundamentally, family welfare was designed to allow mothers to care for their children at home. Despite the professional aspirations they reserved for themselves, Progressive women assumed that destitute mothers would remain homemakers.[3] They lobbied for "widows pensions" for such families, and by 1919 thirty-nine states had complied. When family assistance was included under the provisions of the 1935 Social Security Act, it is not surprising that the norm established by state "widows pensions" would be carried over to the new federal law. As formulated by Progressive women, family welfare conceded two major issues that would bedevil the program in ensuing decades: First, family welfare, a means-tested public assistance program for mothers, was differentiated from the universal pension and unemployment insurance programs aimed at men, the latter providing more generous benefits than the former.[4] Second, while costs would be shared by state and federal governments, eligibility and management of the program would remain the prerogatives of the states. Implicit in the new family welfare program was a norm: the virtuous mother. Edith Abbott, a leader in the family welfare movement, testified that only ideal families would receive benefits—"really nice children and the families are really nice"—limiting eligibility to about 50 percent of those who might need aid.[5] This meant that the brunt of any denial of benefits would fall on the shoulders of minority mothers, especially those in the South where Jim Crow still reigned. Southern welfare officials assumed that, unlike white mothers who could not be expected to leave their children, black mothers were needed as domestics or field hands. Obstructing their eligibility to welfare benefits assured white families low-wage labor, as had the exclusion of domestics and agricultural workers from Social Security.

The dual legacy of race and class evident in family assistance thus determined how the Left would come to understand welfare: It was morally offensive and patently discriminatory. Subsequently, liberals fought to get minority mothers out of the labor market and onto cash welfare, assuring them the same entitlements that had been guaranteed to white mothers. In their 1971 classic, *Regulating the Poor*, Frances Fox Piven and Richard Cloward claimed that the expansion and contraction of relief rolls and welfare benefits was a product of business's demand for low-wage labor countered by civil unrest on the part of the poor. The result was a cycle propelled by social disruption on the part of disproportionately minority workers.[6] Although the social control thesis posited by Piven and Cloward attained cult status on the Left, it was largely impressionistic; the book's many charts illustrated an essentially ideological tract. Almost three decades after its introduction, a rigorous analysis found no relationship between civil disorder and the expansion of welfare benefits, concluding that the Piven and Cloward "thesis simply does not hold up under close empirical scrutiny."[7]

During the early 1980s, Piven and Cloward would enlist two confederates, Fred Block and Barbara Ehrenreich, to counterattack the Reagan administration's assault on the poor.

> The current ideological attack on the welfare state is a continuation of the repeated efforts of the American business elite to limit the gains not only of the most vulnerable but of the majority of working people. In fact, the contemporary arguments against the welfare state are remarkably similar to those that have been employed decade after decade by business interests and their intellectual representatives.[8]

Subsequently, it became politically correct to portray welfare reform as a conservative plot to exploit the minority poor, employing the welfare bureaucracy as the instrument of class, racial, and gender oppression.

Mimi Abramovitz, a feminist and socialist, bowed to Cloward and Piven in the preface to her indictment of welfare, *Regulating the Lives of Women*. The welfare state, Abramovitz alleged, was a manifestation of "patriarchal capitalism."[9] Welfare was less a means for ameliorating insecurity and more a source of oppression; its manifest intent, a public relations scheme on the part of agents representing elites, was subverted by its covert agenda, keeping the minority poor mired in poverty. "From this perspective, the welfare state operates to uphold patriarchy and to enforce female subordination in both the spheres of production and reproduction, to mediate the contradictory demands for women's home and market labor, and to support the nuclear family structure at the expense of all others."[10] Subsequently, Abramovitz excoriated the 1996 Welfare Reform Act as a continuation of patriarchal capitalism's assault on poor women.[11] Yet, Abramovitz's book was more postmodern rhapsody than a demonstration of empirical scholarship. While Abramovitz paid lip service to feminist scholars of social welfare, her attributions were safely interred in the footnotes where they would not intrude on her Leftist platitudes. After all, scholars of "maternalism"—Theda Skocpol[12] and Linda Gordon[13]—had noted that the architects of family welfare (AFDC) were not male capitalists but female Progressives who designed restrictive public assistance in order to keep poor mothers out of the labor market. Rather than being a construct of the patriarchy, family welfare was the inspiration of Progressive women who sought to keep poor mothers at home, even as their advocates—the first generation of women professionals—were carving out an altogether separate niche in the labor market for themselves.

As women entered the labor market in increasing numbers following World War II, the credibility of family welfare suffered. By the 1990s, not only were a majority of working-age women in the labor market, but a majority of mothers—indeed, a majority of mothers with pre-school children—were working, making a maternalist welfare program that supported poor women at home less and less tenable. Accordingly, various strategies to encourage poor mothers to work presaged the 1996 federal welfare reform legislation, notably the 1988 Family Support Act, but these were roundly criticized by the Left as being suspect, an invidious plot to suppress wages of working women. In the end, Abramovitz's deductive approach seemed more interested in scoring ideological points than constructing an empirically based theory of poverty. Yet, this was fashionable among "some so-called radical feminists, who distrusted theory as an imperious assertion of the male intellect," noted Terry Eagleton.[14]

The Left's critique of welfare reform was thus derived from a preoccupation with class, sex, and race, and perforce the outcome had to be negative, even if data might suggest otherwise. Four years after the passage of federal welfare reform, legislation that was embellished by dozens of studies about the economic behavior of welfare mothers, Abramovitz's analysis was conveniently devoid of data. By the late 1990s, for example, welfare researchers concurred that the Earned Income Tax Credit (EITC), which had become significantly larger than family cash welfare, supplemented the wages of welfare mothers who were working; but, Abramovitz failed to recognize its significance. In fact, Abramovitz failed to cite *any* figures on wages, so she elided the reality that earned income coupled to the EITC had lifted many welfare families out of poverty. Similarly, except to note that the public held negative perceptions about welfare, Abramovitz ignored public opinion data indicating wide support for welfare reform. On the eve of welfare reform, a nonpartisan public opinion research group, Public Agenda, conducted a survey revealing that not only did the public favor the most prominent features of conservative welfare reform by significant majorities, but so did African Americans—indeed, so did welfare recipients themselves![15]

That the Left would forgo the data with respect to poverty policy did not go unnoticed by conservative intellectuals. As far back as 1988, Lawrence Mead, a young Turk from the Right, noted the absence of empirical substantiation of Leftist diatribes about conservative intentions on welfare reform. "The best-known radicals in social policy have . . . lost authority because they are no longer doing much research," Mead observed. Leftist "authors have collected no fresh data about the welfare problem, and in an age when most social policy analysis is highly quantitative, that is disqualifying. A purely literary Left can no longer claim the influence it once did on issues of social policy."[16] The Left's preference for ideology over empiricism would effectively remove it from the debate on welfare reform as it evolved during the latter decades of the twentieth century.

The up-shot of this would be perverse: the Left's critique of welfare reform, by presuming that it continued the oppression of poor, minority mothers, got it essentially wrong; rather than diminishing them, welfare reform expanded the opportunities of welfare mothers as a group and therewith enhanced their prosperity. Between the early 1990s and 1999, the number of welfare recipients who were working increased from 7 percent to 33 percent. While the typical wage was only $7.15 per hour in 1999, when supplemented by the EITC, the total income of a typical family of three rose above the poverty level.[17] However tentative that prosperity might have been, welfare mothers perceived it as superior to remaining on public assistance; and as they entered the labor market, the welfare caseload plummeted. Between 1994 and 1999, the number of families on welfare dropped from 4.0 million to 1.8 million, by 55 percent.[18]

MERTON'S CONSTANT

Rather than being attributed to the malevolence of patriarchal capitalism, the catalyst for welfare reform had more prosaic origins: the seeds of the current reform were sown during the War on Poverty. In collaboration with a burgeoning Welfare Rights movement, legal aid attorneys filed successful class action suits challenging capricious state policies—residency requirements and man-in-the-house prohibitions—that barred access to public assistance benefits. In response to yawning breaches in their welfare ramparts which, if not reinforced, would obligate states to divert millions of additional dollars to poor mothers, state lawmakers crafted an effective response: by standardizing benefits and then allowing them to deteriorate in relation to inflation, state legislators effectively brought skyrocketing state welfare expenditures back to earth. In the long run, the strategy would prove remarkably successful: Between 1970 and 1996, the real value of AFDC benefits declined 51 percent.[19] Thus, on the eve of welfare reform, welfare mothers were raising their families on half the cash of those a generation earlier. To be sure, as much as a third of the shortfall would be made-up in in-kind program benefits, especially Food Stamps, yet other forces weighed heavily on welfare families, countering the buffer afforded by non-cash public assistance.

During the 1970s and early 1980s, substantial shifts in demography and capital affected American cities as millions of Americans abandoned older, industrial cities for the suburbs and the "sunbelt." The population loss of several older urban areas exceeded 20 percent, and the residents left behind tended to be minorities; between 1975 and 1985, the minority population of northeastern cities increased from 33 to 42 percent.[20] As the white population fled the industrial metropolis, the economic base of America's cities changed dramatically—blue-collar jobs requiring less education vanished and were replaced by those of the information and service sectors. "In the twenty-year period from 1967 to 1987, Philadelphia lost 64 percent of its manufacturing jobs; Chicago lost 60 percent; New York

City, 58 percent; Detroit, 51 percent," noted William Julius Wilson.[21] The employment prospects of black high school dropouts subsequently plummeted, their unemployment exceeding 50 percent in every region of the United States. Yet, attaining a high school diploma was no guarantee of a job for young African Americans either; the percentage of blacks with high school diplomas who were not working more than doubled after the late 1960s.[22]

As the prospects of poor inner-city minority families dimmed, references to an American "underclass" surfaced in discussions of urban affairs. Rapidly diminishing opportunities for the minority young were expressed by skyrocketing rates of unwed births on the part of women and drug arrests for men. In 1980, the rate of unwed births for black women aged 15 to 44 (81.1 per 1,000 unmarried women) was four times that of whites (18.1); by the early 1990s, however, the rate among white women increased so dramatically that a slightly increasing black rate remained more than double that of white women. Between 1960 and 1995, the number of black female-headed households more than tripled, and the children in single-parent households in which the adult never married increased by a factor of 19.[23] Among young minority males, plummeting opportunity fueled an urban drug war. In the absence of legitimate ways to earn income, illicit drugs became paramount, not only as a source of money, but also as a symbol of oppositional culture. An expanding drug war resulted in a surging arrest rate for black youths, which more than doubled from 683 per 100,000 in 1985 to 1,415 per 100,000 in 1991—nearly five times the white rate. By the early 1990s, it was not unusual if half of young African American males living in an urban neighborhood were in prison, jail, on probation/parole, on bail, or being sought for arrest.[24]

Failing to adjust to newer, more sinister manifestations of poverty, welfare became increasingly untenable and ultimately corrupt as its liberal defenders, chafing under the conservatism that was asserting dominance in social policy, attempted to maintain it. Probably the clearest evidence of the corruption of welfare was the "error rate." In exchange for federal matching funds to state welfare contributions, Washington insisted on accurate payments on the part of state welfare departments; inaccurate payments beyond about 4 percent would result in federal sanctions. Thus, states religiously reported error rates below 4 percent, affirming that more than 96 percent of family welfare payments were accurate. This fiction was exploded by the research of Katherine Edin, whose investigation of the micro-economics of Chicago welfare families revealed that "every single mother supplemented her check in some way, either by doing unreported work, by getting money from friends and relatives, or by persuading someone else to pay a lot of her expenses." In the end, welfare accounted for only 58 percent of family income.[25] Edin and Laura Lein would later amplify these findings through analysis of welfare families in four cities, as would Jason DeParle in his account of welfare reform in Milwaukee,[26] concluding what was obvious to more studious observers of welfare: In the face of a significant decline in the real value of benefits, welfare

mothers supplemented welfare in order to support their children and failed to report it to welfare officials, even if doing so was a felony.[27] The notion that 95 percent of welfare payments were correct was an illusion maintained by state welfare
officials in order to secure federal funds; in fact, virtually *all* welfare payments
were in error.

The interaction of public assistance and the underclass debased welfare as that
institution had been understood. Indeed, the motives and behaviors of welfare administrators, advocates of social justice, and human service professionals were
contorted to the point of tragicomedy. The corruption of institutional welfare vis-
à-vis the poor would parallel the deviancy thesis posited by Robert Merton. In his
classic paper, "Social Structure and Anomie," Merton proposed that society invited
deviancy when structures frustrated the aspirations of its members. The interaction between "cultural goals" and "institutional means" in an open society afforded
a variety of responses, ranging from conformity to rebellion. Merton was realist
enough to recognize that poverty exacerbated frustrations and that the poor often
resorted to "illicit means" when "legitimate" strategies were unsuccessful. The
struggles of parents to reconcile social norms with available means are not lost on
their children, nor are they ignored by similarly fated families. Over time, alienation is institutionalized in a manner that is contrary to traditional norms and
"cultural chaos supervenes,"[28] subverting families and entire communities.

Failing to adjust to newer manifestations of poverty, public welfare became increasingly untenable. Eventually, liberal reluctance to reform welfare contributed
to its association with underclass deviancy. The nature of this reciprocal process
might be labeled "Merton's Constant": in the absence of legitimate institutional
supports, the poor will deviate from conventional norms, inventing opportunities
and exploiting resources illegitimately to get by. In this instance, as the value of
welfare benefits deteriorated, poor disproportionately minority young adults resorted to deviant behavior—unwed pregnancy and drug trafficking—in order to
survive. Ultimately, the integrity of a social institution tends to mirror that of the
population it is designed to serve; the perversion of one subverts the other.[29]

Had the Left taken the trouble to explore the reality of public welfare, it would
have found an institution that was in such disrepair it approximated an oxymoron. Indeed, if liberal intellectuals were reluctant to investigate the experience
of welfare families, they may have had good reason; little light seemed to escape
the black hole of the welfare bureaucracy. Award-winning documentary film
maker Frederick Wiseman graphically depicted the disaster that public welfare
had become in *Welfare*, his portrait of a New York City welfare department of the
early 1970s.[30] In 1980, sociologist Michael Lipsky coined the term "bureaucratic
disentitlement" to describe the tendency of welfare workers to deny benefits to
citizens eligible for aid. The culture of the welfare department assured that "workers on the front lines of the welfare state find themselves in a corrupted world of
service. [They] find that the best way to keep demand within manageable propor-

tions is to deliver a consistently inaccessible or inferior product."[31] Beneficiaries did not perceive welfare as being helpful; often as not, it was simply detested. Theresa Funiciello, a former AFDC recipient, noted as much when she observed that *"there is no accountability in the social service field.* None demanded, none supplied."[32] In 1993, a journalist offered an explanation for the contempt that many beneficiaries felt for public welfare.

> Welfare offices are so understaffed, the workers so burnt out, that some help applicants cheat just to fill unofficial quotas, avoid confrontation, get them out of their hair. It is a system so flawed that the greedy, the lazy, rip and run with ease. The attitude of both sides of the reinforced windows that separate staff from applicants is: Us against Them. The system becomes so cynical that the desperate—the great majority of applicants, by most estimates—are left under a pall of suspicion, clawing even harder to get the help to which they're entitled.[33]

Focus group and organizational analysis of welfare departments revealed welfare mothers eager to escape from the dole yet confronted with indifferent, if not nasty, caseworkers.[34] A 1997 investigation of public welfare in New Jersey revealed that *"the public welfare system itself was the source of the most commonly identified barriers to self-sufficiency,"* including "lacking accurate information; withholding available services; and, disrespecting clients."[35] The acidic ambiance of public welfare comes to the public's attention, if only rarely, as in excerpts from a phone recording presented as evidence in a beneficiary's suit against a California welfare department:

> Yes, Mara Anna Young, this call is for you. This is the Department of Social Services Health and Welfare Agency, and we're in receipt of your letter saying that we have committed blatant fabrication and malfeasance. Miss Young, you're so full of shit. . . . You are not special. You are a piece of shit. That's what the Department of Social Services Health and Welfare Agency thinks of you. So get off your fat, lazy ass, you bitch, because we're sick of you. And guess what? You have already lost your case. We just want to let you know what we think of you. We think you're garbage. Everybody thinks you're garbage. Go somewhere else and leech, you bitch.[36]

For those with intimate familiarity, public welfare had become a *network of negligence,* which had the perverse effect of institutionalizing poverty. Public assistance eligibility required a means test through which applicants had to demonstrate that they had low income and negligible assets in order to qualify for aid. The asset limit, typically $1,500, served as an obstacle for those on welfare who aspired to escape poverty: once assets exceeded the limit, assistance was stopped; future eligibility was contingent on "spending down" below the asset limit. Instead of providing another rung on the ladder of upward mobility, the asset limit effectively left a gap on the ladder, leaving the welfare poor reaching for purchase beyond their grasp. Analysis of length of time on family welfare—spells—confirmed that welfare was becoming a protracted experience for many families. About half of new applicants viewed public assistance as a temporary benefit and terminated benefits within two years. However, long-term recipients of public assistance became more prevalent for the simple reason they did not cycle off public assistance; on the eve of the welfare reform of 1996, a cross-section of the welfare caseload revealed that 50 percent had been on the program eight years or longer.[37]

This posed an enormous strain on local welfare departments. Because welfare was not indexed for inflation, benefits lost value as the cost of living increased, leaving recipients with little choice but to bend the rules on unreported income to sustain precarious family finances. Welfare workers soon learned that short-term recipients tended to leave public assistance as soon as possible and were least problematic, but long-term recipients were another matter. As welfare workers identified self-defeating behaviors on the part of recipients—low self-esteem, erratic work history, substance abuse, multiple pregnancies, family problems—the welfare bureaucracy provided ample means to punish them. The subtle methods of caseworkers drew the ire of Pulitzer prize winner David Shipler:

> The system is also plagued by welfare cheats. They are not people who receive welfare illicitly. The more damaging welfare cheats are the caseworkers and other officials who contrive to discourage or reject perfectly eligible families. These are the people who ask a working poor mother a few perfunctory questions at the reception desk, then illegally refuse to giver her an application form, despite the law's provision that anyone of any means may apply. It is a clever tactic, say the lawyers, because they cannot intervene on behalf of a client who has not applied. The welfare cheats are the officials who design Kafkaesque labyrinths of paperwork that force a recipient of Food Stamps or Medicaid or welfare to keep elaborate files of documents and run time-consuming gauntlets of government offices while taking time off from work.[38]

Welfare rules fueled the contempt of recipients. Long-term beneficiaries accurately perceived their treatment as duplicitous, often railing at unsympathetic caseworkers and inflexible procedures. All too often such disputes resembled pitched battles. No one seemed to appreciate the irony of the situation: the intractably poor not only viewed the institution designed to aid them with hostility, but those employed to alleviate poverty actually aggravated the circumstances of the poorest families.

Little of this was lost on an American public that was rapidly defecting from welfare liberalism. As long ago as 1976, most Americans opposed more spending for social welfare, regardless of age, education, gender, and political affiliation. Significantly, *even those earning less than $10,000 a year opposed additional funding for welfare programs.* Of all the subgroups sampled, only nonwhites approved hiking welfare expenditures.[39] A subsequent National Opinion Research Center poll revealed that while Americans favored aid to the poor, respondents did not favor welfare as the proper conduit for assistance: while 64 percent thought too little was spent on the poor, 41 percent thought too much was spent on welfare. While *Americans favor government action to help the poor,"* concluded Hugh Heclo, *"they generally dislike the subset of government programs that are intended to be targeted on the poor."*[40] A 1988 Public Agenda poll proposed a menu of program improvements, yet found the public disapproving of an expansion of welfare.[41] By the time Public Agenda revisited welfare in a 1996 survey of public opinion about welfare reform, public sentiment was clear. With respect to several scenarios about instituting time limits, the public was increasingly impatient about indefinite receipt of public assistance. "Eight in ten (83%) would even place time limits on the benefits of an applicant sympathetically described as a woman with children who is abandoned by her husband of 15 years, who has never worked, and is running out of money," the study concluded. By contrast, the public was less tolerant of structural causes of poverty; only 11 percent of whites and 15 percent of blacks attributed higher welfare rates among blacks to racism and discrimination. Significantly, the survey included the responses of welfare recipients that paralleled those of the public.[42]

If liberals were out of touch with respect to welfare, the discipline that might have offered the most immediate insight—social work—was off on a tangent of its own. After the War on Poverty, social workers lost interest in poverty, failing to investigate systematically the consequences of welfare for poor families. The clearest evidence of this dereliction is found in *Social Work Research and Abstracts.* Beginning in 1965, articles about social welfare were abstracted for research purposes and cross-referenced to facilitate use. In 1965, the pivotal year of the War on Poverty, 12 articles about poverty were published; the following year, the number jumped to 22. Through the late 1960s and early 1970s, the number fluctuated between 12 in 1969 and 3 in 1970. In 1973, the editors added "the poor" to "poverty" as an entry, and the number of articles jumped to 11. Thereafter, social work's interest in poverty flat-lined for two decades. Between 1974 and 1988, the year in which the first conservative reform of welfare was instituted through the Family Support Act, the number of articles appearing in the social work literature averaged fewer than four per year. What makes this indifference so remarkable was the dramatic increase in welfare expenditures during the period, from $16 billion to $98 billion, a doubling in inflation adjusted dollars. Family aid had expanded significantly, the welfare bureaucracy had become organizational purgatory, and the Right was probing welfare to identify its vulnerable points, but social work, arguably the profession best situated to assess each of these developments, showed minimal interest. Social work had turned its back on the poor.

The confluence of these factors would be terminal for family welfare. Having ignored the horror that public welfare had become for families dependent on it, having dismissed public misgivings about welfare, and having failed to mount a research agenda commensurate with the allocation of public funds, welfare liberals had somehow managed to become functionally ignorant in vital matters relating to public welfare.[43] It was only a matter of time until public welfare would be receptive to *conservative* reform.

THE NEW PATERNALISM

By the beginning of the second term of the Reagan presidency, conservatives were confronted with a public welfare institution best characterized by profound and extensive neglect. Earlier conservative assaults on welfare were not known for their nuance: George Gilder had pontificated that what the poor needed was not more government assistance but "the spur of their own poverty."[44] Martin Anderson had claimed that "the War on Poverty has been won, except for perhaps a few mopping-up operations."[45] Charles Murray had proposed a famous "thought experiment:" scrapping "the entire federal welfare and income support structure for working-aged persons, including AFDC, Medicaid, Food Stamps, Unemployment Insurance, Worker's Compensation, subsidized housing, disability, and the rest."[46]

The Right found a wedge into public welfare with "behavioral poverty," a concept that allowed conservatives to target the deviant poor. Descriptive data from social programs showed that the most intractable welfare dependents were also those with deviant attributes. Conservatives argued that while providing cash to the "traditional" working poor might have been justified because they would use it responsibly, making it available to the "underclass" poor just reinforced their deviance, protracting their poverty; *ipso facto* welfare benefits should be made conditional on behavioral conduct. As AEI's Michael Novak observed, if the poor simply adhered to traditional norms, welfare would be a temporary measure, if it were necessary at all. "It is not entirely a mystery how many climb out of poverty," wrote Novak. "Simply finish high school, get and stay married, get and keep a job." Novak implicated welfare in behavioral poverty. "Existing welfare policy [i]s toxic. Even if welfare policy has not *caused* the widespread behavioral dependency that has now become so highly visible, at the very least existing public policies have done little to remedy the situation."[47]

The solution to behavioral poverty, proposed Lawrence Mead, was to make receipt of welfare conditional on traditional norms. Significantly, the "new paternalism" was directed at middle-class taxpayers as much as at the welfare poor. "From the public's perspective," noted Mead, "the key aim of welfare employment is to change lifestyle—simply to have the welfare adults do more to help themselves. Actually working or leaving aid may be the final goal, but to show effort in

that direction is also an end in itself." The ultimate objective of the new paternalism would be the poorest of the welfare poor: "the long-term recipients [who] remain dependent largely because they do not work regularly and often have children out of wedlock."[48] Given the severe and extenuating dysfunctional behavior
of the poor, the new paternalism invited interventions along a number of fronts,
including work, procreation, education, health, and family life. By addressing all
of these, Mead contended, the "new paternalism" would stop the disabling behavior of the poor and in so doing integrate them into the social mainstream.[49]

So configured, the new paternalism called for a radical resurgence of government in the social affairs of the welfare poor. Mead was unapologetic about the
institutional authority required to thwart further expansion of the underclass; instead of the occasional intrusion of meddlesome caseworkers, Mead wanted to
systematize it. Reversing the social calamity exacerbated by welfare necessitated a
healthy dose of Big Brother.

> Government is moving away from freedom and toward authority as its basic
> tool in social policy. Opportunity is no longer enough to overcome low in-
> come, given the dysfunctional character of serious poverty today. The ghetto
> has become to a great extent self-perpetuating, and, for many residents, there
> remains no alternative to society attempting to redirect behavior. A tutelary
> regime is emerging in which dependents receive support of several kinds on
> condition of restrictions on their lives.[50]

In one of the most rapid transitions from social theory to public policy, the new
paternalism became federal welfare policy via the Family Support Act in 1988,
only two years after the publication of Mead's *Beyond Entitlement*.[51]

The conservative offensive against welfare came in two parts. Less well known
was the Omnibus Budget and Reconciliation Act of 1981, which encouraged states
to seek waivers to experiment with innovative programs that would wean poor
mothers from AFDC in order to become economically self-sufficient. Significantly, waivers granted by the federal government required formal evaluations of
their effectiveness. The more prominent initiative was the FSA, which mandated
that AFDC recipients engage in work but are granted exemptions. FSA incorporated both incentives and penalties for AFDC mothers in relation to work. The
carrot consisted of the Job Opportunities and Basic Skills program that provided
job training and "transitional benefits": the continuation of child care, Medicaid,
and transportation for one year after securing a job. The stick was the termination
of benefits for a mother who refused to participate in "welfare-to-work" and did
not have an exempting excuse, such as a preschool-age child. The act was bud-
geted at a Reaganesque $3.34 billion over five years.

By the early 1990s, evaluative evidence from the first waiver demonstrations
began to appear. At best, welfare-to-work generated modest increased earnings—

less than $1,000 per year—hardly enough to make the typical family independent of welfare. Welfare savings were also modest, optimally sufficient to recover the cost of mounting the welfare-to-work initiative. At worst, earnings were negligible, and the cost of establishing welfare-to-work was never recovered in welfare savings. Curiously, of the welfare-to-work programs established in the 1980s and investigated by the Manpower Demonstration Research Corporation (MDRC), Arkansas's stood out. Of the 13 programs evaluated, *only* Arkansas's work program increased earnings of welfare participants *and* generated sufficient welfare savings to recover its investment in welfare-to-work during the first year after a participant completed the program.[52] Arkansas's governor at the time was, of course, Bill Clinton, who recognized the political capital to be gained by exploiting welfare reform: even though welfare reform produced small increases in earnings and comparable savings in welfare costs on a per-participant basis, the latter, when extrapolated over a large caseload, generated a windfall in the tens of millions of dollars that could be claimed by the astute elected official.

"THE END OF WELFARE AS WE KNOW IT"

After his election, President Clinton moved expediently to reform AFDC. Wary of the influence that would be brought to bear on the two-year time limit by liberal interests (89 liberal advocacy groups had transmitted their objection to time-limited welfare), Clinton adopted a strategy of empanelling a relatively small group of thirty experts, all of whom held positions within the new administration. The charge to the Working Group on Welfare Reform was four-fold: (1) make work pay by increasing the minimum wage and low-income tax credits; (2) dramatically improve child support enforcement; (3) provide education, training, and other services to help people get off and stay off welfare, and (4) institute a two-year time limit.[53] So constituted and charged, the Working Group on Welfare Reform promptly bogged down over time limits. A White House decision to pursue healthcare reform further retarded welfare reform, to the point that it was too late for presentation to a Democratic 103rd Congress.

The results of the 1994 mid-term Congressional elections fundamentally changed the circumstances for any discussion of social policy, let alone welfare reform. To stunned liberals, soon-to-be Speaker of the House Newt Gingrich had telegraphed his intentions with respect to the welfare state in the "Contract with America."

The Great Society has had the unintended consequence of snaring millions of Americans into the welfare trap. Government programs designed to give a helping hand to the neediest Americans have instead bred illegitimacy, crime, illiteracy, and more poverty. Our Contract with America will change this destructive social behavior by requiring welfare recipients to take personal responsibility for the decisions they make.[54]

Many months, and two presidential vetoes later, President Clinton capitulated to conservatives and signed the welfare reform legislation they had crafted; by fulfilling his promise to "end welfare as we know it," Clinton clinched his reelection.

The Personal Responsibility and Work Opportunity Reconciliation Act (PRWORA) was truly radical. It not only terminated AFDC, the 60-year-old entitlement to poor families, but included virtually every component featured in the Contract with America:

- Created Temporary Assistance for Needy Families (TANF) as a state block grant;
- Made TANF a discretionary program while cutting benefits $55 billion over six years;
- Instituted a five-year lifetime limit on receipt of TANF with state option for shorter limits,;
- Held the states responsible for labor force participation of TANF recipients, from 25 percent of recipients working in 1997 to 50 percent in 2002, although states could exempt 20 percent of cases from working;
- Strengthened child support enforcement by denying license renewals to parents in arrears;
- Encouraged states to prepare plans to diminish the "illegitimacy ratio" from 1996 through 2005 with the five best performing states eligible for $20 million bonuses; and
- Denied TANF and Food Stamp benefits to persons convicted of felony drug violations, and prohibited federal welfare benefits to immigrants for the first five years they were in United States.

Liberals were crestfallen; after all, the Congressional Budget Office, whose director had been chosen by the Republican leadership, had projected that "between 2.5 million and 3.5 million children could be adversely affected by the bill's five-year time limit when it is implemented, even after the 20 percent hardship exemption is taken into account."[55] Worse, a Democratic president had signed a Republican welfare reform plan that was infinitely more conservative than anything presented during the Reagan presidency.

WELFARE BEHAVIORISM

With welfare having been devolved to the states, attention immediately focused on the 40-plus states that had been granted waivers for welfare experiments designed to reverse the negative features of behavioral poverty. During the 1990s a considerable literature of research accumulated around various strategies to alter the behavior of welfare recipients by encouraging them to work, avoid out-of-wedlock births, send their children to school, and vaccinate their children against communicable disease, among others. In order to comply with federal waiver requirements, state welfare demonstrations had to mount field experiments where subjects were randomly assigned to test/program or control groups then followed over time to determine any experimental effect. With the exception of a few universities who secured state evaluation contracts, the vast majority of such studies were conducted by private research firms, such as MDRC, Abt Associates, and Mathematica. While such field experiments could not approximate the controlled conditions of a research laboratory, they were marked improvements over the survey methods that had characterized earlier studies. Compared to the ideological formulations of Leftist academics, the welfare waiver studies were not just a radical improvement in providing defensible data for program development, they were revolutionary.

By way of illustration, in 1997, the federal Department of Health and Human Services and the Department of Education, in collaboration with MDRC, released a detailed evaluation of welfare-to-work programs in which participants were randomly assigned to three groups: a Labor Force Attachment (LFA) group that pushed recipients immediately into work, a Human Capital Development (HCD) group emphasizing education and training, and a control group. The evaluators reported on the experience of the different welfare-to-work strategies over two years as implemented in three cities and concluded that the following: HCD cost almost twice that of LFA; both HCD and LFA increased participants' employment and earnings (though those of HCD were smaller); both HCD and LFA reduced welfare outlays (largely as a result of imposed sanctions); both HCD and LFA reduced the proportion of recipients who had been continuously on welfare; and both HCD and LFA generated increased earnings and lower welfare outlays for mothers with pre-school children at home. Inauspiciously, the researchers found that, though the programs evaluated were not operated under the new welfare reform legislation, *none* of the sites evaluated met the enrollment requirements of PRWORA. Increased earnings through LFA were reported from all three sites, slightly over $1,000 over two years, or about $0.25 per hour, an amount unlikely to leverage most families off of public assistance. Only two sites claimed sufficient LFA-attributed savings above the cost per experiment, thus recovering the cost of mounting the program, and then only after the second year.[56]

Similarly, the first formal evaluation of time limits revealed that welfare recipients were unlikely to significantly improve their earnings when confronted with termination of benefits. This study involved recipients terminated from Escambia, Florida's Family Transition Program (FTP). During the last quarter of their second and last year of welfare, the earnings of FTP families eclipsed those of AFDC control families by a statistically significant $207, and their receipt of

AFDC and Food Stamps decreased $169. However, the wages claimed by FTP participants were comparable to the AFDC control group, just over $6 per hour. Six months after termination from welfare, 16 of 25 family heads interviewed were working, although their monthly income had fallen from $913.20 to $756.20. FTP may have reduced welfare dependency, but it did so by cutting benefits, and that exacerbated family poverty.[57]

Outcomes of initiatives designed to reduce teen pregnancy were also tentative. Researchers of Ohio's Learning Earning and Parenting (LEAP) concluded that while the program encouraged 13 percent of drop-outs to return to school, "many of the teens have had additional children since the [advent of the program]."[58] The final evaluation of New Chance revealed that the program "did not reduce the rate of pregnancies or childbearing. Indeed, women in the experimental group were more likely than women in the control group to be pregnant during 9 of the 24 months after [the study began]."[59]

Despite the equivocal results of welfare waivers, conservatives were undaunted. Led by Wisconsin Governor Tommy Thompson, they crafted ever more comprehensive strategies of welfare behaviorism. The most ambitious of Thompson's welfare reform initiatives was New Hope, a multiyear demonstration begun in two high-poverty areas of Milwaukee. New Hope provided a range of health and human services to anyone working at least 30 hours per week: (1) job search for the un- and under-employed, (2) wage supplements for full-time workers that boosted their income above the poverty level, (3) health insurance on a sliding fee scale, and (4) affordable childcare. Importantly, all services were coordinated at one location by a personal case manager.[60] A study of 1,357 New Hope participants concluded that "a package of earnings supplements, health- and child-care benefits, and full-time job opportunities can substantially increase the work effort, earnings, and income of those who are willing to work full time, but need assistance to do so." Of New Hope program supports, 78.0 percent of participants used wage supplements, which increased their income above that of the control group by $1,165 over two years; 47.6 percent elected health insurance; 27.9 percent requested help with childcare; and 32.0 percent needed community service jobs since they were unable to get a private-sector job. New Hope also resembled other comprehensive welfare-to-work strategies in its cost: $7,200 per participant.[61]

The paradox of welfare behaviorism was, of course, that it served to do exactly what welfare liberals had long, but unsuccessfully, advocated: it raised benefits for welfare recipients. Granted, the increases were conditional on the behavioral regime that the Right had scripted into welfare reform, but this was defensible for the primary reason that the income and benefits package extended through welfare-to-work participants was not unlike that of other working Americans. This was also congruent with the precept of Clinton's New Democrats—"Make work pay." Enjoying the latitude to experiment with waivers, governors across the nation found that the formula worked in their states as well. Comprehensive ben-

efits encouraged thousands of welfare recipients to work, and the savings that
states reaped due to cascading welfare rolls could then be reinvested into complementary antipoverty strategies. Welfare behaviorism thus provided conservatives
with their first unqualified triumph in social policy; yet much of their success
could be attributed to a fact that liberal academics might have exploited had they
gone to the trouble of conducting the research: to compensate for benefits that
lost value due to inflation, welfare recipients supplemented family income
through unreported activities; many of them had been working all along.

MOBILITY AND WELFARE

By the late 1990s, conservative proponents of welfare reform were confronted
with a paradox: caseloads were plunging well beyond levels suggested by outcome
research on welfare waivers. The most likely explanation is that a tough welfare-
to-work program clarified what many welfare mothers had long been doing: trying to make ends meet by relying on whatever resources were on hand, with work
featuring prominently among their options. In an analysis of child support,
Kathryn Edin found that more than half of AFDC mothers met paternity requirements by fudging information, a practice she labeled "covert noncompliance."
In her study of 214 families in four cities, she discovered that 57 percent of mothers "either lied about the identity of the father of one of their children or had
hidden crucial identifying information (Social Security number, address, or
current employer) from the enforcement agency."[62] Later, Edin and Laura Lein
documented that virtually all welfare mothers depend on a variety of income
sources—surreptitious child support, non-reported earnings, as well as gifts from
family, friends, and paramours—survival strategies dictated by the meagerness of
welfare benefits. While 5 percent of recipients reported working to welfare officials, this was the tip of a rather larger iceberg. "Approximately two-fifths (39 percent) worked off the books or under a false identity to generate additional income, and 8 percent worked in the underground economy selling sex, drugs, or
stolen goods . . . 77 percent of mothers were currently receiving covert contributions from family, boyfriends, or absent fathers in order to make ends meet."[63]

While such activity was disallowed by public assistance regulations, welfare officials were unprepared to root it out. Their denial of widespread unreported income represented a concession, possibly justified by empathy about substandard
benefits: so long as their official error rate on welfare payments was not elevated
to the point that federal funding was jeopardized, welfare mothers could do whatever was necessary to get by. Once the welfare reforms of the new paternalism
were overlain on the programmatic anarchy that had come to typify public welfare, however, significant efficiencies suddenly emerged. Rigorous case management on the part of welfare workers announced bluntly to current and future ap-

plicants the rules of the new regime: work would be enforced, and there would be certain sanctions for noncompliance. For welfare recipients who were engaged in unreported employment, the response was obvious: enroll in a welfare-to-work program, promptly report the "new" job, and take advantage of the transitional benefits that were available. As might be expected, a significant number of mothers who were already working, but doing so off- the books, realized that more hassle for inadequate welfare benefits was not worth the trouble and simply left public assistance. Another subgroup was diverted from welfare; anticipating the new rules, they simply opted not to apply.

If diversion accounted for the unexpectedly sharp drop in caseload, a valid question remained: was diverting poor families from welfare a way to direct them to comparable or better opportunities than those afforded by welfare, or was diversion a way to purge and churn the caseloads in order to deny benefits to those who were eligible for assistance? Bradley Schiller examined state AFDC caseload data from 1990 to 1996 and concluded that "tough" reform provisions limiting "accessibility to welfare do have their intended caseload effect."[64] Thus, it would appear that in the murky world of welfare administration, discretion has been exercised aggressively enough to cleanse the rolls of malingerers.

There is an ideological corollary to aggressive diversion that has been pursued by conservative proponents of welfare reform, however, and it is that liberals had *under*valued the ways in which the welfare poor exploited opportunities that afforded upward mobility. To the extent that the welfare poor had other means to make ends meet, welfare was less vital. Indeed, the absence of major civil disorder accompanying stridently conservative welfare reform was at least suggestive evidence that welfare families were more resourceful and industrious than liberals had previously thought. The interaction between employers and low-wage workers, for example, showed more upward mobility than was conventionally assumed. Harry Holzer reported that "80–85 percent of employers claim that they would hire welfare recipients or applicants with GED and/or government training."[65] Delving deeper into the labor market, David Howell and Elizabeth Howell constructed a matrix of "job contours" consisting essentially of self-employed, white-collar, blue-collar, and low-wage jobs, and then analyzed the mobility of workers according to race, gender, and immigrant status. During a period of enormous compression in job opportunities due to an influx of immigrants, the researchers found that among workers who had worked at least 20 weeks in the previous year, "male and female African American and female new immigrant workers show[ed] substantial improvements in their employment distribution, shifting from the two 'worst' (secondary) job contours toward the two 'best' (independent primary) contours."[66]

Marriage and work continued to play an important role in the prosperity of welfare families. Dan Meyer and Maria Cancian examined the post-welfare circumstances of 594 women and observed "a trend toward improved economic status over time with the percentage of poor dropping from 56 percent in the first year to 41 percent in the fifth year, and the proportion who have incomes over two times the poverty line increasing from 15 to 23 percent." At year five, more than half, 54.6 percent, of mothers were independent of public assistance altogether, although only one third, 35.8 percent, were above the poverty line on the basis of their incomes alone.[67]

The prospects of employment were further explored in the Post-Employment Services Demonstration (PESD) involving 5,000 welfare recipients in four cities during the mid-1990s. PESD researchers identified several barriers to work: 15 percent evidenced health problems that interfered with work; sometimes boyfriends objected to women's employment; more than one fourth reported transportation difficulties—but the overriding concern related to child care. Despite these problems, mothers who were able to work regularly experienced upward mobility. "Those who were continuously employed were likely to continue to get off welfare during the year, and only a third were receiving welfare by the end of the year," the researchers concluded. Surprisingly, the researchers found that "human capital variables"—education and job experience— had little relationship to the length of employment for welfare mothers who found work.[68]

UNRAVELING WELFARE REFORM

The tale of welfare reform that emerges is convoluted, a product of an expanding labor market, the deceit of welfare mothers, the indifference of social work, savvy conservative think tanks, an opportunistic president, unprincipled welfare administrators, and an alarmed public. The interaction of these disparate elements produced an anomaly in American social policy: The conservatism that produced an incremental welfare reform via the 1988 Family Support Act actually *accelerated* to generate truly radical reform in 1996.

In order to provide for their children under conditions of deteriorating public assistance benefits, many welfare mothers migrated back and forth between welfare and work; "covert work" went unreported to welfare officials.[69] Neither welfare nor work was sufficient to provide for their families, so mothers overlapped and augmented them. This solution was illegal, of course, since welfare regulations required reporting all income; except that mothers had little choice but take the risk in their dealing with a corrupted AFDC program. The extent of such activity might have been appreciated had social work scholars conducted field research on the actual experiences of welfare families. For most social workers, studying welfare families was an unnecessary distraction since public assistance programs were to be a temporary interlude prior to the inevitable deployment of a European-style welfare state that would incorporate a guaranteed annual income for everyone. Ideological nostalgics busied themselves with theorizing about Leftist postmodernism and cultural politics rather than stoop to empirical investigations of the welfare poor. Many social scientists who might have had an interest in poverty research noted the liberal backlash directed at James Coleman and Daniel Patrick Moynihan and demurred from initiating such studies. The resultant vacuum in understanding the worsening economic circumstance of welfare families and their imaginative solutions increased until it was imploded by the research of Kathryn Edin. Faced with official welfare investigators, welfare mothers probably answered questions in much the same way they responded to welfare caseworkers who were gatekeepers for public assistance benefits—they hedged, contrived, and when necessary reworked reality so that it came into some approximation of what they had done to survive—the result more approximating fiction than an empirical reflection of reality as it had been portrayed by the liberal Left. It is likely that the extent to which welfare mothers were engaged in remunerative activity—that they worked—had long been under-reported. Social work's historical interest in welfare would have made it an obvious candidate for documenting the waywardness of family welfare, but it deigned to do so; significantly, the seminal empirical work was conducted by a sociologist (Katherine Edin) and an anthropologist (Laura Lein).

All of this occurred within the context of public policy. As conservative social philosophers became more adept at understanding the rationale and machinations of welfare, they brought the resources of the new policy institutes to bear. Demonstrating masterful control of the means of analysis during the 1980s, conservative ideologues transformed public philosophy on welfare, focusing on the detrimental consequences of behavioral poverty. Within a decade the conditions were right for a radical overhaul of family welfare. By the early 1990s, liberals had already lost the welfare debate; the majority of states had been granted waivers for welfare experiments, one by one opting out of the AFDC program. Formal evaluation of state welfare waivers showed rather consistently that welfare-to-work produced modest income increases for recipients as well as modest welfare savings per participant. (The results of initiatives directed at other aspects of behavioral poverty were, at best, mixed.) Extrapolated over large caseloads, however, modest welfare savings became windfalls to elected officials who further propelled conservative welfare reform.

Stringent welfare-to-work programs succeeded beyond conservatives' wildest dreams. In unexpected numbers, welfare mothers entered the labor market, many of them converting from the informal labor market to its formal counterpart, essentially declaring their availability for employment. Proponents of welfare-to-work, such as Lawrence Mead, later conceded that an unknown number of "smoke-outs" had occurred as a consequence of welfare reform, largely because of the sanctions that had been exacted from welfare mothers' benefits. But it is just as likely that many mothers went "legit" when it was in their interests to do so. When compliance with welfare reform generated more benefits than dodging punitive welfare rules and engaging in deviant behavior (*a la* "Merton's Constant"), welfare mothers entered the labor market with enthusiasm. Over time, many of them eventually escaped poverty altogether.

The great irony of welfare reform is this: Not only did the disaster that welfare liberals had predicted not come to pass; but a new champion of struggling welfare mother emerged—conservative Republican governors who had taken advantage of state waivers to craft a poverty policy more congruent with the circumstances and aspirations of the welfare poor. Thus, when PRWORA was up for reauthorization in 2002, state governors argued for continuing flexibility in welfare rules on the basis that their "laboratories" of welfare experimentation had yielded such compelling outcomes. All this has left liberals on the defensive. No longer contending that welfare reform would be a debacle, generating increases in homelessness and child abuse, welfare liberals reversed field, conceded the virtues of labor market participation, and argued for greater support for "transitional benefits."

Welfare reform provided the Right with its first triumph in social policy, piloting the template for reforming other public assistance programs and suggesting the vulnerability of the social insurances. With the assistance of the second Bush White House, congressional conservatives moved to devolve Medicaid, Food Stamps, and Head Start to the states as block grants. The big enchilada would be Social Security and Medicare, programs strongly defended by the elderly. Just as the Clinton presidency conceded the retraction of family welfare as a cash entitlement, so it also presaged the privatization of Social Security. The Gramlich commission, appointed by Clinton's Secretary of Health and Human Services, proposed different forms of privatizing the nation's public pension program.[70] On two vital fronts—public assistance and social insurance—the Right was making clear headway in containing and restructuring the liberal welfare state.

Yet, the conservative success in welfare reform betrayed a parallel failure, an unwillingness by the Right to address scandalously inferior child welfare. Once again, the response of welfare liberals proved puzzling. While they were quick to condemn conservatives for using welfare reform to consign welfare mothers to the ranks of the working poor, they were deafeningly silent to the catastrophe that was occurring with respect to child welfare. If welfare reform represented social policy as symbolic politics of the benign variety, the collapse of the nation's provision of services to maltreated children represented symbolic politics at its nadir: both Left and Right found ways to systematically ignore the damage inflicted on children through the nation's child welfare program.

WEDNESDAY'S CHILDREN

[Encountering a peasant who was flogging a young shepherd, Quixote brandished his lance and halted the whipping.]

The peasant lowered his head and, without responding, he untied his servant, and Don Quixote asked the boy how much his master owed him. He said wages for nine months, at seven reales a month. Don Quixote calculated the sum and found that it amounted to seventy-three reales, and he told the peasant to take that amount from his purse unless he wanted to die on their account. . . .

"And if you wish to know who commands you to do this, so that you have an even greater obligation to comply, know that I am the valiant Don Quixote of La Mancha, the righter of wrongs and injustices, and now go with God, and do not even think of deviating from what you have promised and sworn, under penalty of the penalty I have indicated to you."

And having said this, he spurred Rocinante and soon left them behind. The farmer followed him with his eyes, and when he saw that he had crossed the wood and disappeared from view, he turned to the servant Andres and said: "Come here, my son; I want to pay you what I owe you, as that righter of wrongs has ordered me to do."

"I swear," said Andres, "that your grace better do the right thing and obey the commands of that good knight, may he live a thousand years; for, as he's a valiant man and a fair judge, heaven be praised, if you don't pay me he'll come back and do what he said!"

"I swear, too," said the farmer, "but because I love you so much, I want to increase the debt so I can increase the payment."

And seizing him by the arm, he tied the boy to the oak tree again and gave him so many lashes that he left him half-dead.

DON QUIXOTE

If welfare reform represents symbolic politics by elevating welfare mothers to the ranks of the working poor, child protection resembles programmatic purgatory. As periodic news accounts of scandals in Florida, New Jersey, and Washington, D.C., attest, the nation's inability to care for abused and neglected children is a striking contradiction to its affluence. Reviewing data from the 1970s and 1980s, British researcher Colin Pritchard reported that the U.S. child homicide rate was more than double that of the second most lethal nation for children: Australia.[1] In a comparison using data from the early 1990s, American researcher Jane Waldfogel calculated that the reported as well as substantiated cases of child maltreatment in the UUnited States are double the rates of Canada or the United Kingdom.[2] Paradoxically, the United Nations Human Development Index consistently ranks the United States among the ten most developed nations in the world.[3]

Contradictions notwithstanding, neither conservatives nor liberals have been eager to reform child welfare. Vulnerable children offer few political gains for conservatives. For the Right, supporting interventions to protect abused children invites violating the sanctity of the family, a primary concern of "traditionalist" or "cultural" conservatives. Furthermore, examining the context of child maltreatment brings into immediate focus the extensive family and community problems that exacerbate family violence—poverty, substance abuse, unemployment—that conservatives have given short-shrift. For liberals, child abuse and neglect are problematic for other reasons. The care of vulnerable children has been entrusted to child welfare professionals for over a century; human service professionals not only populate the ranks of caseworkers but the administration of child welfare programs as well. For liberals, admitting the extent of the damage inflicted on children under the auspices of social programs raises fundamental questions about the capability of a large contingent of human service professionals to say nothing of the integrity of the welfare state. The result is an ideological convergence, a tacit agreement between Right and Left that it benefits neither camp to delve into a children's services calamity that continues to fester. Regardless, journalists across the nation have won Pulitzer Prizes for their exposés of child welfare, chronicling the malfeasance of the very agencies mandated to protect maltreated children.

INSTITUTIONALIZING MALTREATMENT

Among child welfare programs, child protection is distinctive. It is a universal service, available to children regardless of the economic circumstance of their families, and it is public, mandated by law and funded by general revenues. Yet the public is more likely to learn of the program when the Fourth Estate uncovers agency ineptitude that is implicated in a child's death. At some time during the past two decades, the media in virtually every metropolitan region in America has reported a child's death from abuse or neglect after reports had been made to child welfare authorities. Perhaps the most celebrated case was that of Lisa Steinberg, a New York City girl who died after multiple beatings. Subsequently, the horrific death of Eliza Izquierdo resulted in the appointment of special commission, which led to the overhaul of the city's child protection agency.

In 1990, Marjie Lundstrom and Rochelle Sharpe won a Pulitzer Prize for their series, "Getting Away with Murder." Recognizing that official child abuse data do not include child fatalities, Lundstrom and Sharpe conducted an exhaustive review of the practices followed by medical examiners when children die. Their conclusion reflected the general inadequacy of official data on child maltreatment. While government agencies report that three children die each day from maltreatment, Lundstrom and Sharpe observed that "at least three more child-abuse deaths each day are believed to go undetected."[4] Among those culpable of suppressing the child homicide rate were child welfare professionals. Although child protection professionals are sworn to act in the best interests of the child, public policy often obscures what actually happens to abused and neglected children. Social welfare departments, under assault for poor performance, develop the organizational equivalent of paranoia, using agency procedures to thwart the public scrutiny of indefensible policies. "Turf battles are so vicious in some places that social service workers jealously guard their files on murdered children to avoid any public blame," they observed. "In fact, some social workers are forbidden by state confidentiality laws to confirm that a child has been killed, making it impossible for anyone to accurately count the number of child abuse deaths nationwide."[5]

In 2001, the death of a 23-month-old African American infant due to child abuse led reporters from the *Washington Post* to investigate other child deaths. The District of Columbia Child and Family Service Agency (CFSA) was profoundly troubled, so much so that it had the dubious distinction of being the largest public family service agency placed under federal court supervision. Within a year, Sari Horwitz, Scott Higham, and Sarah Cohen had, indeed, identified a problem of imposing proportion. Their research revealed that between 1993 and 2001, 229 children had died as a result of maltreatment in the District of Columbia, but the deaths had gone without proper investigation on the part of the Metropolitan Police Department and the Child and Family Service Agency.[6] Yet the notoriety of being the basis for a Pulitzer Prize only belatedly prompted reforms within the agency. Maryland threatened to return 1,500 District foster children because of inadequate documentation on the part of CFSA.[7] Punctuating CFSA lapses in accountability, the family of one of the children who had died of abuse, a 15-year-old whose deformed spine crushed her internal organs because corrective surgery had not been performed, initiated a $120 million suit against

CFSA. In a perverse action on behalf of the District, attorneys argued that CSFA was not liable because the agency had been placed under federal court supervision![8]

Not long after the *Post* reporters' award was announced, the nation witnessed another illustration of child welfare in disarray: a 5-year-old Miami girl in foster care had gone missing for 15 months, yet Florida child welfare workers were unable to locate her.[9] Although the head of the Florida family service agency admitted that the ineptitude of child welfare workers was "appalling," she had no explanation for the whereabouts of the 374 other foster children whom the state was unable to locate.[10] Florida child welfare workers replicated the performance of those who had been encountered by the prize-winning *Post* reporters: rather than admit the extent of problems in children's services, workers used confidentiality as an excuse to avoid public accountability.

In January 2003, the decomposing body of 7-year-old Faheem Williams was found in a Newark basement; his two brothers had been locked in a nearby room, "emaciated and with burn scars on their bodies."[11] Although Williams had been an active protective services case with the New Jersey Division of Youth and Family Services (DYFS), multiple agency errors failed to save him. Subsequently, the *New York Times* obtained case records on 17 children that documented the deaths of four children and "the sometimes brutal, prolonged abuse of 13 more."[12] As the *Times* would learn, the culture at DYFS conspired to expose children to risk. Rather than redoubling efforts to protect maltreated children, child welfare workers were so intent on closing cases that they often took shortcuts, contravening agency policy and state law. In a grim parody of street slang, workers came to refer to the rush to eliminate cases as "drive-by closings." For years, DYFS used confidentiality to avoid public scrutiny: "One of the most serious offenses committed by [DYFS] over the years has been its ability to keep the full dimensions of its failings secret—from parents of children in its care, from lawyers acting on behalf of children who have been raped or killed, and from legislators seeking to reform the agency's practices." When confidentiality and stone-walling failed to discourage court inquiries into its operations, DYFS simply defied court demands to turn over records![13] Though the exposé of DYFS brought the agency's defensive practices to light, it did little to correct for its malfeasance. Within a year of the Williams tragedy, Matthew Calbi was beaten to death by his mother, despite four investigations of the family during the previous two years.[14]

In October 2003, a New Jersey couple was arrested for starving two boys they had adopted; the oldest was 19 years old, 4 feet tall, and weighed 45 pounds. Despite 38 visits by a DYFS caseworker during the previous two years, no evidence of malnourishment had been reported.[15] Although agency policies called for annual medical check-ups, none of the six children that the couple had adopted had seen a doctor during the previous six years.[16] The case file documented that one emaciated child beseeched his caseworker for food and rooted through the glove box in the caseworker's car in search of something to eat. "When he ate away from home, he begged the caseworkers not to tell his adoptive parents," reported the *New York Times*. "The family was nevertheless allowed to adopt three more children; each came with a government subsidy."[17] In fact, the previous year the couple obtained more than $30,000 in welfare benefits for the children they had adopted and one foster child.[18] Reflecting on a suit her advocacy agency brought against DYFS for its neglect of foster children, Marcia Robinson Lowry, director of a legal advocacy organization, Children's Rights, expressed her exasperation: "Either people were purposely flouting a federal court order or the depths of their incompetence was so profound that people didn't know what they were supposed to do."[19] Immediately, New Jersey Governor James McGreevey announced a two-year plan to right the state's foundering child welfare agency.[20]

In March 2004, Children's Rights filed a suit against the State of Mississippi for exposing maltreated children to further risk. The state had closed 34 child abuse prevention centers, and caseloads of child welfare workers were skyrocketing. While the Child Welfare League of America had suggested that caseloads not exceed 17 per social worker, in several Mississippi counties the number of caseloads had risen to 100 per worker; in Forrest County the caseload exceeded 200. Ominously, services were provided to fewer than half of families in which neglect or abuse had been confirmed. Due to a shortage of caseworkers, the state could assure that only half of reported cases of child maltreatment were even investigated; as a result, in 2004, the percentage of substantiated cases was less than half what it was in 1997.[21] Mississippi would appear to be poised to replicate the debacles that had befallen Florida, New Jersey, and Washington, D.C.

These tragedies reflect the approximately 2,000 children who die annually, the ultimate victims of substandard provision of children's services. While official sources cite a significantly lower child death rate, about 1,100 children, this number is almost certainly depressed as a result of incomplete and inconsistent reporting; a more correct figure may be upward of 5,000. Douglas Besharov, a senior fellow of the American Enterprise Institute and author of a book on child protection, estimated that as many as half of these deaths were cases known to local child welfare authorities.[22] How can publicly mandated interventions become so ineffective? William Epstein posed an explanation for the collapse of child welfare philosophy and practice. Conceding the inevitability of inferior services to vulnerable children, child welfare researchers, caseworkers, managers, and advocates perpetuate an ethic of "social efficiency," caring for children at the least cost regardless of the consequences. The persistent production of substandard information has elided the validity of program initiatives for children, the outcomes of which are indeterminate at best. The result, contended Epstein, is nothing less than "pernicious liberalism," the generation of an appealing rhetoric that hypocritically obscures the institutional neglect that is understood as child welfare.[23] Epstein presented a devastating case.

The applied social sciences and all of their attendant core academic disciplines that together constitute the field of child welfare take a chest-feather
pride in what they know. In truth, "what we know" is a gnomic conceit of
professionalism. The field does not know the rudiments of its operations or
its outcomes and it lacks the self-discipline or largeness of character to find
out. It spends its scarce resources to create a series of factional studies for its
own ideological and political advantage, furthering both the fiction that it
knows what to do and that its preferences are in the interests of maltreated
children. In the most fundamental way, the field has not bothered to find out
what maltreated children need and how those needs can be met.[24]

In 2000, Alvin Schorr, an eminent child welfare scholar, published a critical report, "The Bleak Prospect for Public Child Welfare," concluding that "the system
has faced confusion about its purposes and methods, declining professionalism,
and progressive disorganization."[25] A century ago, advocates for children had
been sanguine about the prospects of an adequate system of care: "In this early
period public child welfare worked toward being an elite service—dedicated to
children, with well-trained staff and high morale," Schorr reflected. "Policies were
family centered; foster care would aim to be a temporary expedient to be used
when a parent faced an immediate problem."[26] Yet the foundation established by
Progressive reformers and New Dealers would prove unstable: "From the 1960s
on, child welfare suffered a series of blows that left this ideology and the program
in shambles."[27] Child abuse and neglect came to be understood as a medical
problem, and less attention was directed at the economic and social deterioration
of poor, disproportionately minority families with vulnerable children. Graduate
degrees in social work were no longer required for Child Protective Services, resulting in the deprofessionalization of children's services. While 62 percent of
child welfare workers possessed a college degree in 1958, only 28 percent did so
in 1988.[28] Reductions in governmental support contributed to high caseloads,
which encouraged veteran child welfare professionals to leave for greener pas-
tures. "The immediate future of public child welfare is relatively clear—child
welfare around the country is in a parlous state," Schorr concluded. "In many
places the debasement of services, the decline of staff, and the absence of sustained citizen engagement are so advanced that it is difficult to see how these may
be reversed."[29]

The nation's misadventure in child welfare was not lost on the philanthropic
community. For decades, the Annie E. Casey Foundation had invested tens of millions of dollars in children's services, identifying and supporting model programs
across the nation. Unfortunately, the exemplary programs it subsidized remained
just that, isolated from the mainstream and failing to catalyze system-wide reforms. In 2003, the Foundation identified a significant impediment to progress:
the human services workforce.

Human services is reaching a state of crisis. Frontline jobs are becoming more and more complex while the responsibility placed on workers remains severely out of line with their preparation and baseline abilities. Many are leaving the field while a new generation of college graduates shows little interest in entering the human services sector. Millions of taxpayer dollars are being poured into a compromised system that not only achieves little in the way of real results, but its interventions often do more harm than good. It is clear that frontline human services jobs are not attracting the kinds of workers we need, and that regulations, unreasonable expectations, and poor management practices mire workers and their clients in a dangerous status quo.[30]

A companion report released by the Brookings Institution echoed the Casey Foundation's conclusions: "Unfortunately, there is a vast gulf between what these human services workers are asked to do and how they are equipped for that task," wrote Paul Light. "Workloads often exceed recommended limits, turnover rates among the most qualified workers are high, and human services employees describe their work as both frustrating and unappreciated."[31]

To the concerned observer, a child welfare system on the verge of implosion might have been expected to undertake a rigorous inventory of staff and funding resources, methods of investigation, and status of information systems, to say nothing of public relations; but this was not to be. Instead of an honest appraisal of its public mandate to protect vulnerable children, child welfare veered off on a postmodern tangent, forsaking empirical demonstration of its effectiveness, pursuing ersatz causes of child abuse, and in the process eliding public accountability. Alvin Schorr described diplomatically what would follow—"remedies . . . dictated by fashion"[32]—yet this fails to account for the casualties that ensued. In their romance with ideological fads, child welfare workers not only placed hundreds of already vulnerable children at risk, but rationalized services that would be implicated in further harm to them and on occasion their deaths.

A POSTMODERN TANGENT

That child welfare, a profession originating in the Progressives' faith in social engineering, would reject the application of empiricism to enhance the common good is perverse, to say the least. The rebuke of the research of Daniel Patrick Moynihan and James Coleman, which was perceived to be critical of liberal social programs and related problems, served as an object lesson to academic researchers. With the rejection of empiricism as a means for exploring social ills, ideology moved to the fore; political correctness soon trumped social science. To be sure, some researchers persevered, insisting that experimental and survey

research offered important clues about the problems experienced by poor, disproportionately minority Americans. Psychologist Arnold Sameroff, for example,
studied the impact of accumulating risk factors on child development. The presence of multiple risk factors—poverty, father's absence, low parental education,
punitive parenting, minority status, parental substance abuse, maternal mental
illness, and large family size—progressively diminish the IQ of 4-year-olds; while
children with three or fewer risk factors score more than 10 points above normal,
the introduction of the fourth drops their scores below normal, and those with
seven or eight risk factors score 15 points below normal.[33] While much of the
damage that is inflicted on children is the product of the long-term deficits in
their lives, illicit drugs and alcohol abuse are often associated with acts, whether
on the part of adults[34] or children,[35] that precipitate a referral to child welfare.
Unaccountably, such promising leads rarely transcended the gap between research study and service application.

Instead of focusing on how to strengthen the empirical basis of service interventions, child welfare professionals were increasingly fascinated by more exotic,
less rational ways to help vulnerable children. To be certain, the infatuation with
postmodernism was not uniformly embraced; indeed, one child welfare scholar
was prompted to complain of "a marked hostility to science. Entire books have
been written on child development, family relations, and so on, by people who
not only have never done any empirical research on these topics themselves but
who also have no familiarity with the relevant empirical research done by others."[36] Yet postmodernism was appealing for a child welfare system struggling to
maintain itself, even if the long-term consequences would prove corrosive. Openness to multiple truths may have incorporated the perspectives of all parties to a
case; but, while this might have been desirable in assessing complicated decisions,
it also served to undercut professional authority. Skepticism about empirical
methods may have functioned to sustain archaic information systems. Identification with clients romanticized the struggles of the minority poor, characterizing
administrators as the personification of an oppressive white patriarchy. In effect,
the postmodern manifesto provided the intellectual cover-up for a child welfare
system that was not only unable to protect abused and neglect children but was
also implicated in their harm. Conveniently, when cases went awry, "confidentiality" served to elide public accountability.

Perhaps the first demonstration of postmodern influence in social welfare was
the flap over trans-racial adoption. After the Civil Rights movement, the number
of African American children placed in foster care and later adopted by white
families steadily increased, provoking the National Association of Black Social
Workers (NABSW) to contend that the culture of the African American community was being destroyed.[37] NABSW accused child welfare organizations who
placed black children with white families of engaging in "cultural genocide."[38]
Subsequently, NABSW convinced child welfare agencies to halt the practice, and

the number of minority children adopted by parents of another race plummeted; by 1968 the number of trans-racial adoptions had been halved. In 1975, the number of trans-racial adoptions numbered only 800 nationwide. Yet, research on trans-racial adoption documented that minority children who were adopted by Anglos grew up without evident impairment. "Our studies show that trans-racial adoption causes no special problems among the adoptees or their siblings," noted Rita Simon and Howard Altstein. "We have observed black children adopted and reared in white families and have seen them grow up with a positive sense of their black identity and a knowledge of their history and culture."[39] Despite such empirical evidence, social work clung to its opposition to trans-racial adoption until federal legislation expressly prohibited the practice of same-race adoption. Instead of basing child welfare practice on empirical evidence, social work promoted ideology. There were at least two casualties in this affair: minority children languished unnecessarily in foster care when Anglo homes were available for placement, and social work cast itself as a discipline that, by virtue of its eschewing empiricism, advocated irrationality. The brouhaha over trans-racial adoption would be relatively benign compared to other postmodern excesses in child welfare, however.

In 1988, Ellen Bass and Laura Davis published *The Courage to Heal,* a how-to book for victims of sexual abuse. Bass and Davis contended that childhood sexual abuse was so traumatic that memory of assaults was repressed for years and could only be recovered under the guidance of a trained therapist. The thesis of Bass and Davis was diabolical in its implications: "Even if you are unable to remember any specific instances . . . but still have a feeling that something happened to you, it probably did."[40] While repressed memories might have been dismissed as a transparent attempt by clever and perhaps avaricious therapists to mine insurance benefits from the worried well, its impact would extend far beyond the parameters of sexual neurosis. Foremost, repressed memories would become the catalyst for a tawdry legacy of incarceration of childcare providers and parents of alleged victims. In the decade following the appearance of *The Courage to Heal,* the McMartin Preschool, Little Rascals Day-care, and Fells Acre Day-care cases would demonstrate the folly of repressed memory: After systematic prodding, children alleged any number of extravagant and contradictory behaviors on the part of adults close to them, resulting in their imprisonment for years.[41] Subsequently, virtually all of the alleged perpetrators have been released.

Perhaps because the repressed memory episode was so embarrassing to the child welfare profession, it failed to register within the professional literature as such. "Like the Salem witch hunt three centuries earlier, the sex panic had no internal brake that could prevent its accusations from racing beyond all bounds of credibility," observed Frederick Crews. Having incorporated postmodern tenets in clinical practice, therapists found it easy to accept recounts of childhood experience, even if these were implausible for the simple reason that children had a valid claim on reality. The plasticity of diagnostic categories invited invention, especially if novelties could be capitalized upon by way of books, seminars, and prestige. Confidentiality served as a means for evading oversight, precluding examination of cases to establish the veracity of the phenomenon. Given the hypersensitivity of the problem, the absence of empirical safeguards created the conditions for psychic mayhem:

> Poorly trained social workers, reasoning that signs of sexual curiosity in children must be "behavioral memories" of rape, were charging parents with incest and consigning their stunned offspring to foster homes. And most remarkably, whole communities were frantically attempting to expose envisioned covens of Satan worshipers who were said, largely on the basis of hypnotically unlocked "memories," to be raising babies for sexual torture, ritual murder, and cannibal feasts around the patio grill.[42]

Of course, social work was not the only profession whose vigilance had been suspended. The recovered memory snafu contributed to a growing dissatisfaction among psychologists about the evidentiary basis of psychological practice, contributing to the establishment of the American Psychological Society. "Many practitioners, because they don't keep up with the scientific literature, may be using suboptimal and, in some cases, even dangerous treatments," said Scott Lilienfeld, who founded the Scientific Review of Mental Health Practice in order to investigate suspect clinical practices. Predictably, therapists and client groups invested in clinical fads reacted with hostility.[43]

The repressed memory phenomenon soon bled into child welfare. Sexual abuse was a criterion for child maltreatment as specified in the 1974 Child Abuse Prevention and Treatment Act. While sexual abuse registered in frequency behind physical and emotional abuse, at 2.1 per 1,000 maltreated children, it was nonetheless a problem of significance.[44] When coupled with emergent psychiatric disorders, such as multiple personality disorder, which were more prevalent among women, repressed memory complemented feminist claims that their emotional needs had been largely dismissed by a psychiatric profession historically dominated by men. If the disregarded problems experienced by adult women could be traced to childhood sexual abuse, then it was important to uncover those events. That most of the therapists who would be assisting in this endeavor were professional women who regarded themselves as feminists added urgency to the project. Since repressed memory therapy permitted therapists to delve into the sexual experiences of adult women, it also allowed them to escape the more pedestrian and unpleasant work in Child Protective Services where sexual abuse was more immediate, yet difficult to address. The use of anatomically correct dolls in working with reticent children, the application of guided imaginary with troubled adults, and the drama of courtroom testimony were decidedly more exciting that the quotidian tasks associated with public child welfare: substance-abusing parents, disordered homes, poverty-stricken neighborhoods, and the like.

In its blatant disregard of the basic rules of logic, however, recovered memory allowed human services professionals to discard even the rudiments of evidence in their work. "Denial is the art of pretending not to know what you know," counseled repressed memory therapist Renee Frederickson. "It is not defeated by logic, insight, information, or confrontation, although all of these play a part in its demise. Denial is overcome only by patient growth in the opposite direction. It eases over time, returning periodically to taunt you with the possibility of your own foolishness."[45] That the source of a client's problem would be found in the shadowy recesses of the unconscious absolved the therapist of investigating the validity of sexual abuse claims. "The therapist has to remember that she is not a fact finder and that the reconstruction of the trauma story is not a criminal investigation," admonished another proponent, Judith Herman. "Her role is to be an openminded, compassionate witness, not a detective."[46] Ripped from its epistemological grounding in experience, recovered memory therapy became an exercise in faith. As such, it was a short distance to the acceptance of sexual abuse as a result of satanic cults.

That child welfare professionals would take seriously the notion that people would be victimized by satanic cults appears, in retrospect, preposterous; yet concomitant with the repressed memory phenomenon, therapists exploited the evil that many clients alleged they had experienced. A critic of recovered memory therapy, Elizabeth Loftus, set the scene. "At the close of the twentieth century, sane and rational people were getting hysterical about rumors that a murderous satanic cult had infiltrated their communities, sacrificed hundreds of aborted fetuses and newborn babies, forced young women to have sex with animals, and programmed the minds of normal churchgoing citizens to erase their memories of evildoing."[47]

Paralleling the repressed memory phenomenon, satanic or ritual abuse was anything but benign, a preoccupation of a handful of eccentrics. In several communities public resources were expended to investigate lurid allegations made by impressionable children, leading to the incarceration of adults who were innocent. As Lawrence Wright would recount in his coverage of the imprisonment of Paul Ingram of Olympia, Washington, satanic abuse bore a striking similarity to the witch hunts of Salem, Massachusetts, centuries earlier.[48]

A more pedestrian case was that of Dale Akiki, a San Diego Sunday school teacher who was incarcerated for sexual abuse in 1993. Akiki was of small stature, in part because he suffered from Noonan's syndrome, a condition typified by a large head, club feet, a concave chest, droopy eyelids, and sagging ears, problems that had required more than a dozen surgeries. A few months after volunteering to supervise a Sunday school class, a three-year-old child told her mother that Akiki had exposed himself to her. Soon, a four-year-old made similar accusations.

Akiki was dismissed as a volunteer, but the allegations multiplied until he was accused of "violent sexual assaults, beatings, animal mutilation, forcing children to ingest urine and feces, abductions to secret rooms at the school, to local hotels and [his] home, and death threats if the 'secrets were revealed.'"[49] Akiki was arrested and jailed without bail, and the children who had accused him of abuse were interviewed by therapists. Meanwhile a county-funded Ritual Abuse Task Force exerted pressure to prosecute the case. At trial, children claimed that Akiki had killed an elephant, a giraffe, and a rabbit in Sunday school, then drank their blood.[50] All told, Akiki spent two-and-a-half years in jail awaiting trial, an experience that presented its own novelties: a murderous street gang protected him from other inmates; upon his acquittal, a group of 25 sheriff's deputies hired a white limo to carry him from the courthouse to his home.[51]

But the Akiki case would be much more consequential than the imprisonment of an innocent man. At pubic expense, it had become a parody of local child protection. The Akiki trial cost San Diego County $2.3 million, of which $350,000 went to therapists through the Victims of Crime Program, almost exhausting the fund. In 1994, Akiki filed a $110 million damage suit against the county. The money might have been better spent elsewhere. Only two years earlier, the local Child Abuse Coordinating Council reviewed child deaths recorded by the Medical Examiner's Office and found that, in 1991, of the 154 children who died as a result of abuse, 56 were known to Child Protective Services.[52]

While satanic abuse might be dismissed to local aberrations associated with overzealous prosecutors, inexperienced therapists, and hysterical parents, the academic community was immersed in the problem, although with divergent experiences. Psychologists Elizabeth Loftus and Richard Ofshe became prominent for critiquing the adherents of recovered memory and satanic abuse. Proponents of repressed memories and ritual abuse launched the *Cultic Studies Journal* through the American Family Foundation in an effort to validate the phenomenon. For all the interest generated by repressed memory and satanic abuse, attempts to empirically validate them would be a minefield, as evident in the experience of Susan Clancy. A Harvard-trained psychologist, Clancy hypothesized that victims of repressed memory would be more likely than non-victims to embellish a short list of words upon recall. For example, Clancy exposed subjects to related words, such as "candy," "sour," and "sugar," then later added "sweet." As suspected, Clancy found that victims of repressed memories were more likely to have seen "sweet" on the original list, the embellishment suggesting the fallibility of those claiming repressed memory. Subsequent to publishing her findings in *Psychological Science*, Clancy was confronted with some objections to her research, among them that victims of repressed memories had had such traumatic experiences that their recall was impaired. In order to replicate her study to address this problem, Clancy had to find a group of subjects who were traumatized by obviously invalid experiences. But whom? Clancy subsequently replicated her study with a group of people who remembered being abducted by aliens, then verified that alien abductees were, like her repressed memory subjects earlier, more likely to imagine errant words associated with those on an original list as compared to a non-abductee control group. But academics and victims of repressed memory were unwilling to leave the issue to empirical adjudication, hectoring and intimidating Clancy until she relented and accepted a research position in Nicaragua.[53]

As the postmodern enthusiasm for repressed memory attests, the absence of professional norms in child protection, especially an appreciation for research, leaves child welfare workers susceptible to ideological fashions. The infusion of cultural diversity into child welfare injected a relativism that confused workers and subverted agency procedures. Judith Marks Mishne summed up the dilemma:

> What is misperceived as "political correctness" has replaced common sense, good judgment and clinical assessment. Of late all too frequent agency practice is tolerance of varied forms of child abuse, because they are supposed [to be] routine disciplinary measures undertaken by various ethnic groups and segments of other groups described as people of color. Such tolerance of reverse racism, I think, actually appears to be part and parcel of cultural awareness training, provided by so-called "ethnicity experts."[54]

Kinship care, an alternative to out-of-family placement of children who have been maltreated, illustrates how political correctness compromised the welfare of at-risk children. An analysis of kinship care in California found that supervising adults were more likely to be single, less educated, more welfare dependent, and poorer than other foster parents. As a way to strengthen minority families, kinship care was strongly endorsed in the African American community, yet questions remained about the benefit of this arrangement for abused and neglected children. "Vulnerable African American children in kinship care, placed with aging relatives who are perhaps unable to provide adequate supervision, may be the unwitting victims of the romance of the autonomous African American community," suspected William Epstein.[55]

During the 1980s and 1990s, a romance with race, ethnicity, and poverty led child welfare professionals to embrace "family preservation" as the intervention of choice when working with abused and neglected children. Proponents of "family preservation" held that short-term crisis intervention could avoid a child's placement outside of the home. Typically, family preservation programs assigned child welfare workers to very small caseloads, but required them to be available round-the-clock for as long as six weeks. When preliminary research revealed that the vast majority of children receiving such services avoided out-of-home placement, the fortunes of family preservation rose. The infatuation with family preservation eclipsed a more comprehensive understanding of how maltreated children were faring, such as the child's health, school performance, and psychosocial development; yet its adherents advanced the movement on a single variable: avoidance of out-of-family placement. In 1990, researchers from the University of Chicago reported that family preservation was more inspiration than substance. The Illinois Family First program had no effect on rates of subsequent reports of maltreatment or on the duration or types of placement, and its impact on improving housing, parenting, and economics was mixed.[56] Family preservation nonetheless led a charmed life, generating the first major injection of federal funds in child welfare in decades in the form of $930 million authorized through the 1993 Family Support and Preservation Program. The dominance of family preservation since the 1990s was due, then, not to a track record validated by research, but rather its timeliness—family preservation not only provided a lifeline for child welfare professionals and public program administrators who were desperate to demonstrate that a social program could produce desirable outcomes at low cost, *and*, in keeping families intact, it promised to neutralize the increasingly strident, antiwelfare rhetoric of the religious Right. That children might be further harmed as family preservation became the signature program in child welfare was simply ignored.

While interventions that lacked empirical substantiation defined child welfare throughout the 1980s and 1990s, postmodernism had yet to run its course. Drawing on the work of psychiatrist Alvin Poussaint, social work professor Joy DeGruy-Leary applied the term "post-traumatic slave syndrome" to describe the "self-destructive, violent, or aggressive behavior" evident among African American youth, a vestige of the "multigenerational trauma" inflicted by slavery.[57] Post-traumatic slave syndrome served as the basis for an eponymous play that was performed at New York City's Henry Street Settlement and received a positive review in the *New York Times*.[58] Although post-traumatic syndrome played well in the theater, it faired less well in the courtroom. On June 30, 2003, an African American man, Isaac Cortez Bynum, beat his son, Ryshawn Lamar Bynum, to death in Beaverton, Oregon. The autopsy revealed that the two-year-old "died of a brain injury and had a broken neck, broken ribs, and as many as 70 whip marks on his legs, buttocks, back, and chest that were of various ages."[59] Bynum's attorney enlisted DeGruy-Leary for the defense, arguing that the father's behavior "in a general way" reflected the way in which slaves were brutalized by their masters. In pretrial testimony, DeGruy-Leary explained that, although she had not examined Bynum, post-traumatic slave syndrome was a plausible explanation for his behavior. "If you are African American and you are living in America, you have been impacted," she stated. Conceding that she would have reported the injuries inflicted on the boy, DeGruy-Leary testified that such punishment is "extremely common" in the African American community. "It falls in the rubric of what they think is normal," she said. Seeking to establish the validity of post-traumatic slave syndrome, the judge contacted the associate director of research for the *Diagnostic and Statistical Manual of Mental Disorders*, who not only had not heard of the term, but that, to his knowledge, no one had proposed its inclusion in the next edition of the book. Subsequently, the judge threw out DeGruy's testimony.[60] Post-traumatic slave syndrome soon became a staple of Internet chat rooms, serving as a convenient target for conservative rants against errant liberalism.

NETWORKS OF NEGLIGENCE

While post-traumatic slave syndrome may have been an extreme manifestation of postmodernism in social welfare, it reflected the impressionistic basis for interventions designed to help children. The received wisdom on child welfare, rather than being constructed systematically from empirical research, was largely the product of common sense compromised by adverse circumstances. That environmental factors contributed to the shabby quality of child welfare could not be dismissed. Services to children exist in a society in which dualism has been and continues to be conspicuous in designating benefits and opportunities, apportioning generously to the affluent, stingily to the poor. Historically, American child welfare has been shaped by class (public services are deployed *de facto* for the poor) and race (families of color have been marginalized from mainstream institutions and therefore have a disproportionate need for services). A primary consequence of dualism, which is usually neglected in examinations of children's services, is that more affluent families obtain services from private, often commercial, providers. This has multiple advantages: The services are superior to those in the public sector and confidentiality provisions assure privacy and anonymity. Except in the egregious examples of child maltreatment in which reports are received by public officials, private children's services allow more affluent families to dodge public child welfare. In allowing the exit option for those who can afford it—an inevitability in a free society—dualism thus subverts broad support for public child welfare.

The children who are presented for child welfare services, of course, are not just those with multiple risk factors, but also those who have experienced a degree of neglect or abuse that has been brought to the attention of authorities; in other words, children who warrant extensive interventions that entail major investments. The quality of services provided to such children, however, tends to be the obverse of what they need. The credentials of child welfare workers are suspect. Professional social work, for example, is of a vocational nature, rarely expecting students to acquire the skills and knowledge typical of the full-status professions (law and medicine) or even the semi-professions (education and nursing). The product of substandard preparation is a "professional" who is eager to follow agency procedures, is compliant with supervision, and is reluctant to use professional research, standards, or ethics as a basis for action. For this reason, strikes of overburdened child welfare caseworkers against public officials who oversee substandard care are virtually unknown in the United States.[61]

If the professional capacity of child welfare caseworkers is problematic, the daily care provided to troubled children by families and institutions offers, with notable exception, little reason for confidence. Families, either those providing foster or kinship care, tend to mirror the socioeconomic status of their charges; as a result, they fail to compensate for the material or relational deprivation associated with the need for care in the first place. Accordingly, child welfare offers minimal care at best. An unpleasant feature of foster or kinship care is *increased* harm to children who have been placed as a result of abuse or neglect. Occasionally, the damage is so extensive that class action suits have been filed on behalf of children in care against heads of children's services departments that are supposed to be helping them. After reviewing research on foster care, Duncan Lindsey concluded that "foster care is often more dangerous than the family the child is removed from."[62] Yet, for their welfare, children *are* often removed and placed in foster care, an intervention that proves of dubious value. As William Epstein reported, half of "permanent" foster placements typically fail.[63] At its best, institutional care tends to be minimal; often care is so substandard that services are placed under court management.[64]

The matter of accountability, or its more consequential version, *liability*, enters the picture only occasionally. Public agencies and their agents might be held liable for negligence, but in 1989, in *DeShaney v. Winnebago County Department of Social Services*, the Supreme Court ruled that neither social workers nor their governmental employer could be held liable, even when caseworkers had ample evidence of harm being inflicted on a child but failed to take any action, when the child was not in the custody of the state.[65] Thus, the *DeShaney* decision exempted public agencies from liability if they had no direct control over a child, as when a child is placed in foster care.

No account of children's services would be complete without an accounting for the projects underwritten by American philanthropy, the industry of foundations that subsidize advocacy activities on behalf of troubled children, as well as particularly meritorious demonstration projects mounted by public and nonprofit agencies. The amount dedicated to children by philanthropy is difficult to pinpoint because of overlapping activities by nonprofit agencies, but it is probably about $3.5 billion.[66] Regardless, it is decidedly *un*politic to question the charitable impulses that drive American philanthropy because rescissions in governmental allocations for public welfare have been compensated for in part by philanthropic activity for children. Yet the philanthropic sector contributes to the disarray in American children's services, primarily by its very voluntaristic nature. Short of violating the canons of tax exemption, philanthropies are free to fund whatever their program officers can convince the allocations committee of the board of directors to subsidize. Unfortunately, there is no way to correct for whim, fancy, or simple caprice in making such awards. In actuality, the careers of program officers, indeed the stature of foundations, are constructed out of the selection

process for meritorious programs, a process that begins with a furtive search for the novel, a slick packaging of same for board digestion, and the celebratory announcement of a grant to the local media. James Garbarino has been candid in his appraisal of the resultant disarray: "We have seen too many programs that don't rock the boat or require us to change ourselves or our institutions in any major way. Based on politically fashionable themes, these are well-meaning but ineffectual programs for which funding is readily available from donors who wish to appear responsible."[67] Absent empirical standards to guide philanthropic giving, the sexiness of today's fashion in children's services may well eclipse yesterday's more proven program. Worse, when foundations prioritize funding in a manner that *disallows* awards for program maintenance, managers of even effective programs are forced to reinvent their programs to get a shot at continued funding.

For six decades the federal government has had, more than any other entity, the mandate to defend maltreated children. Indeed, since the first White House Conference on Children in 1909, advocates for children have lobbied for a strong federal presence in child welfare.[68] Initially with Title IV of the 1935 Social Security Act and subsequent expansions in 1974 for child abuse, 1980 for adoption assistance, 1993 for family preservation, 1997 for child safety, and 2003 for child protection, the federal government has initiated and subsidized a range of child welfare activities, often in collaboration with state government. In 1996, federal appropriations for child welfare totaled $6.5 billion, compared to $6.4 billion in state funds, and $1.3 billion spent locally.[69] Despite the billions of dollars allocated for child welfare, the product has been a Byzantine maze of some 40 categorical federal programs targeted at different subgroups and funded through varying matching formulae.[70] Perversely, a more favorable federal match often dictates a state's focus in child welfare, an administrative practice that has become standard as state health and human service administrators exploit the fungibility of federal revenues. More perplexing is the absence of systematic data on the expenditure of federal funds for children's services. In exchange for the $5 billion in federal funds projected for foster care and adoption assistance in 2000,[71] states are not required to demonstrate service effectiveness, aside from avoiding misappropriation of funds. For the $2.5 billion available for a wide range of services under the Title XX Social Services Block Grant (much of it focusing on children), the federal government did not institute *any* reporting requirements for the states until the mid-1990s, and then the information released by the Federal Department of Health and Human Services was of a cursory nature and often incomplete or sporadic.[72]

In 2003, the federal Administration on Children and Families released an assessment of the performance of 32 states with respect to seven basic outcomes central to child welfare. The program audits included the largest states—California, New York, Pennsylvania, Michigan, Texas, and Florida—so the results summarized the experiences of a large number of vulnerable children. The subsequent report

card documented that a majority of states failed to be in compliance on every outcome measure; on two outcomes, not one state was in "substantial conformity"
(Table 6-1). A year later, little had changed. With respect to the seven standards, significant improvement had occurred on only the sixth when 14 states met the educational standard. *Not one state was able to assure that maltreated children had a permanent and stable living arrangement; not one state was in compliance with regard to
families having improved their ability to care for their children; only one state demonstrated that it adequately met a child's physical and mental health needs.* As a result of
their poor performance, states risked losing millions of dollars in federal funds;
however, this appeared a symbolic threat since it is unlikely that the federal government would step in and assume direct control of services for abused and neglected
children. But there was little reason to expect dramatic improvement in state compliance with the seven standards either: "Many states said they did not have enough
caseworkers to investigate reports of abuse and neglect or to monitor children in
foster care. They have difficulty recruiting and retaining workers because salaries
are low," reported the *New York Times.* "But some states, grappling with what they
describe as their worst fiscal problems in more than 50 years, have cut spending for
some child welfare services."[73]

The federal presence in child welfare has thus become little more than a funnel

TABLE 6-1.

State Compliance on Child Protection Outcomes

OUTCOMES	STATES IN SUBSTANTIAL COMPLIANCE	STATES NOT IN SUBSTANTIAL COMPLIANCE
Children are, first and foremost, protected from abuse and neglect	5	27
Children are safely maintained in their own homes whenever possible and appropriate	4	28
Children have permanency and stability in their living situations	0	32
The continuity of family relationships and connections is preserved for children	5	27
Families have enhanced capacity to provide for their children's needs	0	32
Children receive appropriate services to meet their educational needs	7	25
Children receive adequate services to meet their physical and mental health needs	1	31

Source: "Summary of the Results of the 2001 and 2002 Child and Family Services
Reviews," (Administration on Children and Families, downloaded August 28, 2003).
http://www.acf.hhs.gov/programs/cb/cwrp/results.htm

of revenues that the states exploit in a tangle of program activities. Oversight has been conveniently obviated because of the absence of reporting data. In a half-century of federal activity in child welfare, leadership has become more a testament of bureaucratic adroitness than it is any compelling vision of what troubled children require and a demand that the states perform accordingly.

The states, for their part, have shown a callous disregard for the needs of children. Illustrative of state indifference to child welfare has been the revelation that some 12,700 parents have relinquished custody of their children in order for them to receive needed mental health services. Since the General Accounting Office could access records from only 19 states, the number of such cases is probably more than twice the figure cited. Because of the paucity of mental health and supportive services available in the community, parents of seriously disturbed children have little choice but make their children wards of the state if they are to obtain any care at all. That parents would have to turn their children over to the state may not produce the outcome desired. The fortunate children with severe mental impairments end up in foster care where their foster parents are eligible for state-provided mental health services.[74]

The unfortunate ones become residents of state institutions where care is deplorable even after court intercession. A Justice Department investigation of the Columbia (Mississippi) Training School found that many residents had been institutionalized for status offenses—running away, substance abuse, or probation violations—but that the treatment they received was punitive—residents shackled to poles and restrained in chairs for hours. In the worst instances, "boys and girls were choked, slapped, beaten, and attacked with pepper spray"; misbehaving girls were placed naked in a windowless cell with only a concrete floor to sleep on and a hole to relieve themselves for days or weeks at a time. Paradoxically, a sister institution, the Oakley (Mississippi) Training School, had been the subject of a 1977 federal court ruling that required more staff and less punitive treatment to residents.[75]

PROFESSIONAL INEPTITUDE

The moribund nature of children's services, then, can be attributed to the interaction of several factors. Social dualism allows more affluent families to avoid child welfare so that public services become associated with the minority poor. Children referred for child welfare evidence multiple risk factors that are often exacerbated by abuse and neglect, insults that merit intensive intervention. The case for adequate child welfare, however, is subverted by professional mediocrity—the inability of child welfare professionals to use research, standards, and ethics as a basis for action. Knowledge about child welfare is dictated by ideological fashion as opposed to rigorous scientific inquiry. Typically, programs receive minimal

funds; consequently, surrogate family care and institutional services are normally inadequate and often injurious to children placed in that care. Accountability of public agencies has been compromised by the *DeShaney* decision, protecting governmental agents from liability when a child is not in the custody of the state. The tendency of philanthropy to promote new fashions in programming subverts continuity, especially when promising programs need maintenance funds. Finally, federal officials have been unable to craft a single, unifying template for child welfare, opting instead to maintain a tangle of categorical programs.

How child welfare could have so deteriorated rests largely on the shoulders of human service professionals who have failed to present a convincing case for reform to the public. Instead of acknowledging the structural problems inherent in the present non-system, caseworkers, administrators, and advocates of services to children have effectively rationed care to those most vulnerable. Although some children do benefit from child welfare, an unconscionably large number are left in programmatic limbo, while many others unaccountably suffer permanent injury and even death. Instead of documenting the travesty, child welfare professionals become enchanted with postmodernism, in the process "fall[ing] for a sentimentalist, socialworker theory of morality which disavows the reality of human wickedness."[76] How could such a debacle continue for so long under the tutelage of child welfare professionals?

C. Wright Mills provided an important clue in his classic paper, "The Professional Ideology of Social Pathologists." Mills contended that professional pathologists were the key to understanding how personal troubles become social problems. Essentially, professionals serve as the arbiters of deviancy; as such they function as defenders of the bourgeois status quo. The problem, as Mills saw it, was that professional pathologists were educated to focus on the discreet case of deviance as opposed to the wider systemic dynamics that generated entire cohorts of deviant cases. "Present institutions train several types of persons—such as judges and social workers—to thinking terms of 'situations,'" observed Mills. "Their activities and mental outlook are set within existent norms of society; in their professional work they tend to have an occupationally trained incapacity to rise above a series of 'cases.'"[77] That the professions would engage in reductionism so systematically galled Mills, who was well versed on the promise of social engineering properly understood, having written his doctoral dissertation on pragmatism.

In "The Protection of the Inept," sociologist William Goode suggested that there was something much more malevolent at work here than the myopic detachment of American professionals that concerned Mills. Goode observed that all societies address ineptitude in two ways: establishing means for aiding the vulnerable and defending society from the inept. In this case, Child Protective Services has been deployed to protect maltreated children from abuse and neglect, and child welfare has been professionalized to protect society from quackery.

Although professions commit themselves to advancing the public interest, and secure a state-granted professional monopoly for so doing, there are flaws in the bargain. "All professions, while claiming to be the sole competent judges of their members' skills, and the guardians of their clients' welfare, refuse to divulge information about how competent any of them are, and under most circumstances their rules assert it is unethical to criticize the work of fellow members to laymen," Goode observed.[78] "Few are fired for incompetence, especially if they last long enough to become members of their work group. . . . Clearly the group does not typically expel these less competent members. Instead, in each collectivity there are structures or processes which protect them."[79] Thus, it comes belatedly to public attention that surgeons remove the wrong limbs, police have been bribed, and teachers are deficient with respect to basic knowledge—that much is incontrovertible. The professions, however, are subject to regulation, so the offenses are isolated, their impact minimized.

The novelty of Goode's formulation is not that well-credentialed people do damage, but that it becomes institutionalized. In a society where labor is subjected to market conditions, some work is of relatively little value, a circumstance conducive to "a higher level of ineptitude. The best illustrations can be found at the lower job levels, where few people actively *want* that kind of work," Goode notes. "This type of work is ranked as socially necessary but not important."[80] The result becomes a norm: "People decide they would rather pay little and tolerate ineptitude than pay good wages and thus be able to demand a high level of competence."[81] This circumstance, of course, is associated with stratification; those working with the poor and problematic in education, social services, and corrections typify this. In each of these instances, the public utility model has been deployed not only denying clients the ability to demand better service, but effectively protecting inept service providers as well. "As a consequence, a fairly low, often ritual, level of output is tolerated, and thus there are few pressures to evaluate personnel by reference to the supposed target performance."[82] As a norm of ineptitude becomes institutionalized, it becomes increasingly difficult to improve performance. Organizationally, "the inept create a 'floor,' a lowest permissible level of competence," and this becomes the common denominator of the quality of organizational activity. As Goode noted with scathing accuracy, "to some degree, the mediocre 'need' the really inept."[83]

Under these circumstances, the role of administration consists largely of containing the damage attributed to systemic ineptitude; for high visibility positions where inferior performance becomes pandemic, an executive will make heavy use of a public relations spokesperson. Public administrators who make a career of containing ineptitude are highly valued; hence, superintendents of inner-city school systems, directors of welfare departments, and administrators of juvenile services commonly move from city to city, their mobility contingent on avoiding exposés and expensive litigation. Public administrators who cultivate reputations as "trouble-shooters" rarely benefit the communities that their agencies serve in any substantive way since their primary function is not improving service—though this gets ample rhetoric—but rather damage control. Since public service organizations serve a similar strata of clientele, ineptitude tends to transcend the agencies serving entire communities.

It is not difficult to see how ineptitude has influenced child welfare, contributing to an organizational culture infused with mediocrity. Deprofessionalization of child welfare populates offices with staff not well-trained in human services. The poverty and problems that typify children needing protection tend to diminish public support as it is; but, professional endorsement of questionable interventions, such as repressed memory and satanic abuse, further undermines public confidence in children's services. Rather than subject children's services to the same degree of rigorous field research as has occurred in welfare reform, child welfare interventions are substantiated by sentiment and anecdote. When exposés of the failure of child protection are featured in the media, child welfare administrators cite confidentiality as a way to avoid public scrutiny. The *DeShaney* decision conveniently negates much of the legal liability on the part of child welfare professionals even when they are derelict in their work. Despite decades of subsidies, the federal government has been unable to get little more than incomplete data from state child welfare agencies; what data are reported are damning in the inadequacy of services provided to abused and neglected children. Rather than redouble efforts to develop effective interventions in children's services, the tangle of federal categorical programs encourages states to dispose of children in ways that maximize federal revenues. When foundations have funded innovative children's programs, their efforts are often frustrated by an organizational culture that subverts reform. For all the effort directed at helping vulnerable children, child welfare in America is roughly half as proficient as comparable efforts in Canada and the United Kingdom.

THE FUTURE OF CHILD WELFARE

That the nation's experience with child welfare was launched a century ago is perhaps the ultimate paradox of child protection. The amount dedicated to children—on the order of $20 billion—might be expected to produce a modicum of accountability; yet the battalions of child welfare professionals have failed to craft a credible response to the maltreatment of children, as evident in the federal child and family outcomes reviews. Instead of acknowledging its institutional flaws and developing systematic strategies for their solution, children's service workers have indulged in a series of postmodern fads, ranging from opposing trans-racial adoption to embracing repressed memories and satanic abuse. More substantive investigations of family preservation have failed to validate the enthusiasm of child welfare professionals. The obvious counterpoint has been welfare reform, an initiative that required field experiments, the results of which have been used to better craft and expand services for poor, disproportionately minority women who are entering the labor market. Instead of similarly exploring alternatives for the care of maltreated children, child welfare professionals have retreated to kinship care, a happy, yet unsubstantiated, reconciliation of familial romanticism with low-cost budgeting. Although a handful of critics have called for fundamental reform, their voices have been muffled by a choir of political correctness. As had been the case with welfare reform, the Liberati occupied itself with postmodernism rather than address the real problems experienced by maltreated children. That such foolishness would be allowed to continue over the decades is perhaps best reflected in Saul Bellow's observation, "A great deal of intelligence can be invested in ignorance when the need for illusion is deep."[84]

7

RADICAL PRAGMATISM

If knights, grandees, noblemen, or the high-born were to consider me a fool, I should take it as an intolerable affront; but that scholars who never entered or trod the paths of chivalry should set me down as a madman does not effect me a jot. A knight I am and a knight I shall die, if it please the Most High. Some travel the broad field of proud ambition; others by way of base and servile adulation; others again by way of deceitful hypocrisy, and a few by way of the true religion. But beneath the influence of my star I journey along the narrow path of knight errantry, in which exercise I despise wealth, but not honour. I have redressed grievances, set down fiends. I am in love, only because knights errant are obliged to be so; and, being so, I am not one of those depraved lovers, but of the continent and platonic sort. I always direct my purposes to virtuous ends, and do good to all and ill to none.

DON QUIXOTE

Reflecting their denial of conservative control of social policy, liberals often invoked "the pendulum theory," hoping that a public shift in preferences would be, somehow, self-correcting. Historian Arthur Schlesinger, Jr., hypothesized such a theory based on thirty-year ideological cycles. Drawing on the New Deal of the mid-1930s and the Great Society of the mid-1960s, Schlesinger prophesied the election of the next unapologetically liberal president—and the introduction of the next major expansion of social programs—in the early 1990s.[1] Unfortunately, while Schlesinger was proposing his cyclical vision of social policy, "new Democrats" were busy organizing the Democratic Leadership Council to assure that the pendulum did *not* swing back to the political Left. Any uncertainty about President Clinton's ideological predilections were laid to rest when he

signed the 1996 Welfare Reform Act, subsequently punctuated by his announcement that "the era of big government is over."

In this instance, liberals might have appreciated a different historical cycle, one
posed by Milton and Rose Friedman. The Friedmans posited three "tides" that
shaped social affairs following the Enlightenment: the rise of laissez-faire during
the nineteenth century (Adam Smith tide), the rise of the welfare state during the
twentieth century (the Fabian [Marxist] tide), and the resurgence of free markets
during the next century (the Hayek tide). In naming the last tide after Frederich
von Hayek, the Friedmans recognized a philosopher little known to liberals who
not only foretold the demise of state socialism, but also predicted the globalization of capitalism.[2]

The ascendance of conservatism as public philosophy is significant in several
respects. First, the transformation was executed in less than two decades; galva-
nized by Barry Goldwater's 1964 presidential election defeat, movement conservatives determined to reverse the nation's adherence to liberalism and celebrated the
accomplishment only sixteen years later. Second, the nation's embrace of conservatism was the result of a concerted effort on the part of think tanks that introduced innovative and aggressive marketing of ideas in an environment in which
complacent liberal institutions had been predominant. Third, liberal policy institutes failed to respond in kind, continuing an archaic mode of analysis typified by
impenetrable books, a reflective manner, and a defensive posture. Given liberal
intransigence, conservatism not only dominated social policy during the latter
part of the twentieth century, but appeared well positioned to control domestic
affairs far into the next century too. The consequence for social policy was profound. The conservative triumph in welfare reform coupled with tax cuts made it
unlikely that social insurance obligations to baby boomers would be honored,
portending the demise of welfare liberalism and reorganization of the American
welfare state. Further clouding the prospect of a resurgence of the Progressive tradition in domestic policy was the Left's infatuation with postmodernism.

PROACTIVE RHETORIC

Early in the twenty-first century, it was increasingly evident that the welfare state
no longer provided a valid template for domestic policy among the Western
democracies. Certainly, conservative dominance in social policy during the past
quarter century effectively banished the liberal dream of replicating the northern
European welfare state in the United States. In place of incremental progress in
protecting citizens against insecurities associated with industrialization and capitalism, Americans witnessed a bipartisan effort to alter fundamentally, if not re-
tract outright, the legislation that has served as the foundation for the nation's social policy for more than half a century. Instead of adding benchmarks to the

expansion of the welfare state, liberals were reduced to defending the very social programs that had been the bedrock of contemporary social progress. The evidence was irrefutable. The 1981 Omnibus Budget Reconciliation Act decimated public welfare while inviting states to seek waivers in order to deploy alternatives to Aid to Families with Dependent Children (AFDC). The Family Support Act of 1988 introduced the first conservative imprint on public welfare since the Social Security Act. In 1989, Congress repealed Catastrophic Health Insurance, the first retraction of a social insurance program in the history of the American welfare state.

If the conservative vector in social policy was established by the Reagan and first Bush administrations, the Clinton presidency did little to reverse its momentum. During the first term of the Clinton presidency, the Health Security Act was soundly defeated. In 1996, President Clinton signed the Personal Responsibility and Work Opportunity Reconciliation Act, capping the expenditures for AFDC, devolving the program to the states, and setting time limits on receipt of aid, the most radical change in welfare policy since the War on Poverty. Striking at the heart of the welfare state, Clinton's bipartisan Social Security panel presented three options for salvaging the nation's public pension program, each of which called for varying degrees of privatization. Subsequently, the second Bush presidency moved boldly to the Right. During his first presidential election campaign, George W. Bush advocated restructuring social insurance programs. Rather than avoiding the "third rail" of domestic policy, Bush appointed a commission on Social Security reform that consisted solely of advocates of privatization. Coupled to a massive, ten-year tax cut and the imminent retirement of "baby boomers," fundamental questions loomed about the viability of Social Security and Medicare.

That this had come to pass was more a testament to the choreography of public sentiment than it was an inherent cynicism of Americans toward the needy. Indeed, as far back as the late 1970s, the president of the American Enterprise Institute had pledged to alter public philosophy so that is was more congruent with conservative precepts. During the 1980s, policy institutes from the ideological right—the Heritage Foundation, the Manhattan Institute, and the Hoover Institution—planned and executed a series of maneuvers that succeeded in reversing liberal hegemony in social policy. By the end of the decade, liberals were faced with a paradox. Although Americans supported social insurance programs,[3] conservatives were defining the debate on the future of social policy. How had conservatives become so masterful at employing rhetoric in order to put public opinion to ideological service? What could this suggest for future directions in social policy?

In 1991, Albert O. Hirschman addressed such questions in *The Rhetoric of Reaction: Perversity, Futility, Jeopardy*.[4] Having served on the Ford Foundation's project on the future of the American welfare state, Hirschman was provoked to consider the quite profound impact of the relatively flimsy critiques of American social welfare programs that had been advanced by conservatives. Hirschman drew on T. H. Marshall's three stages of citizenship—civil, political, and social/economic—to assess the inordinate difficulty encountered by liberals in bringing the American welfare state to completion. Using historical material, Hirschman proposed that earlier progress in citizenship—attaining and defending civil and political rights—had also encountered adversity. Moreover, Hirschman concluded that conservative arguments against progressive change could be organized around three theses: perversity, futility, and jeopardy. What made Hirschman's work astute was his observation that these very theses characterize much of the current conservative assault on the American welfare state.

By now the critique of the welfare state trumpeted by the Right has a familiar ring: Rather than alleviating deprivation, welfare programs worsen dependency and contribute to a malignant underclass (it is perverse). Rather than ameliorate conditions of the poor, poverty persists despite the hundreds of billions of dollars spent on social welfare (it is futile). Rather than advance social and economic rights of the disadvantaged, social programs require the elaboration of the state, the expansion of which attenuates freedom and prosperity for all (it is jeopardy). Such arguments are not novel, contended Hirschman; they surface regularly when conservatives wish to sabotage progress.

Although he was able to identify some of sources of regressive rhetoric, such as Charles Murray,[5] Hirschman's work was incomplete. In part, this was due to the omission of other conservative seers, such as Peter Berger and Marvin Olasky, and the intellectual organizations that have promoted conservative philosophy during the past two decades (e.g., the American Enterprise Institute and the Heritage Foundation). In part, it was because Hirschman's book appeared before Bill Clinton's election to the presidency and the failure of the administration's Health Security Act, before the 1994 Republican electoral triumph that was underscored in subsequent congressional elections, and before the welfare reform legislation was signed into law in 1996, to say nothing of the election of George W. Bush—events that further propelled conservatism in America. What, then, were the antecedents of conservative arguments against the welfare state? What are the themes that could serve to direct future social policy?

THE LIBERAL ANTECEDENTS OF REACTIONARY RHETORIC

In targeting social programs, conservatives put liberalism squarely in their sights. Two decades of sniping have clarified the specific theses that conservatives have advanced as well as the liberal counterattack. The success that conservatives have enjoyed in shaping public philosophy can be attributed to their construction and maintenance of a network of policy institutes that have maintained an incessant assault on liberalism and social welfare programs. To compound matters, Left-wing Liberati have embraced postmodernism, which the Right has, with scathing accuracy, roundly disparaged. Conservatives have become so proficient at this rhetorical parrying that they routinely reduce Progressives to ideological carica-ture. Instead of posing an alternative set of theses, liberals have found comfort in defending familiar, shopworn ideas.

Thus, the antecedents to conservative rhetoric have not only provided the fuel for the Right, but they have also become a crutch for the defenders of welfare liberalism—one that offers diminishing support. Probably the best indications of the conservative aptitude for this rhetorical game are the contrasting ambiances that pervade the respective ideological camps. Liberalism, once the font of opti-mism effused by the likes of Pete Seeger and Hubert Humphrey, evinces a pitiable dejection, while the Right, at one time the refuge of spoilsports like Richard Nixon, produces the spirited orneriness of P. J. O'Rourke and Robert Rector. Dur-ing the 1960s, liberals smirked that there weren't any Republican folk songs; but since the 1980s conservatives seem to be having all the fun.

The liberalism that evolved with the New Deal and the Great Society orbited around three poles: adequacy, equality, and regulation. Adequacy was articulated by programs that assured income to those populations marginal to the labor mar-ket. Income-related entitlements were extended to poor workers by creation and elevation of the minimum wage and, upon retirement, the provision of a minimal pension through Social Security. For those outside the labor market, welfare pro-grams such as AFDC, Food Stamps, and Supplemental Security Income (SSI) guaranteed a financial floor. In the half century following passage of the Social Se-curity Act, non-income supports were offered, such as health care (Medicare and Medicaid), prenatal care (the Women, Infants, and Children Supplemental Nutri-tion Program), and housing (Section 8). Behind the adequacy thesis was a liberal assumption that providing basic supports for the poor would free them to use op-portunities, such as education and work, to prosper.

Equality was a direct response to the social and income stratification of Ameri-can culture according to class, race, and gender. The redistributional impulse that at least formally taxed the rich at higher rates in order to provide benefits to workers was advanced by Progressives to ameliorate problems associated with di-verging classes. The Civil Rights Act of 1964 extended social and political rights to African Americans whose opportunities were attenuated by de facto segregation. In order to encourage employers to hire and promote minorities and women, Af-firmative Action was introduced. In advancing equality, liberals argued that gov-ernment's assurance of equal political rights should be extended to the economic and social sectors, as well. The ultimate objective was a society in which class, race, and gender, if not eradicated, would no longer circumscribe opportunity for entire subpopulations.

Regulation served to justify governmental intrusion into the economy in the late industrial period. During the Progressive era, regulation was the instrument of choice to clean up corruption and exploitation in government, the production of food and drugs, commerce and banking, and working conditions for women and children.[6] A more central role for government in markets was sanctioned by Keynesian theory in order to avoid recession. Governmental actions to counter the Depression and defend the nation during the Second World War then the Cold War led Americans to expect federal intervention when America's prosperity and security were threatened. During the post–World War II era, federal initiatives were authorized in order to keep the nation strong in the event of foreign aggression, among them the G.I. Bill, completion of the inter-state highway system, and an extensive student loan program.[7] Much of the liberal activist agenda after 1960s—the Civil Rights Act, the ill-fated Equal Rights Amendment, the Occupational Safety and Health Act, and the Americans with Disabilities Act—were justified by a broad interpretation of the regulatory role of the federal government.

Adequacy, equality, and regulation served liberalism well, effectively orienting American social policy for a half century. The brew was sufficiently potent that even conservative presidents—Eisenhower and Nixon—not only admitted the correctness of liberally inspired policies but also conceded to their extension. By 1980, social program expenditures accounted for more than 57 percent of the federal budget and almost 20 percent of the gross domestic product.[8] In the judgment of most observers, the welfare state had become an institutional fixture in American culture.[9] Conservatives, however, were unwilling to condone a welfare state that hemorrhaged benefits through open-ended entitlements and went to work building a critique of liberal social programs.

THE CONSERVATIVE CRITIQUE

The conservative challenge to welfare liberalism began with a string of policy institutes promoting conservatism as public philosophy. Think tanks, such as the American Enterprise Institute, the Heritage Foundation, the Hoover Institution, and the Manhattan Institute, among others, collected resentment that had accumulated within the corporate sector, the Right wing of the Republican party (as well as some disaffected conservative Democrats), and the grassroots traditionalist movement, catalyzing a fundamental critique of liberal social policy. This ideological offensive was played out much in the way Hirschman described.

Conservatives attacked the liberal adequacy thesis by arguing that its consequences were *perverse*. Rather than assure the poor of a safety net from which they could bounce back into productive activities, welfare insidiously induced dependency, lulling economically marginal families into an underclass from which they could not escape. Charles Murray popularized this thesis in *Losing Ground*, which appeared in 1984. Still, Murray was somewhat uncertain about how to remedy the degeneracy he attributed to welfare, so he obliquely presented his solution as "a thought experiment"—"scrapping the entire federal welfare and income support structure for working-age persons."[10] However elliptically presented, the suggestion of outright elimination of all welfare for working-age Americans was breathtaking. No less astonishing was the relatively weak evidence that Murray offered to substantiate his argument.

This idea that welfare exacerbated poverty led conservative analysts to differentiate a "new" behavioral poverty from the "old" cash poverty.[11] While the income programs of the social safety net might be appropriate for the prudent poor, the problem of behavioral poverty called for a more strategic response. According to Lawrence Mead,[12] the negative effects of welfare could be corrected by making receipt of benefits conditional on mainstream behavior, particularly work. Thus, welfare-to-work featured prominently in the Family Support Act of 1988; in order to receive AFDC, beneficiaries without exempting circumstances would be required to participate in education, training, or job placement services or lose their benefits. Once having found a job, AFDC recipients were entitled to "transitional benefits," the receipt of assistance for child care, transportation, and Medicaid for one year to ease the transition to private-sector employment.[13] By the early 1990s, enforcing Mead's notion of reciprocity among welfare recipients had become fashionable among state governors. Wisconsin introduced "learnfare," the requirement that children on AFDC demonstrate regular school attendance or their family would lose benefits. New Jersey promoted family planning by refusing to increase benefits for additional children born after welfare benefits were granted. Several states took President Clinton at his word for his intent to "end welfare as we know it" by introducing a time limit on receipt of welfare, the termination of benefits being the ultimate form of conditionality. By the time the 104th Congress was prepared to "devolve" welfare to the states in a block grant, some 40 states had already received waivers from the federal government to pilot experiments. State welfare experiments and passage of the Personal Responsibility and Work Opportunity Reconciliation Act of 1996—"welfare reform"—essentially validated the perversity thesis.[14]

The Right also attacked the liberal equality thesis, contending that social programs were *futile* in the face of unalterable societal forces. Foremost, conservatives alleged that poverty had become more intractable even as public welfare expenditures increased. The more benign expression of the futility thesis portrayed class, race, and gender as "deep" structures that were simply immutable. George Gilder, for example, indicated that the interaction of race, gender, and class were too formidable to be transformed by social programs. Accordingly, his solution was to leave the poor to benefit from "the spur of their own poverty."[15] This theme blossomed in *The Bell Curve* by Charles Murray and Richard Herrnstein.[16] According to Murray and Herrnstein, low intelligence contributed to a range of social pathologies: teen pregnancy, welfare dependence, crime, unemployment, school failure, and family break-up. The reproduction of the low-IQ poor assured the growth of a "cognitive underclass," a subpopulation that was unable to benefit from well-intentioned social programs. Rather than improve the conditions of the underclass, welfare benefits maintained the degenerate poor, assuring the replication of persons with low IQs. The growth of the irremediable underclass eventually increased the hazards for intellectuals in the society, so the "cognitive elite" sought security by walling itself off in gated communities. Yet, despite the hazard presented by the underclass, the cognitive elite has been unable to mount credible responses to the threat posed by the low-IQ poor. The result, concluded Herrnstein and Murray, has been an inevitable "dumbing down" of American society.

Finally, conservatives argued that excessive regulation promulgated by liberals extended the role of the federal government to the point that American society was in *jeopardy*.[17] This argument evolved most vividly through the "mediating structures project" of the American Enterprise Institute (AEI), described in Chapter 3. Analysts at AEI contended that the authoritarian impulses of big government must be countered by a protean corporate sector and vibrant mediating structures of the voluntary sector. In the absence of such correctives, big government threatens American civilization itself. Having identified big government as a cultural hazard, the problem of responding to social need remained. The solution to this problem was proposed by the Heritage Foundation's Marvin Olasky, who suggested the revival of mediating structures extant prior to the New Deal. "The more effective provision of social services will ultimately depend on their return to private and especially to religious institutions," he averred. "Most of our twentieth-century schemes have failed. It's time to learn from the warm hearts and hard heads of the nineteenth."[18] By reinvigorating mediating structures, conservatives argued that the jeopardy posed by the social programs of big government could be avoided. Not surprisingly, as welfare reform proposals proliferated in various states, the more conservative governors favored replacing government welfare with voluntary, nonprofit activities, all consistent with mediating structures theory and, of course, the jeopardy thesis.[19]

PROACTIVE RHETORIC

If conservatives have successfully invoked a reactionary rhetoric, is it conceivable to craft a proactive rhetoric that is not a recitation of welfare liberalism? Proactive rhetoric should address flaws in the conservative critique of social programs at the same time it avoids the liberal tendency to retreat to the themes of the past. In a democratic policy, it must propose a vocabulary of possibility that resonates with the current and projected experience of Americans. Perforce, a proactive rhetoric would be as post-conservative as it is post-liberal.

As counterpoint to the perversity thesis (programs exacerbate poverty), a *mo-*

bility thesis would demonstrate how social policy can enhance prosperity. Conservative consequences of the perversity thesis—making receipt of welfare conditional on specific behaviors—is appealing rhetorically, but in practice it is at best ambiguous. Most research on welfare-to-work programs shows that they not only fail to vault many people into economic independence, but they also fall short of saving government substantial amounts in welfare expenditures.[20] As elaborated in Chapter 5, the typical welfare-to-work program increases participants' income, but only by several hundred dollars annually, hardly enough to make families self-sufficient. Moreover, savings to welfare departments are modest. Because of the initial investment needed to mount a welfare-to-work program, it often takes years for agencies to recover that initial outlay and achieve net savings, if ever. Many welfare-to-work enthusiasts regard the Riverside, California, program as a model, yet the results there are far from sanguine: "Even the Riverside program, considered to be the most successful welfare-to-work program evaluated to date, does not promise lasting results. Three years after entering the program, only 23 percent of the participants were still employed and off AFDC," observed Randall Eberts of the Upjohn Institute for Employment Research. "Furthermore, the earnings do little to lift welfare recipients out of poverty. In California overall, only 20 percent of the participants had annual incomes above the poverty rate after three years."[21]

If welfare-to-work disappoints, the implications of other forms of welfare conditionality are just as problematic. Learnfare—the requirement that AFDC children attend school regularly or their families risk benefit reductions—requires a "bean-counting" capability that would be a bonanza to the governmental bureaucracy. An evaluation of Milwaukee's experience with Learnfare concluded that the program failed to produce the outcomes promised by proponents.[22] But the imposition of time limits is most troublesome. Findings of the Institute for Women's Policy Research reveal that over 40 percent of AFDC mothers are either peripherally attached to the labor market, augmenting welfare with wages, or they drift in and out of welfare depending on the availability of work.[23] LaDonna Pavetti of the Urban Institute reports that 56 percent of women leave welfare by the end of the first year, and 70 percent leave by the end of two years; however, 45 percent return to public assistance before the end of the first year off welfare, and 57 percent return by the end of two years.[24] The imposition of time limits puts an abrupt halt to the parallel and cyclical relationship between low wages and welfare. Without public assistance, many poor mothers would simply be unable to support their families.[25]

A mobility thesis would highlight the aspirations of the poor and their climb up the socioeconomic ladder. "Social mobility is the saving fire that redeems society," David Brooks contends.

> Social mobility opens up horizons because people can see wider opportunities and live transformed lives. Social mobility reduces class conflict because

each person can build his own fortune, rather than taking from the fortunes of others. Social mobility unleashes creative energies and keeps everything new and dynamic. It compensates for inequality, because the family that is poor today may become richer tomorrow. It is the very essence of justice, because each person's destiny is somehow related to the amount of talent and effort his or she pours into life. The purpose of government is to ensure that there is, to use Lincoln's words, "an open field and a fair chance" so that everyone can compete in the race of life.[26]

Perhaps the best evidence of this comes from immigration research, which indicates that immigrants have labor force participation rates that eclipse those of native residents.[27] Not only do they create more jobs than they take, but immigrants also show a net contribution to the tax base.[28]

A conceptual illustration of the mobility thesis is the Individual Development Account (IDA) proposal fielded by Michael Sherraden.[29] Noting that most welfare benefits focus on income maintenance but that most poor families become prosperous by accruing assets, Sherraden suggests IDAs to promote upward mobility of the poor. IDAs are tax-exempt accounts providing they are spent on completing an education, buying a home, or establishing a business. An individual's contribution to an account would be matched by an external source, such as philanthropy or government, according to the income of the account holder.[30] IDAs reflect "such widely held values as opportunity, fairness, and the related belief that all people should have a decent chance to achieve self-fulfillment and well-being," noted Larry Brown and Larry Beeferman. "A further shared value is that of initiative: the sense that each of us has strengths and abilities, however different, and that we have an obligation to make a concerted effort on behalf of ourselves, our families, and society. This, in turn, connects to the values of self-reliance, the goal of maximizing personal responsibility, and independence."[31] Subsequently, the Corporation for Enterprise Development undertook an $8 million demonstration of IDAs at 13 sites across the nation as the "Downpayment on the American Dream" project, and IDAs became central to the Assets for Independence Act. Microcredit, sometimes called microenterprise, modeled after the Grameen Bank, is another example of a mobility accelerating program.

An answer to the futility thesis (programs are useless) would be the *empowerment* of the poor. Essentially, conservatives have trumped liberals with the futility thesis because of welfare liberalism's skepticism about markets and its adherence to the public utility model. Because capitalism skews the distribution of resources and opportunities, liberals have argued that the victims should be provided with necessities by government outside of the predatory marketplace, justifying the erection of public monopolies to serve the poor—bureaucracies that segregate the poor economically and socially from the mainstream. One of the ironies of contemporary social policy has been the genius with which some "bleeding-heart" conservatives diverged from conventional conservatism and exploited this opening during the Reagan presidency. Noting the courage of the late Kimi Gray, a welfare mother, in organizing neighbors in a District of Columbia housing project in order to expel drug users, then Secretary of Housing and Urban Development Jack Kemp initiated a program through which tenants could buy their housing units. At the same time, then Secretary of Education William Bennett endorsed the school choice initiative that had been introduced to the Wisconsin legislature by Annette "Polly" Williams. A former welfare mother and director of Jesse Jackson's presidential campaign in Wisconsin, Williams had become so concerned about the quality of public education received by her children that she sponsored the nation's first educational voucher legislation. In the early 1990s, Kemp and Williams teamed up to launch a conservative policy institute, Empower America!

Finally, the Left is beginning to reassess its allegiance to government monopoly. Public housing, for example, "isolate[d] low-income residents in class- and racially segregated developments rather than integrate them into middle-class neighborhoods." Moreover, the standardized benefits, provided through the public utility model, contradicted the virtue of consumer sovereignty. "The left must make especially clear that it sees the government as a partner in solving problems rather than as a boss," conceded Charles Noble. "There would still be safety-net programs and the provision of key primary goods, such as health care. But the focus would be on opportunity and choice, so that people could exercise control over their own lives, rather than on providing everyone with the same amount and quality of valued things."[32]

The *restructuring* of industrial bureaucracies rebuts the jeopardy thesis (new policies subvert previous achievements). The flattening of corporate bureaucracies proceeded with a vengeance during the last two decades of the twentieth century. Firms such as IBM, Sears, and General Motors shed tens of thousands of employees in order to maximize the use of technology, while diverting savings to stockholders through profits and bonuses to executives via excessive compensation packages. Within government, restructuring was promoted by David Osborne,[33] who investigated how governors were adjusting to increasing demand for services yet diminishing federal assistance to the states. Later Osborne teamed up with Ted Gaebler to produce *Reinventing Government*,[34] a book that quickly captured the attention of public administrators. Osborne then consulted with Vice President Al Gore on the National Performance Review, a federal housecleaning initiative that promised to eliminate 252,000 federal employees at an alleged savings of $108 billion.[35] Thus, the industrial-era edifices of the corporate and governmental sectors appear headed to the bureaucratic rendering plant.

Within this broad context of organizational transformation, experimentation in welfare provision has proceeded in the form of state welfare reform demonstrations. As noted earlier, most state experimentation in welfare reform has been aimed at countering the perversity thesis, not eliminating welfare per se. For that very reason, state welfare reforms that reflect a preoccupation with making receipt of welfare conditional on normative behavior require *further* elaboration of the welfare bureaucracy. In a delectable irony that critics of the Right might be quick to point out, such social engineering of the poor contradicts conservative precepts since it attenuates individual liberty while amplifying the functions and costs of government. Conservatively inspired welfare reform thus generates a perversity of its own by expanding the public welfare apparatus. Logically, devolution of welfare from the federal government to the states could be amplified by devolving authority to communities and individuals. This already occurs in two areas: The Community Development Financial Institutions Loan Fund subsidizes the deployment of neighborhood economic development organizations, and the Earned Income Tax Credit provides a refund for low-income workers. Because these initiatives are not part of the conventional welfare paradigm of poverty policy, they are not known as well as traditional programs such as Temporary Assistance for Needy Families (TANF), SSI, and Food Stamps, which are manifestations of the public utility model.

CHANGING THEMES IN SOCIAL POLICY

The themes associated with liberalism, conservatism, and their sequel are depicted in Table 7-1. This scheme of rhetorical transitions suggests that liberalism defined domestic policy roughly from 1935 to 1980, and that conservatism has served a similar function from 1980 to the present. Until Progressives abandon the antiquated rhetoric of welfare liberalism, they will be vulnerable to conservative critique of the welfare state. For liberals, the Right's apprehension about the welfare state was most often associated with Newt Gingrich, whose antipathy for federal social programs permeated the Republican Party: "The decay of the welfare state . . . has reduced citizens to clients, subordinated them to bureaucrats and subjected them to rules that are anti-work, anti-opportunity and anti-property. The welfare state must be replaced, not reformed."[36]

Reservations among Democrats have been less recognized. Ted Kennedy,

TABLE 7-1.
Themes in Social Policy

LIBERALISM	CONSERVATISM	RADICAL PRAGMATISM
Adequacy	Perversity	Mobility
Equality	Futility	Empowerment
Regulation	Jeopardy	Restructuring

speaking before the Women's National Democratic Club as early as 1988, stated, "We now stand between two Americas, the one we have known and the one toward which we are heading. The New Deal will live in American history forever as a supreme example of government responsiveness to the times. But it is no answer to the problems of today."[37] In the shadow of the 1994 Republican electoral triumph, "new" Democrat Al From had been more blunt: "The New Deal Era is over. It was a grand and glorious era for Democrats, but it is over. The nails are in the coffin of New Deal liberalism, and it is dead and buried. It was a great ideology while it lasted—it was the ideology that built the middle class of America—but the policies that built the middle class can no longer earn their support. And we have lost them."[38] Any fantasies about a revival of welfare liberalism were obliterated by President Clinton's signing of the 1996 Welfare Reform Act and George W. Bush's successful reform of Medicare and intentions to privatize social security. The massive tax cuts passed during George W. Bush's first term, coupled with the impending retirement of tens of millions of baby boomers, foretell a slow-motion train wreck that effectively puts an end to welfare liberalism.

RADICAL PRAGMATISM

Twenty-first century America needs a template for social policy that is socially, economically, and technologically dynamic—a format that is radically pragmatic. Mobility, empowerment, and restructuring extricate social policy from the current ideological impasse, which is an artifact of liberalism and conservatism. Historically, the themes of radical pragmatism can be traced to that unique American philosophy, which evolved in the nineteenth century. By exploiting the opportunities implicit in democratic capitalism, pragmatism can be reinvented to provide the basis for radical innovations in social policy. In this respect, radical pragmatism can be distinguished from what Terry Eagleton termed "philistine pragmatism," an orientation to the future that is limited by utilitarian preferences.[39] Accordingly, radical pragmatism has profound implications for the moribund state of social policy. Its application to family and child welfare show how these could be reconfigured.

Bootstrap Capitalism

Poverty policy in the United States consists of two streams of activity. The most well known is public welfare, comprised of the federal Department of Health and Human Services, parallel state agencies, and local welfare departments. The Income Maintenance division of local welfare departments distributes public assistance through TANF, SSI, Food Stamps, Medicaid, and less frequently General Assistance. Cash assistance and the welfare bureaucracy were described in Chapter 5.

Less known is the stream that is overseen by the Treasury Department, which provides a range of tax expenditures, such as the Earned Income Tax Credit (EITC), as well as operating community development initiatives, such as the Community Development Financial Institution (CDFI) Loan Fund. As a result of these dual tracks in poverty policy, paradoxes abound. The EITC, for example, rebates to low-income workers about twice the volume of welfare benefits that are spent through TANF, yet it is not often understood as welfare. As a wage supplement, the EITC would be a valuable benefit for welfare recipients transitioning to the labor market, yet welfare departments rarely help beneficiaries obtain it. While TANF has been converted to a discretionary program in which appropriations are capped, the EITC is open ended; there are no limits on allocations made to eligible tax-payers.

Radical pragmatism would craft a poverty policy congruent with the information age by integrating these streams. Accordingly, bootstrap capitalism relies on three components that are evident in extant programs: wage supplements, asset building, and community capitalism.

Wage Supplements—The primary lesson of welfare reform is that the poor are eager to work, but their wages remain stubbornly low. Since its inception in 1975, the EITC has become the largest wage supplement for the working poor, returning $35 billion annually to low-wage workers. Although the premise of the EITC is sound, it has two flaws. While it could be important for facilitating the transition from welfare to work, too few welfare recipients know about it; an Urban Institute study revealed that only 33 percent of welfare recipients had ever received an EITC refund. Although the EITC can be obtained in a way that encourages financial management as a periodic wage supplement, virtually all recipients elect to get it as a one-sum refund, often through refund anticipation loans that carry extortive interest rates. Other tax credits could benefit the poor by rebating a portion of wages that employers pay them as workers. During the 1990s, the Work Opportunity Tax Credit and Welfare-to-Work Tax Credit provided rebates to employers of low-wage workers, but these too are not used fully.

Asset Building—Middle-class families know that the road to prosperity is paved with assets, however, the nation has not mounted an adequate initiative to encourage the poor to save. For decades, public welfare prohibited the poor from accumulating assets, imposing limits of $1,500 per family. More recently, IDAs have been piloted at a number of localities through the Down-Payment on the American Dream demonstration, and they were featured in the Assets for Independence Act. By 2002, a disparity was increasingly obvious: while federal and state funding for IDAs totaled only $200 million for the poor, the non-poor claimed $300 *billion* in asset-related tax breaks. This was part of a larger picture of economic injustice. As Jacob Hacker argued, the "hidden welfare state" provided disproportionate benefits to the affluent through tax expenditures.[40] With the exception of the EITC, the vast majority of tax benefits—mortgage interest deduction, pension contributions, charitable giving, medical care, and child care—benefit those whose incomes exceed $30,000.

Community Capitalism—Although the affluent are well-versed in financial services, the poor are confronted with a dwindling number of branch banks (due to deregulation) and a plethora of check-cashing outlets (due to predation). Even though the majority of income for the poorest of neighborhoods is derived from wages, massive amounts hemorrhage from low-income communities every month because non-exploitive financial institutions have not been established in them. Since the mid-1990s, however, the Treasury Department has overseen the deployment of dozens of CDFIs, credit unions and community development banks that have become an alternative to the "fringe banking industry" by providing a range of financial services to residents and employers of poor communities. A 2001 survey of CDFIs revealed extensive investments in microenterprise, business, community services, and housing, augmenting the community's capital. CDFIs in operation three years or less averaged capital of $4.6 million, while those in operation at least a decade held $11.6 million.[41] In addition to trapping capital in poor neighborhoods, community capitalism complements faith-based social welfare. In New York City, former congressman Floyd Flake used his position as pastor of the Greater Allen Cathedral to construct a $23 million network of community development ventures. Seeing the future as a social entrepreneur, Flake recognized just how fundamental the change in social policy has been: "Those of us who have made a commitment to stay in an urban community have decided that *this* is our paradise," he observed. "We are going to rebuild that paradise—and we understand that it means some paradigm shifts."[42]

Initially, a poverty policy that promotes bootstrap capitalism would forge direct linkages to established welfare departments. Models such as the Self-Help Credit Union of Durham and the Alternatives Credit Union of Ithaca would be enlisted to demonstrate how capitalism can accelerate the upward mobility of poor families and their communities. Ultimately, community-developed credit unions (CDCUs) would be allowed to bid against welfare departments for client services, or they could replace them altogether through a charter process.[43] Full conversion to bootstrap capitalism would find that welfare departments had been phased out, replaced by CDCUs that provided a range of financial services to poor families. This could be accomplished by capitating income maintenance and reimbursing CDCUs according to the number of welfare recipients they enroll. Services offered by CDCUs would be coordinated by account managers—professionals trained in family economics—and would include the following:

- Account management (checking, savings, and the use of smart cards for access to benefits from automatic teller machines and Food Stamps automatically deducted at the check-out),
- Financial literacy to educate consumers about using different financial products to attain future objectives,
- Tax preparation to optimize refunds to workers, such as the EITC, as well

as to employers through the Welfare-to-Work and Work Opportunity tax credits, and
• Counseling about IDAs for vocational or higher education, buying a home or establishing a business, and long-range financial planning.

CDCUs could generate operating revenues by selling loan portfolios to commercial banks who would find them of value in complying with provisions of the Community Reinvestment Act. Using direct deposit, CDCUs would have substantial sums on reserve that could be used for community development projects, such as microenterprise.[44] Welfare recipients could enroll in a CDCU of their choice; as a result CDCUs would prosper according to the number of welfare recipients they enroll, providing incentives to provide services congruent with member aspirations. Oversight of bootstrap capitalism would be provided by the Treasury Department. Only Treasury-certified CDFIs would be allowed to supplant welfare departments. Propriety of CDCU activities would be reviewed periodically by the Treasury Department, which could sanction CDCUs for poor performance or terminate them if they are found to engage in corrupt practices. A poverty policy emphasizing economic development would retain a collaborative role for state government insofar as states determine eligibility; however, states should not be prohibited from contracting out such functions to CDCUs if they deem this desirable. States would continue to cover their share of the cost of benefits.

How plausible is Community Capitalism as an anti-poverty strategy? In investigating the scope of the fringe economy, Howard Karger has suggested that Americans expend $125 billion annually to check-cashers, payday lenders, pawnshops, rent-to-own stores and the like.[45] Much of this predatory activity exploits the working poor, in the process leeching money from low-income communities. The National Community Capital Association reported in 2001 that a developing CDFI held capital of $7 million.[46] In other words, the American fringe economy would have provided the capital for a network of more than 17,500 CDFIs. Unfortunately, the promise of Community Capitalism has been unfulfilled, a casualty of the inability of welfare advocates to grasp the prospects of social entrepreneurship and the Bush administration's unwillingness to fully fund the program. As a result, significant amounts of capital continue to hemorrhage from poor communities, a circumstance that is as tragic as it is unnecessary.

Reforming Child Welfare

Protecting children from mistreatment has evolved from the noble, if sometimes misplaced, impulses of voluntary agencies over a century ago into a tangle of program activity involving the federal and state governments. Since the 1935 Social Security Act, child welfare has expanded to include some 30 programs under four federal agencies. The largest of these provide federal funds to states for child welfare activities: Title IVE for foster care and adoption and Title IVB for prevention services. Title IVE is essential to child protection because most children who enter foster care do so as a result of having been abused or neglected; however, its funding mechanisms are anything but straightforward. Title IVE funding is open-ended, but only for children who meet the means-test requirements under the old AFDC program, which was replaced by Temporary Assistance for Needy Families in 1996. Under Title IVE, the federal government reimburses states for about half the cost of their child welfare activities, but 75 percent of training costs for child welfare workers. Federal reimbursement to states for a more recent Independent Living Program, which assists foster children who reach the age of majority, is 80 percent. Prevention programs, under Title IVB, are not open-ended nor are they limited to children who are eligible for AFDC, but they require a lower state match of 25 percent. Many states augment child welfare activities through the Title XX Social Services Block Grant, which requires no state match but is capped.[47] In 2004, federal expenditures for child welfare approximated $7 billion: $4.8 billion for Title IVE foster care, $1.6 billion for Title IVE adoption services, and $693 million for Title IVB prevention services.[48]

The child welfare scandals that have rocked Washington, D.C., Florida, and New Jersey are evidence that the collaboration between federal and state governments has been far from successful. Aside from unacceptably high morbidity and mortality rates of mistreated children, 500,000 children receive questionable care as foster children. As noted in Chapter 6, the vast majority of states fail to provide essential services for abused and neglected children; on two basic factors—assuring a permanent and stable living arrangement and enhancing the capacity of families to care for their children—not one state complies. Upon the release of the Pew Commission report on children in foster care, Chairman Bell Frenzel announced, "The nation's foster care system is unquestionably broken."[49] The editors of the *Washington Post* concurred: "The foster-care system is in abysmal shape. On average, children entering foster care languish in the system for three years, shuttled through three different places."[50]

Children's Authority—The crisis in child welfare warrants a Presidential Commission on Child Welfare to review the status of children's services and proposals to reform child welfare. Fundamentally, the commission should define the Children's Authority as a future model of service delivery.[51] By way of illustration, for over a decade the Youth Futures Authority (YFA) of Savannah/Chatham County, Georgia, has pooled categorical funds, outfitted family advocates with laptop computers, and sent them into the field to serve in poor neighborhoods. Since its inception, the YFA has reported outcomes on its program efforts, revealing improvements in several important variables, such as the number of children behind grade in school, the number of teen pregnancies, and the incidence of founded child abuse.[52] Structurally, the YFA is a chartered by state government as an independent authority; in addition, it has a tax-exempt status allowing it the advantages of a private agency.

On a larger scale, the Harlem Children's Zone was established to coordinate 20 health, education, and social service programs to 3,400 inner-city children. Geoffrey Canada established the Zone as a result of his frustration with the fragmentation of traditional approaches; yet, he has insisted on accountability of service providers and outreach to the neediest families. When Canada encountered resistance by teachers unions about upgrading the education for under-performing students, he enlisted the support of the mayor and school superintendent to establish two charter schools. "We've got to really do something radically different if we're going to save these kids," observed Canada.[53]

In El Paso County, Colorado, David Berns, then director of the Department of Human Services, integrated public welfare with children's services and built bridges to community-based providers in order to enhance services to poor, troubled families. "The Department sought to integrate its child welfare and TANF agencies so that they would provide seamless, family-centered services—regardless of how the families came to the attention of the Department."[54] Between 1998 and 2003 the number of children in out-of-home placements declined 22 percent.[55] Despite budget reductions of $7.6 million for 2003, the Department served 4,00 more families.[56] Critical to Berns's strategy was conflating federal categorical programs channeled through the state so that funding would conform to the needs of El Paso County families. Pooling of funds in this manner had been long advocated by conservatives who championed block grants, just as it has been resisted by welfare liberals who feared cuts in social programs. However, an analysis conducted by Rutledge Hutson on behalf of the National Governors Association, the Hudson Institution, and the Center for Law and Social Policy, suggested the "federal statutes and regulations do not prevent states and localities from developing comprehensive, integrated services for children and families."[57]

Much as the Treasury has the authority to designate CDCUs, the Department of Health and Human Services, in consort with parallel state agencies, would be responsible for designating each Children's Authority. In order to qualify for the designation, a Children's Authority would have to be chartered by the state as a quasigovernmental entity and secure tax-exempt status. Federal and state government would agree to pool categorical funding to finance activities of the Children's Authority. Ongoing funding would be performance-based; agencies continuing inferior service provision would be sanctioned. So long as the Children's Authority provided state-of-the-art services, funding would be open-ended.

Empowering Families and Providers—Services provided by a Children's Authority would be comprehensive. Significantly, investigation for child abuse and neglect would be transferred to the local police department, where special investigative units comprised of police officers and social workers would be formed. Family support, foster care, adoption, and prevention services would be coordi-

nated by a team of family advocates who would have their own unit budget to
draw from in paying for services. Unless indicated otherwise, family advocates
would presume that families are competent to make decisions for themselves. Accordingly, families would be issued vouchers with which to purchase services such
as counseling, child care, and legal assistance. Already, education and training
vouchers have been authorized through the Chafee Foster Care Independence
Program, providing up to $5,000 in assistance to youth aging out of foster care.[58]
Through a child welfare voucher program, families would formally evaluate service providers and their assessments would be posted publicly for reference by
other families. Service providers rated by families as providing inferior service
would be terminated from the Children's Authority network. The Children's Authority would have to offer staff insurance that includes a "whistle-blower" provision, protecting child welfare professionals who identify unethical practices from
administrative reprisal, including reimbursement for legal costs.

Optimizing Information Technology—Data collection would be central to
monitoring a Children's Authority. Each Children's Authority would have to institute a validated risk assessment instrument for helping troubled families. Data
would be integrated with a management information system that would not only
collect data for internal use, but also transmit information to federal agencies. In
addition, it would allow agencies to follow families and abusers across jurisdictions. Monthly reports from the Children's Authority would allow continual up-
dating of a nationwide data set from which exemplary and under-performing
agencies could be identified. In addition, it would facilitate the construction of an
annual report on child welfare, similar to Kids Count of the Annie E. Casey Foundation and the Child Well-Being Index developed by Duke University and the
Foundation for Child Development.[59] All data relating to child morbidity and
mortality would be forwarded to the Centers for Disease Control and Prevention.
A related requirement of Children's Authority designation would be to open public access to records of cases where children have been seriously injured or killed
after being placed under agency care.

Reforming Professional Education—Nationwide deployment of the Children's
Authority model requires reform of professional education. Foremost, a national
certification should be created for Children's Authority team leaders, which includes training in forensics, investigative techniques, family and juvenile law,
management information systems, research, and ethics. In order to generate research on management of the Children's Authority and identify optimal interventions, educational institutions in receipt of child welfare training funds would be
required to conduct state-of-the-art research in child welfare, especially field experiments designed to demonstrate the effectiveness of various interventions.
Currently, schools of social work receive Title IVE training funds; if such programs are unable to generate research up to contemporary methodological standards, federal funds should be diverted to other disciplines that can.

REINVENTING SOCIAL POLICY

As these scenarios demonstrate, the public utility paradigm of social welfare can be reinvented by employing the themes of radical pragmatism. The agencies that are generated tend to be organizationally flat (as opposed to hierarchical) and market receptive (versus public monopolies), and they tend to embrace locality (instead of control by superordinate jurisdictions)—features that are congruent with the information age. So configured, radical pragmatism would be prophetic with respect to social policy because stakeholders—clients, professionals, and taxpayers—have such misgivings about existing social programs and are receptive to alternatives that more clearly advance the public interest. Public disaffection from public welfare should be reason enough for liberals to reconsider the welfare state project, but they have been loath to do so. Liberal intransigence, as Larry Brown and Larry Beeferman observed, has fatal consequences in a dynamic policy environment: the failure "to offer a new vision at all."[60]

As evident during the twentieth century, the genius of pragmatism was its capacity to adapt to political, economic, and technological change that buffeted a mature industrial society. Despite its accomplishments in facilitating the evolution of the American welfare state, pragmatism was vulnerable on several counts. It was ideologically promiscuous; it failed to adequately account for power; and, paradoxically, it underestimated its own capacity to reshape public philosophy. Yet, if pragmatism was capable of providing the philosophical rationale for an industrial order, a revved-up pragmatism would appear to be a good candidate for doing the same in a post-industrial information age, but only if it addressed adequately three central concepts: values, power, and reflexivity.

8

RENAISSANCE

My judgment is now clear and free from the misty shadows of ignorance with which my ill-starred and continuous reading of those detestable books of chivalry had obscured it. Now I know their absurdities and their deceits, and the only thing that grieves me is that this discovery has come too late, and leaves me no time to make amends by reading other books, which might enlighten my soul. I feel . . . that I am on the point of death, and I should like to meet it in such a manner as to convince the world that my life has not been so bad as to leave me the character of a madman; for though I have been one, I would not confirm the fact in my death.

DON QUIXOTE

By its very nature, a society predicated on pluralism invites multiple stakeholders to engage in public endeavors. With respect to social welfare, the governmental sector, the voluntary sector, and the for-profit sector have all been involved in addressing the extensive needs of citizens. History has witnessed the rise, consolidation, and fall of structural interests that have, at various times, dominated American social welfare. For most of the twentieth century, the liberal paradigm of social policy, the welfare state, prevailed, providing an effective and accountable response to the needs of citizens. Since the 1980s, however, welfare liberalism has been under assault by conservatives who have slowed, then reversed, the liberal vector in social policy. The Right has employed multiple strategies with respect to the welfare state: proposing faith-based services as an alternative to public social programs, co-opting established programs like Medicare, and reducing vital revenues through tax cuts. While liberals have watched the conservative juggernaut, aghast not only at the impact on select social programs but the integrity of the welfare state as a whole, there was little prospect for a recrudescence of welfare liberalism.

That there was a political calculus to the Right's orchestration of social policy could not be doubted. "The righteous disdain for taxation is clearly part of a broader backlash against the government's 'greedy hand,'" wrote James Surowiecki in the *New Yorker*. "It is politically expedient, since lower tax revenues can be used to justify sharp cuts in entitlement programs, whose beneficiaries tend to vote Democratic."[1] Lower tax revenues during a period of escalating national security expenditures have driven the federal budget into deficit, an outcome that is quintessentially congruent with the Right's long-term objectives. "Rising deficits will inevitably force Congress to starve those 'wasteful' social programs," suggested economic columnist Jeff Madrick.[2] Conservative ambitions reach well beyond their conventional attempts to contain discretionary spending and pare back welfare expenditures. At the end of the day, the Right has set social insurance—Social Security and Medicare—in its sights. By cutting off essential revenues for social programs, conservatives force liberals into a fiscal corner: "to choose either to increase taxes by unimaginably huge amounts to keep benefits flowing or to cut benefits off and watch the elderly become the poverty class," speculated Roger Altman, deputy Treasury secretary under the Clinton administration.[3]

The figures generated by the Congressional Budget Office are convincing: Between 2003 and 2013, the nation's debt will have risen to $4.3 *trillion*.[4] Since money previously earmarked for Social Security has been used for national security, social insurance programs will face $25 *trillion* in unfinanced obligations. The impending retirement of 77 million baby boomers will put extraordinary pressure on social insurance programs. "Many of the Bush Administration's giveaways, such as the cut in dividend taxes and the abolition of the estate tax, are 'backloaded,' which means the really big handouts won't get distributed until 2008 or later. As it happens, 2008 is also the year that the aging of the population will start to deplete the Treasury," observed economist John Cassidy. "In 2008 the first boomers will be able to pick up their Social Security checks; three years later, they will become eligible for Medicare. Unless the retirement programs are reformed (and there's little sign of that happening), the aging of the boomers will have a crushing effect on the federal government's finances."[5] The compression effect will present a dilemma for liberal Democrats. Facing the insolvency of Social Security and Medicare, the public will be asked to either ratify a doubling of withholding taxes or converting social insurance programs to welfare. Once social insurance is converted to welfare, the liberal welfare state project is finished.

For conservatives, the purpose of social policy is to reverse the dominance of government in the lives of citizens and allow them to do more for themselves. At best, the Right contends, government consumes tax revenues that could be otherwise used for personal purposes; at worst, social programs not only inflict acute damage on individuals but long-term harm on society as well. The inverse relationship between citizen autonomy and government social programs is at the heart of the conservative social policy strategy. By favoring autonomy, tax cuts provide individuals with discretionary income with which they can choose the services they desire. This is shrewd politics. "By repudiating the Washington-knows-best legacy of the New Deal, Republicans will empower the people, and the people will empower Republicans," noted Jonathan Rauch: "If the Democrats dig in their heels and fall back on stale rants against greed, inequality, and privatization, so much the better. The voters will know whom to thank for empowering choices that Republicans intend to give them."[6] Having seized on the strategy, the Right has been ruthless in its application. Movement conservatives such as Grover Norquist have promised a new tax cut every year of George W. Bush's presidency.[7] Ultimately, conservatives intend to amplify the strategy through control of state and federal legislatures, eventually securing "an era of Republican dominance."[8] In all this, the administration of George W. Bush has not only veered further to the Right, but has shown more organizational discipline in pursuing its objectives than even the avatar of contemporary conservatism, Ronald Reagan.[9]

As conservatives of a generation ago faced disarray after the failed Goldwater presidential candidacy, so liberals are confronted with a rhetoric gone flaccid. Certainly, socioeconomic circumstance provides ample material for fashioning a new and compelling lexicon: Income disparities between the rich and poor are at all-time highs; job losses leave older cities vulnerable to problems associated with economic downturn; yet, social programs constrict. In light of deteriorating conditions, the liberal reflex has not been to entertain a "proactive rhetoric," however, but to defend the social programs of the past, the manifestations of the American welfare state. "The Democrats have generally spent their energy defending past accomplishments, from Social Security to Medicare, rather than seeking to refocus that basic commitment to the working class and the poor into ideas that reflect how the nation has changed since those laws were passed," concluded a journalist covering a meeting of the Democratic Party.[10] That George W. Bush's administration is even more stridently conservative than his predecessors suggests that this is ineffective. Liberals have watched with dismay as anachronistic policies of the New Deal and the War on Poverty, which are anchored in an industrial vision of social welfare, are dissembling with accelerating rapidity. "American liberalism, as both a body of ideas and a political coalition, is a shadow of its former self," noted two British journalists. "It is remarkable how far the best liberal thinkers have been reduced to reacting to conservative arguments."[11] Having lost public credibility for envisioning a proactive confident role in social affairs, liberals have been reduced to defensive pessimistic postures, their prescriptions scripted for the next recession or another cohort of social and economic casualties. Liberalism "is no longer a self-confident governing philosophy capable of rising above self-interest of those pressure groups or the self-indulgence of the angry Left."[12]

Yet, both Right and Left have been responsible for the demise of the welfare state paradigm, though in divergent ways. Conservatives have been most visible in their attempts to restructure and de-fund social programs; yet, in proposing an alternative based on individual responsibility supported by "faith-based" initiatives, the Right fails to comprehend the sheer magnitude of the social and economic problems besetting the nation. Despite the transparent inadequacy of their approach, the conservative error is one of commission. Liberals, however, are culpable of errors of omission. Program researchers inhabiting liberal policy institutes and research departments of major universities have continued to assess the performance of existing programs, insistent on maintaining a reflective posture and unwilling to risk proposing fundamental policy reforms. Their assumption is that the American welfare state is on autopilot and that it simply requires tinkering to keep it on course. By contrast, the Liberati have concocted a postmodern portrait of social programs, characterizing them as oppressive institutions maintained by authoritarian human service professionals who do the bidding of social elites. In their frivolity, the Liberati have effectively subverted the welfare state.

PUBLIC PHILOSOPHY IN TRANSITION

The public philosophy that guides social policy in a democratic polity changes glacially, but the consequences of such transformations are enormous. The welfare state was the policy paradigm that liberals used to elaborate social welfare during the twentieth century. As such, it served as moral philosophy as well as pragmatic theory: the just society was one in which the federal government assured unconditional, open-ended entitlements for essential goods and services as a right of citizenship; the means toward its realization depended on progressive taxation, a cadre of ideologically sympathetic professionals, and a needy, but docile, cohort of clients. Beginning with the New Deal and its capstone, the Social Security Act of 1935, and elaborated during the War on Poverty of the mid-1960s, the American welfare state was a work in progress, the ultimate objective being a European-style exemplar. Despite major structural faults—the tendency of public assistance programs to be operated by the states and the absence of universal health care—the vision remained essentially intact. Over the decades, the American welfare state would be evident in a mammoth governmental welfare bureaucracy, the annual consumption of hundreds of billions of dollars in benefits, the emergence of entire disciplines working to maintain it, the identification of special institutes that evaluated its programs and proposed incremental modifications, and the dependence of millions of citizens on its benefits. In its heyday, the welfare state enjoyed enormous popularity, so much so that even Republican presidents endorsed its expansion.

By the late 1970s, however, visible cracks were evident in the foundation of the

American welfare state. No longer content at lobbing op-ed broadsides at social programs, conservatives mobilized their quite ample resources and established a nationwide network of think tanks, the purpose of which was to counter the prescriptions of liberal policy institutes such as the Brookings Institution and the Urban Institute. With the election of Ronald Reagan in 1980, conservative policy institutes were ascendant; the American Enterprise Institute and the Heritage Foundation became regular features in the nations' newspapers, while the Hoover Institution, the Manhattan Institute, the Hudson Institute, and the CATO Institute played critical supporting roles. By end of the millennium, conservative policy institutes had scored an unprecedented accomplishment: They had effectively transformed public philosophy from liberalism to conservatism. In the process, they not only ended the family welfare entitlement, but they also set their sights on restructuring Medicare and privatizing Social Security.

For liberals, the reversals experienced at the end of the twentieth century were incomprehensible. The Left looked back on a century of progress in advancing social justice through a series of movements benefiting workers, minorities, women, and homosexuals, much of which had been codified in federal legislation. Having overcome oppression and delivered at least a measure of equity through federal social programs, the end game of the liberal project was filling in the gaps in the welfare state. All of this was predicated on the political support gained from aggregating aggrieved groups under the banner of the Democratic Party; during the expansionary phases of the welfare state during the 1930s and 1960s, the politics of welfare liberalism showed no sign of abating. The last decades of the twentieth century, however, dimmed the prospects of liberal Democrats. "Instrumental, liberal politics is being abandoned not only because it is seen as ineffective, it is also being deserted because it is seen as corrupting and empty of a genuine sense of orientation," observed William Sullivan in the mid-1980s. Ultimately, diminishing political support would weaken the welfare state:

> Public cynicism is growing about the peculiarly American politics of liberalism. That tradition of politics, beginning in the New Deal, has both sanctioned the pursuit of economic self-interest in the context of free enterprise and sought to temper it by a degree of income redistribution and expert bureaucratic fine tuning by the federal government.[13]

Proponents of welfare liberalism perceived the setbacks engineered by the Right as temporary, aberrations in the quest for a full-scale American welfare state. Until the true import of social programs registered with the electorate, liberals would simply wait until the public came to its senses.

Liberal complacency would prove costly. "The liberal response to the New Right's—and Reagan's—domestic policies was, for the most part a shameful silence," wrote Barbara Ehrenreich,

Many prominent liberal political figures and intellectuals took a public stand against the administration's antilabor and antiwelfare policies, but there was no concerted, ideological rebuttal of the right's economic premises, and no challenge to the fundamental hypocrisy of right-wing populism. In fact, many erstwhile liberals of the middle class moved as quickly as possible to distance themselves from the concerns that had defined liberalism since the sixties.[14]

By appealing to the economic and political interests of a broad spectrum of Americans, conservatives effectively pulled the rug out from under liberals.

If the Left couldn't beat the Right at the polls, it could nonetheless highlight the nefarious consequences of conservative public policy. Liberals took it at face value that the data supported their cause. For liberals the sum of all equations told them that conservatives were worsening the circumstances of those reliant on social programs; according to their calculus, many social welfare indicators worsened as a result of conservative dominance in domestic policy. Data analysis served liberals well—after all, it was the long suit held by policy analysts—particularly since the conservative assault on the welfare state was initially executed largely on ideological grounds. The liberal Center on Budget and Policy Priorities established itself as a clearinghouse for data on what was detrimental about conservative social policy, providing the ammunition for liberal advocacy organizations such as the Children's Defense Fund and the Center for Law and Social Policy.

By century's end, however, conservatives had developed their own data capability, and the results were sobering.

- During the 1980s, conservatives criticized the poverty rate, contending that it inflated the number of poor families by failing to include the value of welfare benefits; once social programs were "cashed out," the poverty level fell by about 30 percent. Thus, the liberal contention that the poverty level failed to adequately reflect the true circumstances of the nation's poor, an orthodoxy since its creation in the 1960s, was challenged.[15]
- The gender wage gap, conventionally holding that women earned about 74 cents of a dollar earned by men, was refuted by data showing that women ages 27 to 33 in similar positions, with comparable work experience and educational background as their male counterparts, earned 98 cents for a dollar earned by men. These data suggested that not only were younger women virtually erasing the gender wage gap, but that much of it was explained by women's volition—their choice of occupation or interrupting work for family reasons.[16]
- An analysis of educational performance revealed that, rather than being disadvantaged by a male oriented education system, girls had eclipsed boys with respect to the number of twelfth graders taking advanced placement

tests, participation in extracurricular activities, the percentage of high
school sophomores arriving prepared for studies, the percentage of time
spent on homework, and enrollment in institutions of higher education.
Among the largest discrepancies was the finding that African American
women were five times more likely to attend graduate school than African
American men.[17]

Over time, the Right began to use data to refute the received wisdom that liberals
had scripted on matters relating to poverty, gender, and race.

Capitalizing on these statistical skirmishes, the Heritage Foundation scored
what is arguably the most significant analytic coup among think tanks, liberal or
conservative. Realizing that social policy was increasingly data-driven, the Heritage Foundation integrated several of the largest federal data sets from the Census
Bureau, the Bureau of Labor Statistics, the Commerce Department, and the National Assessment of Educational Progress, among others, through its Center for
Data Analysis. In an attempt to correct for what had been perceived as a liberal
bias in the media, Heritage began providing free tutorials for journalists who
wanted to become more data savvy. The suggestion that the Center's purpose was
crudely ideological drew a swift rebuttal from its director, Mark Tapscott: "Heritage has sufficient confidence that our perspective on the issues corresponds to reality."[18] Thus, on matters relating to data, the Center for Data Analysis has allowed the Heritage Foundation to shed its reputation for ideological hack work
and become fully competitive not only with respect to liberal policy analysis organizations, but the federal government as well. In an increasingly data-driven
policy environment, this is an advantageous position, indeed. Recognized as a
bastion of conservative ideology, Heritage had moved confidently into the realm
of formal quantitative analysis.

In response to growing the conservative momentum in the 1980s, an insurgent
group of Democrats pulled their party hard right, searching for a posture that
avoided their characterization as "tax-and-spend liberals." Charles Peters, the iras-
cible editor of the *Washington Monthly*, provided the entree by introducing
"neoliberal" to the political lexicon. Differentiating among prefixes that proliferated during the 1980s, Peters observed that "a neoconservative is someone who
took a long hard look at where liberalism went wrong and became a conservative;
a neoliberal is someone who took that same hard look at what was wrong with
liberalism, and decided to correct it, but still retain his liberal values."[19] For
Peters, much of what was wrong with the Democratic Party was its reflexive support of the welfare state and opposition to the military and business, and he proposed a radical reorientation:

We want to eliminate duplication and apply a means test to these programs.
As a practical matter the country can't afford to spend money on people who

don't need it . . . As liberal idealists, we don't think the well-off should be getting money from those programs anyway—every cent we can afford should go to helping those in real need. Social Security for those totally dependent on it is miserably inadequate, as is welfare in many states.[20]

The neoliberal disenchantment with the welfare state in general and its welfare provisions in particular resonated with younger Democrats in Congress whose suffering was acute during the first term of the Reagan presidency. The apparent irrelevance of liberalism with respect to domestic policy, compounded by a series of failed presidential candidacies, provoked several prominent Democrats to found the Democratic Leadership Council (DLC). The DLC hired Al From as its director, and then established a think tank, the Progressive Policy Institute (PPI) under the direction of Will Marshall. The DLC scored major victories in 1992 and 1996 with the election of Bill Clinton and Al Gore, both DLC founders. Significantly, as a new Democrat, Bill Clinton trumpeted themes—opportunity, community, responsibility—that diverged from the notion of individuals' unconditional entitlement to benefits of the welfare state. While the DLC and PPI made impressive in-roads against welfare liberalism, the neoliberal movement foundered during the 2000 presidential election. Gore's loss was widely attributed by "new Democrats" as his having reversed field, rejecting the DLC legacy and embracing paleo-liberalism.

In the United States, the diminishing fortunes of welfare liberalism caused a reappraisal of the welfare state. Noting the complementary relationship between government social programs and private sources of provision, Neil Gilbert observed the emergence of the "enabling state" as the successor to the welfare state:[21] "By emphasizing the responsibility of local private units for the delivery of social services, the enabling state encourages a solidarity that is linked to membership in law-abiding, community-based, voluntary associations, which fosters the accumulation of social capital."[22] So formulated, the enabling state was not unlike Amitai Etzioni's communitarianism.[23] But, as Gilbert realized, the concession to capitalism presented fundamental problems. "As it has evolved since the early 1990s, the enabling state generates no counterforce to the capitalist ethos, no larger sense of public purpose that might be served beyond increasing productivity, no clear idea of public service, and dwindling support for the goals of social protection and security."[24] Although the enabling state had reached an accommodation to capitalism, it would not be a happy reconciliation.

Much as Ronald Reagan caused a major reordering of the Democratic Party, so Margaret Thatcher effectively revised British Labor. Anthony Giddens charted the Third Way beyond the conventional parameters of liberalism and conservatism. In so doing, Giddens quite aptly identified a middle ground between the assumptions that had characterized Right and Left. "Social democrats have to shift the relationship between *risk* and *security* involved in the welfare state, to develop a so-

ciety of 'responsible risk takers,'" he observed. "People need protection when things go wrong, but also the material and moral capabilities to move through major periods of transition in their lives."[25] In charting new philosophical territory, Giddens favored an economic premise to social policy by defining *positive welfare* as a product of activities of individuals, government, and private agencies, all necessary for "wealth creation." Optimally, positive welfare is reflected in "investment in *human capital,*" Giddens averred. Reconceived in this manner, social programs reflected a new paradigm for domestic policy. "In place of the welfare state we should put the *social investment state*, operating in the context of a positive welfare society."[26]

The European version of welfare-state restructuring moved quickly into the international arena. Under the "Berlin Communique," heads of 14 governments endorsed a three-point agenda in order to reconcile social obligations with global markets. First, education and work training were promoted in order to make the welfare and working poor economically self-sufficient. Second, civil society would be strengthened by reinforcing citizen responsibility, opposing hate crimes, and employing technology to fight crime. Finally, an international compact was proposed focusing on free trade, buffered by debt relief for developing nations. Although important facets of domestic policy, such as the environment and information technology, had yet to be addressed, the drafters of the Berlin document were convinced that they had the outline for a post-welfare state formulation for domestic policy: "[We] have brought stability to public finances, tackled social exclusion, pioneered reform as well as investment in public services and are now engaging with the construction of a reformed European social model."[27]

Two decades of cogitating about a Third Way seemed to have been enough for all but the most obsessed policy wonks. Despite the artful phraseology, the ideological parsing, and the not so subtle piety, Third Way thinking on matters of social policy proved caustic to the trans-Atlantic welfare state accord. Unfortunately for welfare liberals in the United States, the exhaustion of the European welfare state was contagious. Across the Western democracies, the Third Way provided a platform for voters to abandon the welfare state in favor of more basic values, those aped by conservatives. Redoubling their efforts to find traction among defecting voters, the critics of conservatism continued to migrate to the center—in the words of David Milband of British Labor, a "commitment to social justice through collective action enriched by a commitment to individual freedom and local empowerment."[28] Altogether, welfare liberal preferences seemed increasingly nostalgic, if not quixotic: "I am only at pains to convince the world of its error in not reviving that most happy age in which the order of chivalry flourished," the Knight of the Woeful Countenance might well have said had he the chance to reflect on the end of the grand and noble welfare state experiment. "But our depraved times do not deserve to enjoy so great a blessing as did those in which knights errant undertook and carried on their shoulders the defence of

kingdoms, the protection of damsels, the succour of orphans and wards, the chastisement of the proud, and the rewarding of the humble."[29] In the end, the Third Way was sounding vaguely like a centrist, compassionate conservatism. The trans-Atlantic welfare state accord was coming apart at the seams.

SYNTHESIS

Among the most intriguing concepts of American social analysis has been "opportunity structure," a term coined by Robert K. Merton to describe how societies control the means by which citizens attain upward mobility.[30] In some instances, opportunity structures have been among the most celebrated success stories in social policy, as evident in the G.I. Bill, which allowed millions of World War II veterans a shot at a university education when they otherwise would have been limited by a high school diploma that all but assured their candidacy for dead-end factory work. By introducing the term, Merton was quite sympathetic to the "socially disinherited" who had little choice but to adapt or rebel.[31] Thus, Merton anticipated that the absence of opportunity for African American youth would be manifested by high rates of unwed pregnancy among girls and high rates of incarceration for males, both expressed through an oppositional subculture that is celebrated by a distinctive cultural form—"Rap."

But opportunity structures were not understood by most people as a polemic, Merton suggested; rather, people adjust their expectations and behavior according to the ebb and flow of experience. What happens when experience affirms a lack of control over circumstances? Here again Merton was instructive, invoking "luck" as a factor: "The doctrine of luck serves the psychological function of enabling [individuals] to preserve their self-esteem in the face of failure."[32] Insofar as luck becomes a regular part of daily life—a doctrine—it is related to opportunity structure, or the lack thereof; an appreciation of luck emerges, indeed becomes necessary, only when structures of opportunity have become so corrupt that, as perceived by their participants, they become structures of subordination. One of the quintessential ironies of American social welfare is that one of the most obvious structures of subordination masquerades as an opportunity structure: the lottery is an instrument of the state.

A casualty of the Liberati's infatuation with European philosophy, Merton's seminal thinking would be discredited by postmodernism as a social construction of patriarchal, white American sociology. Ironically, "opportunity structure" would have gone the way of sociological oblivion, had it not been rescued by—of all people—Newt Gingrich, the conservative provocateur, who pirated the term to illustrate the virtues of social policies advocated by the Right in his 1994 Contract with America.

As a conduit for upward mobility, the concept of opportunity structure was eminently congruent with the American pragmatic tradition, with its emphasis on how individuals test the immediate environment for ways to realize their aspirations. The proliferation of diverse populations makes the term even more seductive since ethnic groups collectively fashion their own solutions to problems associated with assimilation, many of them prospering despite major obstacles. In this respect, opportunity structure reprises the pragmatic philosophical tradition that viewed the environment as a context that could be exploited as people tested it vis-à-vis their desires. During the twentieth century, pragmatists aimed to construct optimal environments through social policy and political reform that would allow people to prosper. Unlike static philosophies, pragmatism conceded that environments themselves were in constant flux as a result of the relentless drive of humans to improve their circumstances.

By the beginning of the twenty-first century, a moribund welfare state was the most compelling evidence that pragmatism's promise had faded. Pragmatism proved a fickle mistress, abandoning liberalism for a more enterprising and robust conservatism; pragmatism failed to account for the divergence of program capability that emerged within social policy, as evident in well-provisioned *industrial complexes* operating parallel to inferior *networks of negligence*; in resting on its scholarly laurels, pragmatism assumed a reactive stance with respect to societal needs instead of exploiting its capacity to catalyze social reform. Simply put, in order to be relevant to the information age, pragmatism needed an upgrade. Three factors are essential to reasserting pragmatism's relevance in social affairs: values, power, and reflexivity.

Values

Fundamentally, social policy is institutionalized morality; as such it is the manifestation of moral philosophy. A democratic polity uses representative government to implement moral philosophy, patterns of which suggest adherence to a public philosophy, a set of precepts that are preferred by lawmakers and, by inference, voters. That public policy tends toward ambiguity, discontinuity, and transience goes without saying. Nonetheless, beneath the rhetoric, bickering, and outright hostility that accompanies democratic decision-making, a common understanding about the purpose of the activity, a general agreement of the public interest, can be discerned, one reflecting core values. Ultimately, a civilized society is grounded on essential values. The moral foundation of a democratic polity is constructed of the clear articulation of values and the definition of their parameters, while accommodating change. Ultimately, specific values become the common denominator of a democracy.

Martha Nussbaum has proposed a moral foundation for social policy. A feminist philosopher, Nussbaum studied under Nobel Prize–winning economist

Amartya Sen, who is noted for his prescient observations that freedom is indispensable to progress insofar as democratic governments have not only avoided famine but have also been unwilling to wage war against one another. Subsequently, Sen proposed a "capability" approach to poverty, arguing that even in the most dire regions of the Third World, people enjoy at least some freedom in defining their circumstances and therefore their futures. Rejecting economic indicators of development as unacceptably simplistic, Sen emphasized "the expansion of the 'capabilities' of persons to lead the kind of lives they value—and have reason to value."[33] A primary inhibitor in realizing full capability is deprivation, of course, inadequate institutions that deny education, health, and recreation to the disadvantaged. In arguing for a "support-led process," Sen diverged with proponents of an economic model in which income was primary and health, education, and labor benefits were viewed as secondary:

> The success of the support-led process as a route [to development] does indicate that a country need not wait until it is much richer (through what may be a long period of economic growth) before embarking on rapid expansion of basic education and health care. The quality of life can be vastly raised, despite low incomes, through an adequate program of social services. The fact that education and health care are also productive in raising economic growth adds to the argument for putting major emphasis on these social arrangements in poor economies, *without* having to wait for "getting rich" first.[34]

Just as inadequate resources cripple the poor, so do simplistic conceptualizations of poverty hamper the prospects for advancing social justice.

In *Women and Human Development,* Nussbaum asserted the philosophical rationale for an absolute standard of social justice for the most chronically oppressed among the world's poor: women. "The core idea is that of the human being as a dignified free being who shapes his or her own life in cooperation and reciprocity with others, rather than being passively shaped or pushed around by the world in the manner of a 'flock' or 'herd' animal," Nussbaum argued. "A life that is really human is one that is shaped throughout by these human powers of practical reason and sociability."[35] Optimal development was, thus, not only freedom from want but also the amplification of a range of social and political opportunities. Nussbaum identified ten elements of a capability approach to development:

1. Life: enjoying full longevity.
2. Bodily health: having good health, including reproductive freedom.
3. Bodily integrity: appreciating freedom of movement, security from assault, and pleasure in sexual relations.
4. Senses, imagination, and thought: using the mind to explore rational and emotive bases for life as well as to enhance them.

5. Emotions: enjoying attachments to others that are not controlled nor censored by others.
6. Practical reason: forming a conception of what is desirable and planning for one's life.
7. Affiliation: respecting and living with others without fear of discrimination.
8. Other species: living in harmony with all features of the environment.
9. Play: enjoying activities that are entertaining and rejuvenating.
10. Control over one's environment: owning property and engaging politically in order to prosper.[36]

By focusing on individual capacity, Nussbaum portrayed people, regardless of the severity of their circumstances, as rational and independent—inherently capable. Oppressive economic, political, and gender forces may be quite real, but this did not deprive individuals of their ability to act; indeed, by posing freedom as integral to the development calculus, Nussbaum refuted not only the classical dualisms (predicated on class, gender, and race) but their postmodern variant (a male capitalist elite controls people of color through a global network of exploitive organizations) as well. Contrary to dualistic formulations that portray individuals as incapacitated or victimized, Nussbaum offered an altogether different credo: presume competence.

The ten values proposed by Nussbaum provide a foundation for a social policy agenda that could attract broad public support. Significantly, Nussbaum's list is neither liberal nor conservative. While health and education have been traditional liberal themes, security and property have been central to conservatism. In her wisdom, Nussbaum notes that a society that truly values its members must address concerns that have been the preoccupation of both ideological camps. Similarly, there is no prescribed mechanism for building a humane and just social order; given the variability of the human condition, it may be the governmental, voluntary, or corporate sectors, or possibly collaborations among them.

By incorporating liberalism and conservatism, the capability approach requires a rethinking of their role in social affairs. If people are encouraged to make decisions about their own welfare, to freely associate with others, and to be politically active, it is conceivable that they may develop private, community-based cooperatives to advance their well-being as opposed to governmental social programs. If significant investments in health, education, and employment are necessary to construct healthy communities, it follows that the wealth of the affluent is justifiably redistributed, even if doing so attenuates the consumption prerogatives of the rich. The elegance of Nussbaum's formulation is its receptivity to multiple ways through which social needs can be addressed; its genius is her conscription of divergent ideologies to advance the common good.

Power

Concentration of influence is inevitable in a democratic-capitalist political economy. Markets invariably skew the distribution of resources and opportunities, which social policy only partially corrects. A society's openness facilitates the ability of groups to organize networks of influence. Customarily, such networks are typified by their power. C. Wright Mills used the term "power elite" to describe the interlocking directorate comprised of elected officials, corporate executives, and military officers. The validity of Mills's formulation was underscored by Dwight D. Eisenhower who, upon leaving the presidency, warned of the increasing influence of the "military industrial complex."[37] Virtually forgotten, Mills also chronicled the emergence of an elite that managed the welfare state. "During the New Deal the corporate chieftains joined the political directorate [to administer] the New Deal as a system of power . . . essentially a balance of pressure groups and interest blocs."[38] Later, as corporations transformed American health care from a public utility to a social market, Arnold Relman, editor of the *New England Journal of Medicine*, voiced alarm about the burgeoning influence of the "new medical-industrial complex."[39] The power structures that evolved after World War II cemented the position of *industrial complexes* that became synonymous with unaccountable influence as a result of their association with pivotal institutions: the military industrial complex with the Pentagon, the medical industrial complex with the Department of Health and Human Services.

Pierre Bourdieu has developed a formulation that is particularly apropos of the ambiguous and transient nature of power. Bourdieu's analysis is not dissimilar to early American pragmatism, presuming two givens: the *habitus* of people within an *arena* of activity. *Habitus* refers to the customs and norms that form and maintain culture; the arena provides the space where collectives compete in redefining society according to their mastery of three forms of capital: social capital, consisting of personal networks; cultural capital, command of language, practices, and credentials; and economic capital, control of money. By nature, social change is reflexive, mirroring the fortunes of competing parties; "Classes and other antagonistic social collectives are continually engaged in a struggle to impose the definition of the world that is most congruent with their particular interests."[40] It follows that arenas populated by those with little social, cultural, and economic capital will fare far worse than those enjoying a surfeit of such resources. From Bourdieu's perspective, it is easy to review the rise and fall of interests within the welfare state: the replacement of traditional providers of the voluntary sector by welfare bureaucrats of the welfare state. By the same token, it is not difficult to extrapolate the succession of welfare bureaucrats by CEOs who manage the burgeoning system of human service corporations.

Less evident has been the evolution of *networks of negligence* that are sustained by under-funding, substandard professional preparation, and syndicates promot-

ing an ideology that rationalizes inferior services, such as those provided to maltreated children and welfare families. For the same reasons that mutually assured
inferiority characterizes the services provided to these populations—which not so
coincidentally are traditionally associated with public welfare—one could just as
easily expect the same deplorable level of care provided to the seriously mentally
impaired, the disabled elderly, and pupils of inner-city schools, among other
groups. What makes this of such concern is the unconscionably negligent nature
of care they receive, a level of care that is in inverse relationship to their need.
While a truly compassionate society would assure that the most troubled among
us could expect more help, *networks of negligence* function to generate the ratio-
nalizations not only for delivering less care, but often for turning away when injury and death are inflicted. Typically, *networks of negligence* exist below the
threshold of public awareness, except when reporters make headlines exposing
the squalor, morbidity, and mortality typically generated by chronically substandard care. One of the ironies of social reform is that the distance separating the
Fourth Estate and the professionals who maintain *networks of negligence* is such
that media exposeés of human service debacles rarely enter the professional literature even when such reports have been awarded Pulitzer prizes.

Bourdieu proposes a proactive reflexivity to reorder social affairs more justly:
"Our objective is not only to invent responses, but to invent a way of inventing responses."[41] Invariably, the project becomes theoretical. Noting specifically the
value of theory in "the conservative revolution," Bourdieu notes the failure of its
opponents to take theory seriously enough: "One of the theoretical and practical
errors . . . has been the failure to take account of the power of theory. We must
no longer make that mistake. We are dealing with opponents who are armed with
theories, and I think they need to be fought with intellectual and cultural
weapons."[42] Ultimately, the challenge is to institutionalize the incubation of a
corpus of theory that counters the status quo. For Bourdieu, power is contingent
on the capacity to "institutionalize reflexivity in mechanisms of training, dialogue, and critical evaluation."[43]

Theory being the catalyst of the information age, it is incumbent on Progressives to employ the means of analysis in order to format bold innovations in social policy. But to do so brings an unavoidable obligation: critically reviewing the
outcomes of social policies that have been engineered as part of the welfare state.
Such an inventory would reveal the persistent neglect and extensive damage that
is often inflicted on the most troubled Americans in the name of helping them.
Until this occurs, the public will remain leery of social policy; instead of consenting
to higher levels of taxation for social programs, a skeptical public is more likely
to reason that it is better off supporting those initiatives in which it has more
familiarity and confidence by way of charitable contributions. In this respect,
conservative tax cuts have served as a referendum on the welfare state. That tax cuts
are proposed with increasing frequency indicates the depth of voter antipathy

about established social programs. As a thought experiment, it is tantalizing to speculate what could be accomplished if the billions of dollars appropriated for program benefits and administration, the thousands of managers and staff, and the millions of beneficiaries were reconfigured in a manner more congruent with the information age. Undertaking that task requires an appreciation for empirically based theory—a capacity that is beyond the interest of the Liberati.

Reflexivity

Proactive reflexivity—anticipating future social problems, critiquing current policies while crafting alternatives to them, and marketing preferred policy options to the public and lawmakers—has become the distinctive hallmark of conservative think tanks. With few exceptions—the Progressive Policy Institute, a neo-liberal think tank that has been deployed to counter welfare liberalism within the Democratic Party; the New America Foundation, a "radical centrist" policy institute; the Center for American Progress, a newly established liberal think tank—liberal policy intellectuals have been *reactively* reflexive, reluctant to invent bold proposals to future needs. Content to analyze past accomplishments of traditional liberalism manifested in the social programs of the American welfare state, liberal policy institutes have essentially conceded the future to the Right. Meanwhile, the Liberati, battened in the academy, has essentially excused itself from the social policy debate, more intent on explorations of victimhood than rigorously assessing the needs of mainstream Americans. Having gained control of the means of analysis, conservatives are busy shaping the next generation of social policies.

One of the most provocative thinkers about diversity, freedom, and progress has been George Soros. An eastern European Jew who escaped the Nazis to eventually acquire billions of dollars through financial speculation, Soros has turned his attention to nurturing "the open society."[44] As Soros saw it, any society is subject to strangulation by dogma, hence his concern for creating and maintaining pathways of illumination in closed systems. Toward that end, he created the Open Society Institute in order to promote ideas that counter complacency and entropy. For Soros, the oppression of society by the state, as evident in Communism, was matched by the social control exercised by the modern corporation. Accordingly, Soros has undertaken an ambitious plan to make capitalism more socially relevant.

Central to Soros's argument is the concept of "reflexivity." Unlike the natural world where elements interact independent of human agency, the social world is a creation of thought and action. As Terry Eagleton observed, "Reflecting critically on our situation is part of our situation. It is a feature of the peculiar way we belong to the world."[45] Of course, people vary with respect to their capability to shape not only their world but also the circumstances of others. Embedded in reflexivity are differing levels of consequence. Obviously, many events simply fail to merit deliberation and intervention, as in the parking ticket issued despite a broken meter—negotiating the judicial labyrinth is simply not worth the effort. Most reflexivity is of a pedestrian manner and is related to daily requirements, as in "my job is hopeless"—so a new one is sought. Then there are events that are monumental in their consequences. Historical reflexivity occurs when an event actually redefines the world, as in the Civil War and slavery, Darwin's theory of evolution and theology, or September 11 and national security—each instance serves as a benchmark to gauge future thinking and action. "A truly historic event does not just change the world," notes Soros, "it also changes our understanding of the world—and that new understanding, in turn, has a new and unpredictable impact on the course of events."[46]

Reflexivity is implicit in social change. Society is a product of institutional infrastructure, the socialization of people into institutional roles, and the resulting reality is validated by self-perpetuating norms, of course. But what happens when the "self-validating and self-reinforcing" become "self-defeating"? Soros might well have been referring to the American welfare state when he suggested that

> such a process can drive prevailing views and the actual state of affairs quite far apart from each other without any assurance that they will ever be brought back together again. Normally, mistakes tend to get corrected, but when views are self-validating it does not become apparent that they are mistaken until much later in the process—and by that time, the underlying reality has also changed.[47]

That people shape their environment is incontrovertible; it is an innate feature of homo sapiens, the basis of human culture. Indeed, historic events—wars, discoveries, creations—are crafted toward particular ends, their significance often appreciated retrospectively after the true breadth and depth of the consequences can be fully comprehended. Yet, conventional understanding of such events is that they are reactive; social change occurs as a response to a regnant status quo. What makes Soros's conception of reflexivity novel is his proactive use of the term; reflexivity accounts for the deployment of responses in anticipation of future events. This, of course, is what differentiates the liberal from conservative think tanks—in their reflective stance, the former assess events post hoc, the latter contriving solutions in anticipation of future requirements. The implications of reflexivity for social policy are profound. Liberals have been intent on defending past legislative accomplishments evident in the New Deal (a reaction to the Great Depression) and the War on Poverty (a response to the discovery of poverty commensurate with the Civil Rights movement). Meanwhile, conservatives have not only been developing alternatives to existing social programs (enterprise zones and welfare reform) but have also been proposing a set of initiatives in anticipation of the retiring baby boomers (Medical Savings Accounts and the privatization of Social Security).

By controlling the means of analysis, policy institutes on the Right have institutionalized the ability to fashion policy options for events that have yet to occur. At the same time they have discredited liberal social programs, conservative intellectuals have marketed their prescriptions to lawmakers as well as the public. By means of think tanks, conservative intellectuals have converted social intelligence from a public utility to a market commodity, one that is traded in the marketplace of ideas. Like any product, social intelligence is subject to constant revision with respect to its provisions, receptivity, and impact; like good marketing firms, think tanks on the Right have cued up a series of options for various circumstances. And, having learned the importance of evidence in a data-driven policy market, they are developing unprecedented sophistication in marketing their policy products.

The organization of intelligence to advance the common good was a precept of American pragmatism and conservatives have apprehended this idea, using the private sector to achieve its ends. That conservatism has become the nation's public philosophy attests to the ability of the Right to tap into primary themes that resonate with the public. But a question nags: Are these valid? History is littered with syndicates of intellectuals who have manipulated institutional networks for purposes of social progress and which have enjoyed wide public support—fascism and communism most conspicuously. What, Soros has asked, are the social consequences when "theories [have been] effective without being valid'?[48] This is the fundamental flaw of pragmatism, and it is addressed by the value system presented by Nussbaum. Proactive reflexivity within socially just values provides the means for grounding social policy in the public interest.

DIVERSITY

In the fall of 2001, David Brooks contrasted a wealthy suburban county of Washington, D.C.—Montgomery County, Maryland—with rural Franklin County, Pennsylvania. Seeking to plumb the depths of class resentment, Brooks queried Franklin County residents of their animosity toward the "haves" of Washington, D.C. The response was unexpected: "When they are asked about the broader theory [of class resentment], whether there is class conflict between the educated affluents and the stagnant middles, they stare blankly as if suddenly the interview were being conducted in Aramaic," Brooks reported.

> I got only polite, fumbling answers as people tried to figure out what the hell
> I was talking about. When I rephrased the question in more general terms, as
> Do you believe the country is divided between the haves and the have-nots?,
> everyone responded decisively: yes. But as the conversation continued, it be-

came clear that the people saying yes did not consider themselves to be among the have-nots. Even people with incomes well below the median thought of themselves as haves.[49]

The conclusion that Brooks drew was classically sociological: People do not identify themselves with respect to their class position by comparing themselves with an affluent elite; instead "they compare themselves with their neighbors."[50] What emerged from Brooks's reportage was a restatement of the American creed that de Tocqueville first inscribed: "the idea that a person is not bound by his class, or by the religion of his fathers, but is free to build a plurality of connections for himself." Then, concluding in the best of the pragmatic tradition, Brooks intoned, "We are participants in the same striving process, the same experimental journey."[51]

That Americans belong to self-affirming groups has long been a distinctive feature of our culture. The freedoms inscribed in the Bill of Rights allow citizens to congregate according to a variety of preferences—race, nationality, sexual orientation, or, for that matter, taste for piquant Cajun cuisine or affinity for Harley Davidson motorcycles. Sociologically, this is the "melting pot" phenomenon, a short-hand for the pluralism that distinguishes the American identity. That Americans would retain ancestral identification is not surprising for a nation populated overwhelmingly by immigrants. Indeed, the infusion of immigrants continues to define the population as a whole (Table 8-1):

Despite important contradictions—slavery and xenophobia—pluralism has complemented, rather than subverted, the forging of a national community.

During the "culture wars" of the 1990s, however, pluralism was pushed aside by the Left in preference for multiculturalism, which viewed aggrieved groups as the victims of patriarchal, neocolonial politics. As ideology, multiculturalism portrayed pluralism as a quaint and anachronistic representation of an inherently oppressive society. This inflamed conservative and liberal intellectuals alike. Regarding the former, Roger Kimball opposed "the ideology of multiculturalism [where] the politics of ethnic and racial redress is allowed to trump the sustaining unity."[52] From the other end of the ideological continuum, Russell Jacoby criticized the emergence of "a new provincialism [which] feeds a separatism that is turning prickly and hostile. At the end of multiculturalism a primitivism returns, thinking by blood, race, and sex."[53] Multiculturalism would subsequently serve as pretext for the deployment of a civility police at American colleges and universities, which went to inordinate ends, including dictating speech codes and mandating sensitivity training for students and faculty, to assure that the feelings of oppressed groups were not hurt.

While multiculturalism was being hotly disputed on American campuses, business perceived diversity rather differently, assuming that products should simply conform to consumer preferences. Accordingly, commercial researchers began

TABLE 8-1.
American Ancestry: 2000 (First or Only Choice)

COUNTRY OR CONTINENT	MILLIONS
Africa	33.7
Germany	30.2
Mexico	20.6
United States	20.6
Ireland	19.3
England	16.6
Other Hispanic	14.7
Italy	12.9
Asia	10.0
Other British	8.2
Scandinavia	7.0
France and French Canadians	6.7
Poland	6.3

Source: Andrew Hacker, "Patriot Games," *New York Review of Books* (June 24, 2004), p. 30.

developing sophisticated profiles of American subgroups. Perhaps the most intriguing application of pluralism to commerce appeared in cluster analysis, the creation of demographic groups based on lifestyle differences along several dimensions. Michael Weiss, a demographer and journalist, has portrayed America through 62 socioeconomic clusters. Implicit in cluster analysis is a rejection of the crude dualism that has been characteristic of the industrial era; the postindustrial era is decidedly more nuanced in its orientation toward consumers:

Forget sex. Forget race, national origin, age, household composition, and wealth. The characteristic that defines and separates Americans more than any other is the cluster. From sea to shining sea, clusters reflect the diverse patterns of how Americans live, what they buy, and where they share the same lifestyle with others around the country.[54]

The clusters that Weiss identified ranged from the "Blue Blood Estates" (middle-aged professionals, who were moderate Republicans, averaged $113,000 in annual income, and comprised 0.8 percent of the population) to "Southside City" (southern African Americans with little education, who were liberal Democrats, averaged $15,800 in annual income, and comprised 2.0 percent of the population). Blue Blood Estates belonged to country clubs, preferred imported wine, subscribed to the *Wall Street Journal*, listened to classical radio, and drove expensive foreign cars; Southside City preferred three-way calling, purchased instant grits, subscribed to *Ebony*, listened to urban contemporary radio, and drove cheap imported cars.

Cluster analysis offered illuminating insights about social policy. "For the first time, the poorest neighborhoods in America are found outside the nation's largest metros, in Southside City, a cluster of midsized city districts where blue-collar African Americans have an income . . . barely above the poverty line . . . ," wrote Weiss. The residents of Southside City, like the inhabitants of Hard Scrabble, Family Scramble, Hispanic Mix, and Inner Cities, enjoyed freedom to exercise their preferences—shopping at Wal-Mart, consuming fast food, reading popular magazines, driving inexpensive vehicles, and having political preferences toward the middle-of-the-road—but their economic circumstances were tenuous. Citing the impact of globalization and the decline of long-term labor contracts, Weiss found that the prospects of the working poor were deteriorating. In contrast to the notion that a rising tide lifts all boats, the minority poor remained in precarious circumstances; not even assured of a life raft.[55]

The ebb and flow of opportunity, sometimes modulated by social policy, eased or exacerbated minority relations. With the ascendance of Hispanics as the largest American minority, their status vis-à-vis African Americans has been of particular concern. Hispanics represent 28 percent of the labor force, yet command only 19 percent of aggregate wages, while African Americans are approaching parity with whites.[56] Between 1980 and 1995, African American family income grew by $4,576—almost that of whites at $4,845—compared to $269 for Latinos.[57] The denial of public assistance benefits to immigrants under provisions of the 1996 welfare reform would, in all likelihood, widen the income gap between Hispanics and African Americans. Thus, empirical research and cluster analysis illuminated critical differences between minority groups.

The use of cluster analysis represented the application of empirical methods in the pragmatic tradition. Essentially, cluster analysis was the quantified version of focus groups, a concept introduced by Robert K. Merton in the 1950s. Focus groups have become ubiquitous, institutionalized through the election cycle. By late summer in any election year, political consultants begin to conduct focus groups in order to refine candidates' messages; by mid-fall, focus groups reach a crescendo anticipating the culmination of the campaign season. Focus groups are used for more quotidian purposes, as well. Telemarketing firms have been so persistent, calling consumers seeking to complete surveys on a variety of products and services ranging from toothpaste to insurance, that their intrusiveness has been curtailed by "do not call" registries. Thus, in the more competitive sectors, research is used to solicit individual desires in order to shape production. As evident in cluster analysis and focus groups, applied pluralism has been standard fare for marketers, political scientists, and journalists as well.

By measuring the degree to which minority groups prospered, cluster analysis exposed the superficiality of multicultural analysis. In its adherence to the postmodern rejection of empiricism on the grounds that it was a means by which elites oppressed marginal populations, multiculturalism forfeited the capacity to gauge the circumstances of the minority poor. This would prove enormously consequential in the social policy debate: The Liberati's preoccupation with multiculturalism, which eschewed Truth, demonstrated empirically or otherwise, effectively absolved the Right of its role in generating increasing inequality, among other social calamities.[58] "The champions of Enlightenment are right: Truth indeed exists," concluded Terry Eagleton, even if its consequences were "monstrous."[59]

Crafting social policy with regard to pluralism would place it in bold contrast to welfare liberalism, but doing so would make it congruent with the American ethos. In arguing for universal, standard benefits, welfare advocates have blithely ignored the lifestyle preferences of low-income families, deploying benefits irrespective of individual circumstances while requiring them to conform to a welfare bureaucracy that is often detested. Under these circumstances, is it any wonder that only about half of families eligible for public assistance actually receive benefits? The insistence on standardized benefits and the public utility model places welfare liberals in the unenviable position of defending the provision of second-class services to second-class citizens.

Conservative critics of welfare are quick to point out that liberal poverty programs are nothing less than the Left protecting a public monopoly that subordinates the poor, while assuring welfare bureaucrats a plethora of jobs. In rebuttal, welfare liberals often cite the successes of social insurances, especially Social Security and Medicare, largely because they have avoided the stigmatization of public assistance. A cursory examination of the social insurances reveals that they evidence fundamental flaws. Traditionally, neither Social Security nor Medicare has permitted that benefits be shaped according to the preferences of retirees. Liberal claims about the virtues of social insurance are largely rhetorical, defeated by their meager provisions. Anyone vaguely familiar with Social Security would have to concede that it offers little more than poverty-level retirement. Medicare entails a significant deductible for the elderly suffering from acute illness and covers long-term care only minimally, resulting in the pauperization of many older Americans who enter nursing homes. That liberals would predicate their defense of the welfare state upon inadequate social insurance programs is flawed to say the least.

THE FUTURE OF SOCIAL POLICY

The future of social policy is contingent on acknowledging the needs and aspirations of Americans and assuring that basic goods and services are available to them by means that respect their choices and amplify their prosperity. Citizen empowerment, upward mobility, and government restructuring are themes that are congruent with this vision. This orientation to social policy offers the promise of developing a sequel to a welfare state ideal that has been corrupted by the excesses of *industrial complexes* and the inferiority of *networks of negligence*. As social policy reform, radical pragmatism goes beyond a distinctively American philosophy—it is radical because it gets to the root of fundamental social needs, pragmatic because it insists that collectively citizens can craft solutions to their problems. Social policy congruent with radical pragmatism immediately introduces ideas that have been given short shrift by welfare liberals as well as compassionate conservatives:

- Social insurance should allow beneficiaries to experiment with adequate benefit packages, the funding of which could be derived from progressive reforms of social insurance programs;
- Cash benefits should be indexed for inflation at the same time they are adjusted for regional variations in the cost of living;
- The poverty line should be updated and complemented by a "parity in tax expenditures" indicator, measuring the extent to which tax expenditures for the poor compares to tax forgiveness of the affluent;
- When jurisdictions develop the capacity to manage social programs effectively, program authority and funding could be devolved to them, contingent on achievement of specific outcomes, their performance subsequently publicized by "report cards"; and
- Because future social policy depends on the collaboration of governmental, nonprofit, and corporate sectors, a social compact could be forged and updated periodically, which optimizes the functional capacity of each.

As these examples suggest, radical pragmatism provides an orientation to social policy that is as post-liberal as it is post-conservative; accordingly, it challenges existing orthodoxies. Radical pragmatism rejects the liberal preference for standardization and the mammoth bureaucracies necessary to dispense universal benefits. If liberals are to reassert their presence in social policy, they will have to embrace the capabilities of program beneficiaries, deconstruct the welfare bureaucracy, and build opportunity structures for the disadvantaged. Such an initiative would rejuvenate a foundering ideology that has been eclipsed by an ascendant Right. Indicative of their investment in the status quo, welfare liberals have been fixated on defending existing social programs, despite their defects, hoping for the eventual replication of the northern European welfare state in the United States. Instead of exploring new formulations to advance social justice, welfare liberalism is a captive of the welfare state ideal; at best, liberals have become prisoners of their ideological nostalgia; at worst, the Liberati indulges in a Pecksniffian condescension to victim groups. For the Right to evolve a social policy agenda that is more than the sentimental rhetoric evident in the evocation of compassionate conservatism, conservatives will have to take the preferences of the disadvantaged at face value, admit the defects of market strategies, and appropriate funds commensurate with the task at hand. That the Right prefers massive tax cuts that benefit the wealthy while executing Draconian budget cuts in social programs benefiting less affluent Americans, instead of proposing an adequately funded alternative to existing social programs, is evidence that the conservative position on social policy is essentially symbolic.

Radical pragmatism could also jumpstart a moribund discussion about social policy. The debate of the past two decades has been characterized by competing, but antiquated, visions of the public good: the liberal orientation featuring universal and unconditional entitlements as a right of citizenship, financed through progressive taxation, and dispensed through a government bureaucracy *versus* the conservative vision focusing on individualized benefits predicated on equity, paid for by elective contributions, and dispensed through a corporate bureaucracy. There is ample evidence that many Americans, *if* they are covered through government or corporate programs, find their benefits unreliable or inadequate; often they are resentful about the services and benefits they do receive. Originating in the industrial era, neither welfare capitalism managed by corporations nor the welfare state administered by government is congruent with the post-industrial era.

Beyond party and ideology, radical pragmatism challenges philosophers to explore the terrain outside their respective ideological boxes. Daniel Patrick Moynihan, the late dean of American social policy, understood this over a decade ago: "The issues of social policy the United States faces today have no European counterpart nor any European model of a viable solution. They are American problems, and we Americans are going to have to think them through ourselves."[60] To engage in that exploration in a manner that honors a democratic society requires that ideologues (practitioners of the art of moral philosophy) engage with researchers (practitioners of scientific empiricism) in developing the intellectual infrastructure that harnesses control of the means of analysis to advance the public good. The twenty-first century, then, opens a window into the future of generosity; Americans can greet the opportunity with a renewed respect for philosophy, theory, and research—in which event the project will better approximate the historical period that evolves before them—or they can defer to interests that emerged during an earlier epoch—in which case American social policy will increasingly appear exactly what it is—at best retrograde, at worst Quixotic.

Assuming the increasing diversification of America, a social policy that is relevant to the twenty-first century would investigate the circumstances of groups, craft benefits that are consistent with their requirements, and construct bridges that amplify opportunity. As E. J. Dionne, Jr., has observed, the circumstances confronting contemporary America are not unlike those of the Progressive era,[61] that remarkable episode when intellectuals of divergent ideological stripes united to advance the common good by experimenting with novel ways to address pressing social problems of the day. What we now understand as a conservative vector toward that objective took the shape of welfare capitalism, consisting of wage-related benefits that are overseen by corporations. What we now understand as the liberal trajectory took form as the welfare state, comprised of social programs that are administered by government. Having dominated the social policy debate for most of the past century, the liberal trajectory has faltered; an ascendant conservatism is evidence that the social momentum that underwrote the construction of the New Deal and its articulation during the War on Poverty has run its course. While intellectuals of the Right have demonstrated perspicacity in critiquing government social programs, they have failed to propose an alternative that addresses fully the magnitude of need in America.

Ultimately, the purpose of social policy is to bind together the disparate elements of an open society by alleviating the destitution of those who do not produce, the alienation of those who do not belong, the apathy of those who do not participate, and the narcissism of those who do not contribute. Humility comes with recognizing that there are no panaceas in this endeavor, integrity in conceding that approaches of the past are no longer valid, wisdom in realizing that the venture cannot be forsaken. In all this, September 11, 2001, proves a watershed event. By affirming the import of absolutes, it put an end to the Liberati's postmodern romance with relativism and the negation of the American project; the subsequent shift in priorities from *social* to *national* security effectively halted any residual momentum behind the liberal welfare state. While the Right has adroitly employed pragmatism to replace liberalism with conservatism as the nation's public philosophy, its social policy prescriptions range from the symbolic to the negligent. A post-welfare state template for social policy that addresses the full measure of American needs and aspirations remains to be crafted.

EPILOGUE

I think we have come to an ending point in a long transition that began in 1968. During that time, the old Roosevelt Democratic majority coalition has creaked and cracked away under various kinds of racial, religious, social and international forces, and this election was the end point in that transition. I think we live in a country that is majority Republican.

DON FOWLER,
former Democratic Party chairman, commenting on the 2004 election

The 2004 election cemented conservative control of the federal policy process. George W. Bush not only won reelection, but the Republican Party also made substantial gains in the House and Senate. Beyond control of the executive and legislative branches, President Bush will have several nominations to the Supreme Court, furthering conservative influence in the judiciary. White House intentions during the second term are commensurately ambitious: "We'll reform our outdated tax code. We'll strengthen the Social Security for the next generation," the President proclaimed in his victory speech.[1] A second term for George W. Bush proved that the conservative vector in domestic policy would continue unabated.

Dismayed Democrats sorted through the post-election debris, wondering how they had failed to unseat a president who was vulnerable on so many fronts. The 2004 election, initially viewed as a test of the Bush presidency, became instead a referendum on American liberalism. A *Washington Post* editor characterized the Democrats' defeat as "a bitter loss that raises serious questions about the Democratic Party's purchase on a broad national identity."[2] The liberal postmortem of the conservative election route attributed the loss to a variety of issues: public befuddlement about the War on Terror, voter angst about same-sex marriage, and the Democratic candidate's Brahmin aloofness. Regardless, the ramifications were profound: If George W. Bush had engineered No Child Left Behind as education reform, manipulated passage of the Medicare Modernization Act, engineered four tax cuts, and waged two wars during his first term *without* a mandate, imagine what could transpire during the second *with* a mandate? "American liberalism is going into a deep internal exile," concluded *The New Republic's* Peter Beinart.[3] Summing up liberal apprehensions, Tom Toles drew a cartoon depicting Senator Kerry locking up a shop for the night that featured a "Going Out of Business" sign in the window; ominously, the store marquee reads "The New Deal," the caption: "Good Closer."[4] In search of credibility with mainstream Americans, prominent Democrats announced the creation of Third Way to recast an outmoded liberalism that had been rejected by voters, mimicking earlier gestures that established the Progressive Policy Institute and the Center for American Progress [5]

Pundits widely attributed the Republican victory to "moral values." Conservative voters, it was alleged, were mobilized because they feared the erosion of values that were perceived to be fundamentally American: Religious icons were being stripped from public display, popular culture was increasingly coarsened, and homosexuals were making a mockery of marriage. Unfazed, liberals puzzled over why so many voters would forsake their own economic self-interest by supporting a Right-wing agenda that was so "retro." After all, wasn't liberal commitment to social justice the very impulse behind the redistribution of resources from the rich to social programs that benefited low-income Americans? Underlining the paradox, former Clinton domestic policy advisor Bruce Reed pointed out that "of the 28 states with the lowest per capita income, Bush carried 26. An administration whose overriding motive has been to protect the rich was just given a second term by the very people who will suffer most for it."[6] Even in states where economic reversals would have encouraged hard-pressed Americans to vote their pocketbooks and embraced liberals, they defected to Republican candidates. "From the Democratic perspective," observed Richard Cohen dryly, "what this country needs is a good recession."[7]

If the 2004 election left Democrats the party of dour pessimism and Republicans imbued with rosy optimism, the future for the Right is not without hazard. Military adventures in the Middle East necessitating the construction of U.S. military bases there may incite an intractable conflagration pitting Islamic insurgents against American troops. A sputtering economy hamstrung by debt could lead to further hemorrhaging of jobs and capital overseas. The battening of industrial complexes and avaricious CEOs fed by public appropriations for education, retirement, healthcare, corrections, and of course defense could provoke the ire of voters. Domestic initiatives, such as "compassionate conservatism," which seem long on rhetoric but short on appropriations, may be exposed as cynical exercises in the manipulation of public sentiment for political gain. Strong-arm tactics by congressional Republicans, so conspicuous in the passage of the 2003 Medicare reform, invite Democratic reprisals. Finally, recent history has not been kind to second-term Republican presidents—their experiences ranging from disappointing (Reagan) to disastrous (Nixon). If the Right views the 2004 election as the consolidation of conservative dominance in public policy, ushering in a period of permanent governance, it will have to proceed with considerably more finesse than has been evident to date.

Beyond the political fallout, the 2004 election revealed a degree of ideological polarization that shredded the nation's philosophical fabric. Leading up to the election, the Liberati conducted an insurgent campaign of innuendo and guilt by association, most conspicuous in *Fahrenheit 9/11*. That Michael Moore's movie achieved such notoriety was due less to its adherence to traditional standards of muckraking journalism and more to its symbolism of a partisan on a frail craft sailing directly at the conservative juggernaut. For two decades, the Right had treated liberalism as a joke; Ronald Reagan's patronizing references to "tax and spend liberals" segueing to rants by Rush Limbaugh, taunts by Ann Coulter, and the mendacity of Swift Boat Veterans for Truth. Surely, liberals thought, it was time to sling some mud in the other direction.

Superficially, the political theater of the 2004 election, pitting the literary left against the religious right, represented little more than old-fashioned, bare-knuckled ideological combat. Beneath the surface, however, a more insidious development had emerged: the renunciation of rationality in public discourse. The symptoms of public irrationality were evident from both the Left and the Right. Since the apogee of the Civil Rights and Women's movements, liberals had clung to Affirmative Action as a means to advance social justice for populations that suffered under the yoke of slavery and patriarchy. Within the past two decades, however, evidence threatened the validity of Affirmative Action. Increasing diversity and intermarriage strained policies favoring discreet groups on the basis race and ethnicity. The prosperity of some groups justified their exclusion from Affirmative Action, while others lagged behind. Instead of conceding that a new policy regarding social opportunity may be in order, the Liberati has employed identity politics to rail against those who have called for a new approach to redistributive justice, accusing them of racism and sexism.

The Left holds no monopoly on irrationality, of course. Since the rise of the Christian Coalition, the religious right has attempted to contort science so that it conformed to spiritual precepts. In an attempt to discredit evolutionary biology, "creationists" placed their hypothesis on the shelf of high school science classrooms next to Darwin's and claimed comparability. This hubris conveniently disregarded entire libraries of research confirming the essential features of evolutionary theory without enlisting anything more than metaphysics in support of creationism. To historians, the debate was reminiscent of the Scopes trial, judicial theater that exposed the incompatibility of religion and science. A monumental contradiction of the religious right was its opposition to stem-cell research, which "destroyed life," while supporting the death penalty and the invasion of Iraq. Life presumes independent viability, a condition not even remotely applicable to a stem cell; yet the Right effectively used its irrational righteousness as a cudgel against scientific research that promised significant advances in health care. "A growing number of

scientists, policy makers, and technical specialists both inside and outside the government allege that the current Bush administration has suppressed or distorted
the scientific analyses of federal agencies to bring these results in line with administration policy," cautioned the Union of Concerned Scientists.[8] Immediately after
the 2004 election Jerry Falwell announced the rebirth of the Moral Majority as the
Faith and Values Coalition to further the "evangelical revolution," an initiative unlikely to seek reconciliation with the scientific community.[9]

Historically, pragmatism has provided the philosophical means for resolving
disputes about public purpose while avoiding such irrational extremes. From the
crafting of social insurance through the Social Security Act and the creation of the
G.I. Bill to the interstate highway system, pragmatism has provided the inspiration for bold projects that have been milestones in the life of the nation, innovations that have enjoyed consistent bipartisan support. For all their encomia, these
achievements were products of industrial America; as such, their implementation
presupposed a bureaucracy that became programmatically rigid, freighted with
administrators, and indifferent to consumer preference. It is for this reason that
"radical pragmatism"—emphasizing citizen empowerment, social mobility, and
government restructuring—is more congruent for a post-industrial information
age.

What would radical pragmatism suggest for what is arguably the greatest social
policy challenge: the impending Social Security crisis? There is bipartisan agreement that the current course of Social Security is untenable. In 2008, the first of
77 million baby boomers will begin to retire, placing unprecedented demands on
Social Security, the reserves of which have already been diverted to other activities. Four tax cuts in as many years have driven the federal budget into a precipitous deficit that raises doubts about Social Security's solvency, essentially pitting
future retirement benefits against discretionary expenditures that most Americans would perceive as essential. Without a major correction, Social Security will
be unable to honor its current benefit obligations. Either the withholding tax will
have to be doubled or the retirement age delayed significantly, options that will be
effectively vetoed by the Chamber of Commerce and AARP, respectively. In the
worst case scenario, Social Security, a victim of deficits and demographics, will
be reduced to a welfare program—only the poor elderly need apply.

In 1935, Social Security promised an important measure of economic protection for American workers, but nearly seven decades later, Americans' confidence
in the program is eroding. During the latter decades of the twentieth century, the
percentage of Americans who thought they could count on Social Security fell
from 88 percent in 1974 to 46 percent in 1997. During the 1990s, the number of respondents who were "very confident" about the future of Social Security fell from
18 percent in 1990 to 7 percent in 1998, while those who were "not at all confident"
rose from 15 percent to 26 percent. Social Security's relatively low benefits compounded the loss of public faith in the program. In 2002, the average new Social

Security award for a retired worker was $914 per month, an amount that most Americans would deem insufficient to meet the requirements of most pensioners. Many Americans, especially younger workers, are acutely aware of this, and their ambivalence about Social Security reflects the long decline in confidence in the nation's public pension program.

Reforming Social Security requires assuring the solvency of the program while providing investment options for workers. First, the fiscal integrity of the program would be guaranteed by making the withholding tax progressive and removing the cap on taxable income. Hypothetically, minimum-wage workers would receive a significant payroll tax cut if the current FICA, 7.65 percent, were reduced to 3 percent; median-wage workers a more modest reduction at 6 percent; upper-income workers would pay a bit more at 9 percent. However, that 9 percent would apply to all income, not just the first $90,000. Removing the cap on taxable income would thus bring Social Security in line with that portion of the payroll tax, 1.45 percent, that goes to Part A of Medicare, hospitalization insurance, which is assessed on all income.

Second, today's workers would be allowed to supplement their payroll tax contributions with private investments. This investment option would include Individual Development Accounts (IDAs), matching accounts for purchasing a first home, completing vocational school or college, or establishing a business. IDAs were featured in the 1998 Assets for Independence Act, but funded at a paltry $125 million over five years, suboptimal appropriations to say the least. Dedicating the estate tax to match IDA deposits would assure more adequate funding while redistributing wealth.

Complementing Social Security with an IDA initiative has two virtues. By encouraging Americans to accrue assets, IDAs would provide the best way for low-income Americans to escape poverty and attain middle-class prosperity. Thus, IDAs would address directly the widening chasm of economic inequality in America. In 2001, the net worth of the top quintile of households averaged $1.6 million, while that of the bottom quintile was *minus* $8,200. The present distribution of wealth not only leaves lowest income families in chronic debt, but it also exacerbates minority poverty. While the net worth of white households increased 17.4 percent between 1996 and 2002, it fell 16 percent for black families.

Encouraging investment through Social Security would also help reverse the dramatic erosion of savings in the United States. In 2003, the net savings rate fell to 1.2 percent of national income, one-sixth of what it had been in 1981. The corollary of low savings has been hyperconsumption, spending that does little to buffer families against economic downturns while diminishing the nation's capital investment pool.

So configured, Social Security can be updated in a manner that incorporates liberal concerns about the program's regressive tax structure as well as conservative insistence on an investment option. Such a plan stands in stark contrast to regressive tax reform plans floated immediately after the Bush reelection victory. The economic security of the welfare and working poor would be jeopardized by either of the primary candidates for tax reform: The burden of a flat tax or a national sales tax would not only fall disproportionately on low-income Americans, but either would also delete important tax credits for poor households, especially the Earned Income Tax Credit.[10]

Sensible reform of Social Security would also restore integrity to the public policy process. The deceit of the Bush administration's strategy for privatizing Social Security was revealed in a January 3, 2005 memo by White House advisor Peter Wehner, who admitted that a colossal shortfall in revenues might sabotage the plan. "If we borrow $1-2 trillion to cover transition costs for personal savings accounts and make no changes to wage indexing, we will have borrowed trillions and will still confront more than $10 trillion in unfunded liabilities," Wehner conceded. "This could easily cause an economic chain-reaction: the markets go south, interest rates go up, and the economy stalls out."[11] Wehner calculated that the replacement of wage indexing with price indexing would soften the plan's precipitous funding shortfall, however, it meant cutting future Social Security benefits significantly. That slight-of-hand provoked opposition from both sides of the political aisle; even Peter Ferrara, a long-time advocate of Social Security privatization, called it a "bait-and-switch" tactic.[12] Undaunted, George W. Bush remained intent on allowing workers to divert a portion of their payroll tax to private accounts, figuring that the long-term ideological gains would eclipse the short-term political fall-out. "[Conservatives] believe that Bush can do for Republicans what Franklin D. Roosevelt did for Democrats when he proposed [Social Security] more than seven decades ago: create a generation of voters who see them as the guardian of their retirement program," observed journalists of the *Washington Post*.[13] That ideology was trumping the public interest in Bush's effort to privatize Social Security was evident in Wehner's memo:

> Democrats and liberals are in a precarious position; they are attempting to block reform to a system that almost every serious-minded person concedes needs it. They are in a position of arguing against modernizing a system created almost four generations ago. Increasingly the Democratic Party is the party of obstruction and opposition. It is the Party of the Past.[14]

However fiscally irresponsible the Social Security privatization plan advanced by the Bush White House, it did provide a measure of poetic symmetry to the debate: exposing workers' retirement contributions to greater risk placed the nation's economy at risk as well.

Industrialization blessed America with unprecedented prosperity, yet the price of affluence was inequality. The necessity of bridging the yawning chasm between classes, races, and ethnic groups led to bipartisan efforts to not only redistribute income and opportunity more broadly, but also do so according to precepts of sound government. First, Progressives, under the banner of the Republican Party, followed the leadership of Theodore Roosevelt in regulating rampant capitalism, introducing federal regulatory authority, and piloting government programs to protect vulnerable families. Later, Democratic liberals instituted the New Deal at the urging of Franklin Delano Roosevelt and its sequel, the Great Society, under Lyndon Johnson, thus providing the infrastructure for the American welfare state. Philosophically, pragmatism served as the foundation for American social policy, providing a means for reconciling ideological differences, demonstrating how science can enhance the public interest, and encouraging new initiatives for resolving social problems.

An ascendant conservatism is evidence that the paradigm governing social policy for the better part of the past century, the welfare state, is due for an overhaul. With the advent of the information age, a transformation of social policy is inevitable; yet the creation of a new social policy paradigm that enhances the public's interest remains elusive. Already, social industrial complexes have emerged to shape social policy in a manner that places self-interest over that of the public; policy institutes have used control of the means of analysis to constrict options so that social policy enhances not the general welfare but the interests of those who subsidize think tanks. As counterpoint to such distortions, Robert K. Merton proposed "opportunity structures" as a basis for social policy. Unfortunately, the edifices of the industrial era—corporate and government bureaucracies—have too often suffocated opportunity, thwarting the desires of citizens. For that reason, a philosophical renaissance is in order, a rebirth of public philosophy. By empowering citizens, accelerating mobility, and restructuring government, radical pragmatism not only promises to amplify the aspirations of Americans but offers the template for a new paradigm of social policy as well.

NOTES

INTRODUCTION

1. U.S. Department of Commerce, *Statistical Abstract of the United States: 2002* (Washington, D.C., author: p. 305).

2. Peronet Despeignes, "Report Warns of Chronic US Deficits," *Financial Times* (May 29, 2003), p. 1.

3. John Micklethwait and Adrian Wooldridge, *The Right Nation* (New York: Penguin, 2004), pp. 380–81.

4. Peter Peterson, "Deficits and Dysfunction," *New York Times Magazine* (June 8, 2003), p. 18.

5. Kevin Phillips, *Wealth and Democracy* (New York: Broadway Books, 2002).

6. N. Gregory Mankiw, "Deficits and Economic Priorities," *Washington Post* (July 16, 2003), p. A23.

7. Paul Krugman, "Stating the Obvious," *New York Times* (June 8, 2003), p. A27.

8. John Micklethwait and Adrian Wooldridge, "For Conservatives, Mission Accomplished," *New York Times* (May 18, 2004), p. A25.

9. Barbara Ehrenreich, *Fear of Falling* (New York: Harper Collins: 1989), p. 192.

10. Russell Baker, "Mr. Right," *New York Review of Books* (May 17, 2001), p. 6.

11. Peter Lindert, *Growing Public, Vol. 2* (New York: Cambridge University Press, 2004), p. 79.

12. Walter Wallace, *The Logic of Science in Sociology* (Chicago: Aldine: 1971).

13. Terry Eagleton, *After Theory* (New York: Basic Books, 2003), p. 2.

14. Quoted in Robert K. Merton, "On Sociological Theories of the Middle Range, in *Robert K. Merton: On Social Structure and Science,* Piotr Sztompka, ed. (Chicago: University of Chicago Press, 1996), p. 48.

15. Sztompka, *On Social Structure and Science.*

16. Merton, "Theoretical Pluralism," in *On Social Structure and Science,* p. 35.

17. Miguel Cervantes, *Don Quixote,* translated by Edith Grossman (New York: Harper Collins, 2003), p. 21.

18. James Wood, "Knight's Gambit," *The New Yorker* (December 22 & 29, 2003), p. 153.

19. E. J. Dionne, Jr., *They Only Look Dead* (New York: Simon & Schuster, 1996).

CHAPTER 1

1. Amy Goldstein and Mike Allen, "Budget Sharply Boosts Defense," *Washington Post* (December 4, 2003), p. A1.

2. John Micklethwait and Adrian Wooldridge, *The Right Nation* (New York: Penguin, 2004), p. 259.

3. Thomas Kuhn, *The Structure of Scientific Revolutions* (Chicago: University of Chicago Press, 1962).

4. Harold Wilensky, *Rich Democracies* (Berkeley: University of California Press, 2002).

5. Miguel de Cervantes Saavedra, *The Adventures of Don Quixote* [translated by J.M. Cohen] (New York: Penguin, 1950).

6. Harold Bloom, "Introduction," in Miguel Cervantes, *Don Quixote*, [translated by Edith Grossman] (New York: HarperCollins, 2003), p. xxxii.

7. David Landes, *The Wealth and Poverty of Nations* (New York: Norton, 1998), p. 180.

8. Richard Tarnas, *The Passion of the Western Mind* (New York: Ballantine, 1991), pp. 35, 105.

9. Chris Rohmann, *The World of Ideas* (New York: Ballantine, 1999), p. 116.

10. Landes, *Wealth and Poverty of Nations.*

11. Tarnas, *Western Mind,* p. 273.

12. Kuhn, *Structure of Scientific Revolutions.*

13. Don Martindale, *The Nature of Sociological Theory* (Boston: Houghton Mifflin, 1960), p.56.

14. Tarnas, *Western Mind,* pp. 369–70.

15. Rohmann, *World of Ideas,* p. 346.

16. William Epstein, *The American Policy-Making Process: Social Welfare as Ritual* (unpublished manuscript).

17. John Zammito, *Kant, Herder, and the Birth of Anthropology* (Chicago: University of Chicago Press, 2002), p. 15.

18. Martindale, *Sociological Theory,* pp. 217–19.

19. Stephen Ambrose, *Undaunted Courage* (New York: Touchstone, 1996).

20. Edmund Morgan, *Benjamin Franklin* (New Haven: Yale University Press, 2002).

21. Joseph Ellis, *Founding Brothers* (New York: Knopf, 2001), p. 6.

22. Joanne Freeman, *Affairs of Honor* (New Haven: Yale University Press, 2001).

23. Louis Menand, *The Metaphysical Club* (New York: Farrar, Straus, Giroux, 2001), p. 61.

24. Menand, *Metaphysical Club,* p. 63.

25. Menand, *Metaphysical Club,* p. xi.

26. Menand, *Metaphysical Club,* p. 353.

27. C. Wright Mills, *Sociology and Pragmatism* (New York: Oxford University Press, 1966).

28. Jane Addams, *Twenty Years at Hull House* (New York: MacMillan, 1910), p. 91.

29. Allen Davis, *American Heroine: The Life and Legend of Jane Addams* (New York: Oxford University Press, 1973).

30. Charles Noble, *The Collapse of Liberalism* (Lanham, Md.: Rowman & Littlefield, 2004), pp. 58–59.

31. Quoted in Edmund Morris, *Theodore Rex* (New York: Random House, 2001), p. 508.

32. Quoted in James Chace, "TR and the Road Not Taken," *New York Review of Books* (July 17, 2003), p. 38.

33. Justin Kaplan, *Lincoln Steffens* (New York: Simon and Schuster, 1974), pp. 50–51.

34. H. L. Mencken, *Minority Report* (New York: Knopf, 1956), p. 153.

35. Quoted in Martindale, *Sociological Theory,* p. 64.

36. Edwin Black, *War Against the Weak* (New York: Four Walls Eight Windows, 2003).

37. John Lukacs, "The Obsolescence of the American Intellectual," *The Chronicle of Higher Education* (October 4, 2002), p. B8.

38. Michael Ignatieff, *Isaiah Berlin* (New York: Henry Holt, 1998), p. 226.

39. John Hope Franklin, *From Slavery to Freedom* (New York: Free Press, 1980).

40. Theda Skocpol, *Protecting Soldiers and Mothers* (Cambridge, Mass.: Harvard University Press, 1992).

41. Linda Gordon, *Pitied but Not Entitled* (Cambridge, Mass.: Harvard University Press, 1994).

42. Kenneth Davis, *FDR: The New Deal Years 1933–1937* (New York: Random House, 1983), pp. 454–55.

43. Edward Berkowitz and Kim McQuaid, *Creating the Welfare State* (New York: Praeger, 1980).

44. Donna Franklin, *Ensuring Inequality* (New York: Oxford University Press, 1997), p. 55.

45. Jonathan Rauch, "The Accidental Radical," *National Journal,* 35, 30 (July 26, 2003), p. 1.

46. John O'Connor, "U.S. Social Welfare Policy," *Journal of Social Policy,* 27: 48–49.

47. Roy Lubove, *The Professional Altruist* (New York: Atheneum, 1969).

48. Amitai Etzioni, ed., *The Semi-Professions and Their Organizations* (New York: MacMillan, 1969).

49. Barbara Ehrenreich, *Fear of Falling* (New York: HarperCollins, 1989), p. 35.

50. U.S. Department of Commerce, *Statistical Abstract of the United States* (Washington, D.C.: U.S. Government Printing Office, 2002), pp. 320, 340.

51. Harold Wilensky, *Rich Democracies* (Berkeley: University of California Press, 2002), p. 345.

52. T. H. Marshall, *Class, Citizenship and Social Development* (Chicago: University of Chicago Press, 1964).

53. Harold Wilensky and Charles Lebeaux, *Industrial Society and Social Welfare* (New York: Free Press, 1965), p. 127.

54. Wilensky, *Rich Democracies,* p. 247.

55. Richard Titmuss, *Commitment to Welfare* (New York: Pantheon, 1968), p. 127.

56. James Midgley, "The American Welfare State in International Perspective," in Howard Karger and David Stoesz, *American Social Welfare Policy,* 3rd ed. (New York: Longman, 1998), p. 444.

57. Leon Ginsberg, *Conservative Social Welfare Policy* (Chicago: Nelson Hall, 1998), p. 70.

58. Arthur Schlesinger, Jr., *The Cycles of American History* (Boston: Houghton Mifflin, 1986), p. 47.

59. Walter Trattner, *From Poor Law to Welfare State* (New York: Free Press, 1999), ch. 13.

60. Cass Sunstein, "We Need to Reclaim the Second Bill of Rights," *Chronicle of Higher Education* (June 11, 2004), p. B9.

61. Ehrenreich, *Fear*, p. 45.

62. John Micklethwait and Adrian Wooldridge, *The Right Nation* (New York: Penguin, 2004), p. 63.

63. Theodore Lowi, *The End of Liberalism*, 2nd ed. (New York: Norton, 1979), p. 200.

64. Reynolds Farley, *The New American Reality* (New York: Russell Sage Foundation, 1996), p. 66.

65. Albert O. Hirschman, *The Rhetoric of Reaction* (Cambridge, Mass.: Harvard University Press, 1991).

66. John Patrick Diggins, *The Promise of Pragmatism* (Chicago: University of Chicago Press, 1994), p. 3.

67. Mills, *Sociology and Pragmatism*, pp. 69, 71.

68. Milton Greenberg, "How the GI Bill Changed Higher Education," *Chronicle of Higher Education* (June 18, 2004), p. B9.

69. "The GI Bill." Available at http://www.gibill.va.gov/education/GI_Bill.htm. [Accessed July 24, 2003]

70. U.S. Department of Commerce, *Statistical Abstract*, pp. 133, 139.

71. David Bromwich, "Blinding Blandness," *New Republic* (August 18 and 25, 2003), p. 30.

72. Robert K. Merton, *On Social Structure and Science* (Chicago: University of Chicago Press, 1996).

73. In his biography of Mills, Irving Horowitz identified Mills as a "radical pragmatist."

74. Rick Tilman, *C. Wright Mills* (University Park: Pennsylvania State University Press, 1984), p. 57.

75. Aage Sorensen and Seymour Spilerman, *Social Theory and Social Policy* (Westport, Conn.: Praeger, 1993), p. 5.

76. Daniel Patrick Moynihan, "The Negro Family: The Case for National Action" (Washington, D.C.: Department of Labor, 1965).

77. Paul Jargowsky, *Poverty and Place* (New York: Russell Sage Foundation, 1997), p. 189.

78. William Julius Wilson, *The Truly Disadvantaged* (Chicago: University of Chicago Press, 1987).

79. Quoted in Diggins, *Pragmatism*, p. 416.

80. Richard Rorty, *Achieving Our Country* (Cambridge, Mass.: Harvard University Press, 1997), p. 99.

81. Cornel West, *The American Evasion of Philosophy* (Madison: University of Wisconsin Press, 1989), p. 230.

82. West, *Philosophy*, p. 239.

83. Micklethwait and Wooldridge, *Right Nation*, p. 356.

CHAPTER 2

1. John Hope Franklin, *From Slavery to Freedom* (New York: Knopf, 1979), p. 288.

2. Walter Trattner, "The First Days of Social Security," *Public Welfare* (Fall 1985).

3. Jacob Hacker, *The Divided Welfare State* (New York: Cambridge University Press, 2002), p. 22.

4. Hacker, *The Divided Welfare State*, p. 51.

5. Robert Alford, *Health Care Politics* (Chicago: University of Chicago Press, 1975), pp. 14, 17.

6. Murray Edelman, *The Symbolic Uses of Politics* (Urbana: University of Illinois Press, 1962), p. 4.

7. Allen Bloom, *The Closing of the American Mind* (New York: Simon & Schuster, 1987), p. 249.

8. Robert Bellah, et al., *Habits of the Heart* (New York: Harper & Row, 1985).

9. Roy Lubove, *The Professional Altruist* (New York: Atheneum, 1969).

10. National Association of Social Workers, *Social Casework: Generic and Specific* (Silver Spring, Md.: NASW, 1974).

11. Murray Weitzman, et al., *The New Nonprofit Almanac & Desk Reference* (San Francisco, Ca.: Jossey-Bass, 2002), p. 8.

12. Weitzman, *Nonprofit Almanac*, pp. 94, 112.

13. "The 2001 United Way of America Annual Report," (Alexandria, Va.: United Way of America, 2001).

14. Weitzman, *Nonprofit Almanac*, p. 54.

15. Weitzman, *Nonprofit Almanac*, p. 82.

16. Weitzman, *Nonprofit Almanac*, p. 57.

17. Weitzman, *Nonprofit Almanac*, p. 109.

18. Diana Milbank, "Bush Links Faith and Agenda in Speech to Broadcast Group," *Washington Post* (February 11, 2003), p. A2.

19. Richard Morin, "Nonprofit, Faith-Based Groups Near Top of Poll on Solving Social Woes," *Washington Post* (February 1, 2001), p. A19.

20. Lena Sun, Sarah Cohen, and Jacqueline Salmon, "Much of Sept. 11 Charity Remains to Be Disbursed," *Washington Post* (June 11, 2002), p. A1.

21. David Chen, "After Weighing Value of Lives, 9/11 Fund Completes Task," *New York Times* (July 16, 2004), p. A1.

22. Lisa Belkin, "Just Money," *New York Times Magazine* (December 8, 2002).

23. Jacqueline Salmon, "Nonprofits Show Losses in the Public's Trust," *Washington Post* (November 9, 2002), p. A2.

24. Jacqueline Salmon, "Confidence in Nonprofits Loses Boos from Sept. 11," *Washington Post* (August 15, 2002), p. B2; Gregg Winter, "Charitable Giving Falls for the First Time in Years," *New York Times* (October 27, 2003), p. A11.

25. Robert Alford, *Health Care Politics* (Chicago: University of Chicago Press, 1975), p. 204.

26. Lubove, *Professional Altruist*, p. 197.

27. Alford, *Health Care Politics*, p. 2.

28. *Social Security Bulletin, Annual Statistical Supplement* (Washington, D.C.: Social Security Administration, 1999), p. 140.

29. *The National Performance Review. Available at http://govinfo.library.unt.edu/npr/.* [Accessed July 30, 2003]

30. U.S. Department of Commerce, *Statistical Abstract of the United States—2002* (Washington, D.C.: U.S. Government Printing Office, 2002), p. 296.

31. Weitzman, *Nonprofit Almanac*, p. 16.

32. U.S. Department of Commerce, *Statistical Abstract*, p. 340.

33. David Osborne, *Laboratories of Democracy* (Boston: Harvard Business School Press, 1988).

34. Amy Goldstein and Jonathan Weisman, "Bush Seeks to Recast Federal Ties to the Poor," *Washington Post* (February 9, 2003), p. A1.

35. David Obsborne and Ted Gaebler, *Reinventing Government* (New York: Addison Wesley, 1992).

36. Obsborne and Gaebler, *Reinventing Government*, p. 199.

37. Daniel Bell, *The Coming of Post-Industrial Society* (New York: Basic Books, 1976), p. 130.

38. U.S. Department of Commerce, *Statistical Abstract*, p. 105.

39. U.S. Department of Commerce, *Statistical Abstract*, p. 474.

40. *The Unsolved Challenge of System Reform* (Baltimore: Annie E. Casey Foundation, 2003), p. 2.

41. U.S. Department of Commerce, *Statistical Abstract*, pp. 368, 373, 377.

42. Robert Barker, "Private Practice Primer for Social Work," *NASW News* (October 1983), p. 13.

43. A. Goleman, "Social Workers Vault Into a Leading Role in Psychotherapy," *New York Times* (April 3, 1985), p. C1.

44. Margaret Gibelman and Philip Schervish, *The Social Work Labor Force as Reflected in the NASW Membership* (Washington, D.C.: National Association of Social Workers, 1997), p. 69.

45. John O'Neill, "Private Sector Employs Most Members," *NASW News* (February 2003), p. 8.

46. U.S. Department of Commerce, *Statistical Abstract*, p. 101.

47. U.S. Department of Commerce, *Statistical Abstract*, p. 101.

48. Karen Neuman and Margaret Ptak, "Managing Managed Care through Accreditation," *Social Work*, 48, 3 (July 2003), p. 385.

49. Donald Light, "Corporate Medicine for Profit," *Scientific American* 255 (December 1986), pp. 81–89.

50. Howard Karger and David Stoesz, *American Social Welfare Policy*, 4th ed. (New York: Longman, 2002), p. 191.

51. Donald Barlett and James Steele, *Critical Condition* (New York: Doubleday, 2004), p. 73.

52. Bill Brubaker, "Magellan Files for Chapter 11 to Reduce Debt," *Washington Post* (March 12, 2003), p. E1.

53. Barlett and Steele, *Critical Condition*, p. 84.

54. Stephanie Strom, "In Charity, Where Does a C.E.O. End and a Company Start?" *New York Times* (September 22, 2002), p. BU1.

55. Robert Alford, "The Political Economy of Health Care," *Politics and Society* (1973), pp. 127–64.

56. Marc Bendick, "Privatizing the Delivery of Social Welfare Services, in *Working Paper 6: Privatization* (Washington, D.C.: National Conference on Social Welfare), pp. 1–73.

57. J. O'Connor, *The Fiscal Crisis of the State* (New York: St. Martins, 1973), p. 34.

58. Arnold Relman, "The New Medical Industrial Complex," *New England Journal of Medicine,* 303, 17 (1980).

59. "Paying to Make a Point," *Washington Post* (March 19, 2002), p. A11.

60. Ceci Connolly, "Drugmakers Protect Their Turf," *Washington Post* (November 21, 2003), p. A4.

61. Amy Goldstein, "Medicare Bill Would Enrich Companies," *Washington Post* (November 24, 2003), p. A1.

62. E. J. Dionne, Jr., "Medicare Monstrosity," *Washington Post* (November 18, 2003), p. A25.

63. Dana Milbank and Claudia Deane, "President Signs Medicare Drug Bill," *Washington Post* (December 9, 2003), p. A1.

64. Robert Samuelson, "Medicare as Pork Barrel," *Washington Post* (November 24, 2003), p. A21.

65. Jonathan Cohn, "Careless," *New Republic* (December 15, 2003), p. 18.

66. Robert Pear, "Health Industry Bidding to Hire Medicare Chief," *New York Times* (December 3, 2003), p. A1.

67. Robert Pear, "Medicare Chief Joins Firm with Health Clients," *New York Times* (December 19, 2003), p. A20.

68. Judy Sarasohn, "Special Interests," *Washington Post* (June 24, 2004), p. A23.

69. Robert Pear, "Agency Sees Withholding of Medicare Data from Congress as Illegal," *New York Times* (May 4, 2004), p. A17.

70. Sheryl Stolberg and Robert Pear, "Mysterious Fax Adds to Intrigue Over Drug Bill," *New York Times* (March 18, 2004), p. A1.

71. Amy Goldstein, "Foster: White House Had Role in Withholding Medicare Data," *Washington Post* (March 19, 2004), p. A2.

72. Cheryl Stolberg, "2 Decline to Testify on Drug Cost," *New York Times* (April 2, 2004), p. A15.

73. Amy Goldstein, "A Dire Report on Medicare Finances," *Washington Post* (March 24, 2004), p. A1.

74. Russell Banker, "In Bush's Washington," *New York Review of Books* (May 13, 2004), p. 25.

75. Theodore Lowi, *The End of Liberalism,* 2nd ed. (New York: Norton, 1979), p. xii.

76. Alice O'Connor, *Poverty Knowledge* (Princeton, N.J.: Princeton University Press, 2001), p. 214.

77. Colbert King, "A City Lost to Shame," *Washington Post* (June 26, 2004), p. A23.

78. Howard Karger and David Stoesz, *American Social Welfare Policy,* 4th ed. (Boston: Allyn&Bacon, 2002), ch. 13.

79. Richard Stevenson and Steven Greenhouse, "Plan for Illegal Immigrant Workers Draws Fire from Two Sides," *New York Times* (January 8, 2004), p. A20.

80. Alan Elsner, "America's Prison Habit," *Washington Post* (January 24, 2004), p. A19.

81. Harry Specht and Mark Courtney, *Unfaithful Angels* (New York: Free Press, 1994).

82. David Stoesz, "From Social Work to Human Services," *Journal of Sociology and Social Welfare* 29 (December 2002), pp. 19–37.

83. Howard Karger and David Stoesz, "The Growth of Social Work Education Programs 1985–1999," *Journal of Social Work Education*, 39.2 (Spring/Summer 2003), p. 284.

84. Marjie Lundstrom and Rochelle Sharpe, "Getting Away with Murder," *Gannett News Service* (1990), p. 1.

85. Cliffort Levy, "For Mentally Ill, Death and Misery," *New York Times* (April 26, 2002), p. 34.

86. Levy, "For Mentally Ill," p. 34; see also, Clifford Levy, "Here, Life Is Squalor and Chaos," *New York Times* (April 29, 2002), p. A1; Clifford Levy, "Voiceless, Defenseless, and a Source of Cash," *New York Times* (April 30, 2002), p. A1.

87. David Fallis, "As Care Declines, Cost Can Be Injury, Death," *Washington Post* (May 23, 2004), p. A15.

88. Fallis, "As Care Declines," p. A16.

89. Fallis, "As Care Declines," p. A15.

90. Katherine Boo, "Forest Haven is Gone, But the Agony Remains," *Washington Post* (March 14, 1999), p. A1; Katherine Boo, "Residents Languish; Profiteers Flourish," *Washington Post* (March 15, 1999), p. A1; Katherine Boo, "System Loses Lives and Trust," *Washington Post* (December 5, 1999), p. A1.

91. Sari Horwitz, "Williams Fires Five Overseeing Retarded," *Washington Post* (January 19, 2000), p. A1.

92. "An Opaque Clarification," *Washington Post* (May 6, 2002), p. A20 (editorial).

93. Sari Horwitz, Scott Higham, and Susan Cohen, "Protected Children Died as Government Did Little," *Washington Post* (September 9, 2001).

94. "Living Well off the Poor," *Washington Post* (April 25, 2004), p. B6.

95. Jerry Markon, "Ex-Chief of Local United Way Sentenced," *Washington Post* (May 15, 2004), p. A1.

96. Henri Gauvin and Theola Labbe, "Accord Names Overseer for D.C. Youth Services," *Washington Post* (May 15, 2004), p. B1.

97. Fred Siegel, *The Future Once Happened Here* (New York: Free Press, 1997), p. 98.

98. Siegel, *Future*, p. 242.

99. Robert Alford, *Health Care Politics* (Chicago: University of Chicago Press, 1975), p. x.

CHAPTER 3

1. Ted Halstead and Michael Lind, *The Radical Center* (New York: Doubleday, 2001), p. 12.

2. John Micklethwait and Adrian Wooldridge, *The Right Nation* (New York: Penguin, 2004), p. 49.

3. Even Marx, who used a two-part classification, conceded the existence of a "lumpen-proletariat," although he did little to develop the concept.

4. Dexter Dunphy, *The Primary Group* (New York: Appleton-Century-Crofts, 1972), pp. 42–44.

5. Sam Verhovek, "Elder Bill Gates Takes on the Role of Philanthropist," *New York Times* (September 12, 1999), p. 22.

6. Dan Bloom and Kay Sherwood, *Matching Opportunities to Obligations: Lessons for Child Support Reform from the Parents' Fair Share Pilot Phase* (New York: Manpower Demonstration Research Corporation, 1994).

7. Kevin Phillips, "The New Face of Another Guilded Age," *Washington Post* (May 26, 2002), p. B2.

8. *Overview of Entitlement Programs* (Washington, D.C.: U.S. Government Printing Office, 2000), p. 1312.

9. Thomas Shapiro and Edward Wolff, eds., *Assets for the Poor* (New York: Russell Sage Foundation, 2001).

10. Lawrence Mishel, Jared Bernstein, and Heather Boushey, *The State of Working America, 2002/2003* (Washington, D.C.: Economic Policy Institute, 2003), p. 281, 284.

11. Asena Caner and Edward Wolff, "Asset Poverty in the United States," *Public Policy Brief* 76A (Annandale-on-Hudson, N.Y.: Jerome Levy Economics Institute, 2004), p. 4.

12. Ray Boshara, ed., *Building Assets* (Washington, D.C.: Corporation for Enterprise Development, 2001), p. 2.008

13. W. Michael Cox and Richard Alm, *Myths of Rich & Poor* (New York: Basic Books, 1999), p. 73.

14. Bradley Schiller, *The Economics of Poverty and Discrimination*, 7th ed. (Upper Saddle River, N.J.: Prentice Hall, 1998).

15. Bradley Schiller, "Moving Up: The Training and Wage Gains of Minimum-Wage Entrants," *Social Science Quarterly* 75 (1994), p. 629.

16. Schiller, "Moving Up," p. 634.

17. Bradley Schiller, "Relative Earnings Redux," *Review of Income and Wealth*, series 40, no. 4 (1994), p. 447.

18. Daniel McMurer and Isabel Sawhill, *Getting Ahead* (Washington, D.C.: Urban Institute, 1998), p. 33.

19. First established in 1944, PACs are political organizations that are regulated by federal law:. Individual candidate contributions are limited to $5,000 per election; contributions to other PACs are restricted to $5,000 annually; and funding of national party committees cannot exceed $15,000 annually. Because of these restrictions, "soft money"—contributions outside the prohibitions of the Federal Election Campaign Act—have become more prominent in federal elections.

20. Charles Noble, *The Collapse of Liberalism* (Lanham, Md.: Rowman & Littlefield, 2004), p. 33.

21. Noble, *Collapse of Liberalism*, p. 36.

22. "15-month Fundraising Figures of Major Parties Detailed," (Washington, D.C.: Federal Election Commission, June 5, 2000), p. 1.

23. Noble, *Collapse of Liberalism*, p. 34.

24. "Overall Campaign Finance Statistics," (Washington, D.C.: Common Cause, June, 11, 1999).

25. "The Power of 'Soft Money,'" *Washington Post* (February 13, 2002), p. A25.

26. Ruth Marcus and Mike Allen, "Democrats' Donations from Labor Up Sharply," *Washington Post* (July 17, 2000), p. A1.

27. "The Power of Soft Money," p. A25.

28. Ken Auletta, "Pay Per Views," *New Yorker* (June 5, 1995), p. 56.

29. Nancy Gibbs, "Where Power Goes . . ." *Time* (July 17, 1995), p. 21.

30. Micklethwait and Wooldridge, *Right Nation*, p. 258.

31. Mike Allen, "GOP Takes in $33 Million at Fundraiser," *Washington Post* (May 15, 2002), p. A1.

32. Thomas Edsall, Sarah Cohen and James Grimaldi, "Pioneers Fill War Chest, Then Capitalize," *Washington Post* (May 16, 2004), p. A1.

33. "Democrats' Secret Patriots," *Washington Post* (May 25, 2004), p. A16.

34. Juliet Eilperin, "After McCain-Feingold, A Bigger Role for PACs," *Washington Post* (June 1, 2002), p. A1.

35. Thomas Edsall, "Study Suggests Law on Campaign Finance Will Benefit Liberals," *Washington Post* (June 10, 2002), p. A19.

36. Thomas Edsall, "GOP Creating Own '527' Groups," *Washington Post* (May 25, 2004), p. A15.

37. Thomas Edsall, "Republican 'Soft Money' Groups Find Business Reluctant to Give," *Washington Post* (June 8, 2004), p. A21.

38. Hedrick Smith, *The Power Game: How Washington Works* (New York: Random House, 1988), p. 254.

39. Quoted in William Safire, *Safire's New Political Dictionary* (New York: Random House, 1993), p. 840.

40. Charles Peters, *How Washington Really Works*, rev. ed. (Reading, Mass.: Addison-Wesley, 1983), p. 112.

41. See, for example, Sheldon Danziger and Daniel Weinberg, *Fighting Poverty* (Cambridge, Mass.: Harvard University Press, 1986).

42. Peters, *How Washington Really Works*, pp. 101–102, 116.

43. David Ricci, *The Transformation of American Politics* (New Haven, Conn.: Yale University Press, 1993), p. 125.

44. Smith, *The Power Game*, p. 152.

45. C. Wright Mills, *The Sociological Imagination* (New York: Oxford University Press, 1959), p. 57.

46. Alice O'Connor, *Poverty Knowledge* (Princeton, N.J.: Princeton University Press, 2001), p. 15.

47. Thomas Kuhn, *The Structure of Scientific Revolutions* (Chicago: University of Chicago Press, 1970), ch. IV.

48. David Stoesz, "Policy Gambit: Conservative Think Tanks Take On the Welfare State," *Journal of Sociology and Social Welfare* 16 (1989), pp. 8–16.

49. David Stoesz, "The New Welfare Policy Institutes." Unpublished manuscript, School of Social Work, San Diego State University, 1988.

50. David Broder, "Thanks to Two Think Tanks," *Washington Post* (May 8, 2002), p. A2.

51. David Von Drehle, "Liberals Get a Think Tank of Their Own," *Washington Post* (October 23, 2003), p. A29.

52. Michael Katz, *In the Shadow of the Poorhouse* (New York: Basic Books, 1986), p. x.

53. Bruce Jansson, *The Reluctant Welfare State* (Belmont, Ca: Wadsworth, 1988).

54. Brigitte Berger and Peter Berger, *The War over the Family* (New York: Anchor Press, 1983), p. 38.

55. Ricci, *Transformation*, pp. 188, 189.

56. Cited in Barbara Ehrenreich, *Fear of Falling* (New York: HarperCollins, 1989), p. 157.

57. Terry Eagleton, *After Theory* (New York: Basic Books, 2003), p. 52.

58. Peters, *How Washington Really Works*, p. 111.

59. Smith, *Power Game*, p. 24.

60. Mills, *Sociological Imagination*, p. 55.

61. Ricci, *Transformation*, p. 163.

62. O'Connor, *Poverty Knowledge*, p. 243.

63. William Baroody, Jr., "The President's View," *AEI Annual Report 1981–1982* (Washington, D.C.: American Enterprise Institute, n.d.), p. 2.

64. Peter Berger and John Neuhaus, *To Empower People* (Washington, D.C.: American Enterprise Institute, 1977).

65. Berger and Berger, *War Over the Family*

66. Michael Balzano, *Federalizing Meals on Wheels* (Washington, D.C.: American Enterprise Institute, 1979), p. 37.

67. Michael Novak, *Toward a Theology of the Corporation* (Washington, D.C.: American Enterprise Institute, 1981), p. 5.

68. Novak, *Toward a Theology*, p. 50.

69. Novak, *Toward a Theology*, p. 28.

70. James Smith, "Foreword," in Sally Covington, *Moving a Public Agenda* (Washington, D.C.: National Committee for Responsive Philanthropy, 1997), p. 1.

71. Smith, "Foreword," *Power Gap*, p. 1.

72. Burton Pines, *Back to Basics* (New York: William Morrow, 1982), p. 254.

73. Micklethwait and Wooldridge, *Right Nation*, p. 168.

74. Karen Paget, "Lessons of Right-Wing Philanthropy," *The American Prospect* (September–October, 1998), pp. 92, 94.

75. Paget, "Lessons," pp. 91, 92.

76. E. J. Dionne, Jr., *They Only Look Dead* (New York: Simon and Schuster, 1997), pp. 187–91.

77. Enhrenreich, *Fear of Falling*, pp. 164–65.

78. Jon Micklethwait and Wooldridge, *Right Nation*, pp. 160–61.

79. Quoted in Ricci, *Transformation*, p. 171.

80. William Beach, et al., "The Economic and Fiscal Effects of the President's Growth Package" (Washington, D.C.: Heritage Foundation, 2003), p. 16.

81. Laura Blemenfeld, "Sowing the Seeds of GOP Domination," *Washington Post* (January 12, 2004), p. A1.

82. Micklethwait and Wooldridge, *Right Nation*, p. 22.

83. Quoted in Philip Gourevitch, "Fight on the Right," *New Yorker* (April 12, 2004), p. 37.

84. Donald Abelson, *Do Think Tanks Matter?* (Montreal: McGill-Queens, 2002), pp. 91, 93.

85. Peter Peterson, "Deficits and Dysfunction," *New York Times Magazine* (June 8, 2003), p. 18.

86. Michael Tanner, "Social Security and Medicare," presentation at the CATO Institute, March 2, 2004.

87. Alan Wolfe, "Paths of Dependence," *New Republic* (October 24, 2002), p. 41.

88. Tucker Carlson, "Memo to the Democrats," *New York Times Magazine* (January 19, 2003), p. 38.

89. Russell Jacoby, *The Last Intellectuals* (New York: Basic Books, 2000), p. 183.

90. Albert O. Hirschman, *Shifting Involvements* (Princeton, N.J.: Princeton University Press, 1982), p. 132.

91. Micklethwait and Wooldridge, *Right Nation*, p. 382.

92. Peter Bachrach and Morton S. Baratz, *Power and Poverty* (New York: Oxford University Press, 1979), p. 7.

93. For a review of the CAP experience, see Daniel Patrick Moynihan, *Maximum Feasible Misunderstanding* (New York: Random House, 1973).

94. Michael Lipsky, "Bureaucratic Disentitlement in Social Welfare Programs," *Social Service Review* 33, no. 4 (March 1984), pp. 81–88.

95. Quoted in Robert Kuttner, *The Economic Illusion* (Boston: Houghton Mifflin, 1984), p. 86.

96. Ellen Dunbar, "Future of Social Work," *NASW California News* 13, no. 18 (May 1987), p. 3.

97. Harris Chaiklin, "The New Homeless and Service Planning on a Professional Campus" (University of Maryland, Chancellor's Colloquium, Baltimore, December 4, 1985), p. 7.

98. "Willie's Vision for Chicano Empowerment," *Southwest Voter Research Notes* 2, no. 3 (June 1988), pp. 1.

99. "Deconstructing Distrust," The Pew Research Center. Available online.

100. Quoted in E. J. Dionne, Jr., "Poor Version of Democracy," *Washington Post* (June 11, 2004), p. A25.

101. Dale Russakoff, "Cut Out of Prosperity, Cutting Out at the Polls," *Washington Post* (October 24, 2000), p. A12.

102. David Broder, "The 30 Million Missing Voters," *Washington Post* (July 16, 2000), p. B7.

103. John Micklethwait and Adrian Wooldridge, "For Conservatives, Mission Accomplished," *New York Times* (May 18, 2004), p. A25.

104. Matt Bei, "Fight Club," *New York Times Sunday Magazine* (August 10, 2003).

105. Ehrenreich, *Fear of Falling*, p. 194.

106. Micklethwait and Wooldridge, *Right Nation*, p. 169.

CHAPTER 4

1. Terry Eagleton, *After Theory* (New York: Basic Books, 2003), p. 13.

2. Candace de Russy, "Professional Ethics Begin on the College Campus," *Chronicle of Higher Education* (September 19, 2003), p. B20.

3. Russell Jacoby, *The Last Intellectuals* (New York: Basic Books, 2000), p. 184.

4. David Lodge, "Goodbye to All That," *New York Review of Books* (May 24, 2004), p. 39.

5. Lodge, "Goodbye," p. 39.

6. Roger Kimball, *Tenured Radicals* (Chicago: Ivan R. Dee, 1998), p. 4.

7. Stephen Carter, *The Emperor of Ocean Park* (New York: Vintage, 2002), p. 109.

8. Philip Roth, *The Human Stain* (New York: Vintage, 2001), pp. 330–331.

9. Aileen Kelly, "In the Promised Land," *New York Review of Books* (November 29, 2001), p. 45.

10. Chris Rohmann, *A World of Ideas* (New York: Ballantine, 1999), p. 310.

11. Zygmunt Bauman, "Sociology and Postmodernity," *Sociological Review* (1988), p. 798.

12. Steven Connor, *Postmodernist Culture* (Cambridge, Mass.: Basil Blackwell, 1989), p. 9.

13. Quoted in Frederic Jameson, *Postmodernism* (Durham, N.C.: Duke University Press, 1991), pp. 378–379).

14. Andrei Codrescu, *The Disappearance of the Outside* (Reading, Mass.: Addison Wesley, 1990), p. 96.

15. Jameson, *Postmodernism*, p. xiv.

16. Jameson, *Postmodernism*, p. 5.

17. Jean-Francois Lyotard, *The Postmodern Condition* (Minneapolis: University of Minnesota Press, 1989), p. 48.

18. Madan Sarup, *Post-Structuralism and Postmodernism* (Athens: University of Georgia Press, 1989), p. 80.

19. Jerome Wakefield, "Foucauldian Fallacies: An Essay Review of Leslie Margolin's *Under Cover of Kindness*," *Social Service Review* (December 1998).

20. Leslie Margolin, *Under Cover of Kindness* (Charlottesville: University Press of Virginia, 1997), p. 2.

21. Steven Pinker, *The Blank Slate* (New York: Viking, 2002), part I.

22. Dorothy Van Soest, "Multiculturalism and Social Work Education," *Journal of Social Work Education*, 31, 1 (Winter 1995), pp. 59, 60.

23. Stanley Witkin, "Writing Social Work," *Social Work*, 45, 5 (October 2000), p. 390.

24. Stanley Witkin, "Reading Social Work," *Social Work*, 46, 1 (January 2001), p. 6.

25. Witkin, "Reading Social Work," p. 6.

26. Ann Weick, "Hidden Voices," *Social Work*, 45, 5 (October 2000), p. 398.

27. Weick, "Hidden Voices," p. 400.

28. Weick, "Hidden Voices," p. 401.

29. J. Carter, "Postmodernity and Welfare," *Social Policy and Administration*, 32 (1998), p. 104.

30. Pauline Rosenau, *Post-Modernism and the Social Sciences* (Princeton, N.J.: Princeton University Press, 1992), pp. 8–9.

31. Murphy, "Making Sense of Postmodern Sociology," p. 609–610.

32. Dennis Saleeby, *The Strengths Perspective in Social Work Practice*, 2nd ed. (White Plains, N.Y.: Longman, 1997), p. 4.

33. Saleeby, *Strengths Perspective*, p. 3.

34. Saleeby, *Strengths Perspective*, p. 3.

35. Marlys Staudt, Matthew Howard, and Brett Drake, "The Operationalization, Implementation, and Effectiveness of the Strengths Perspective," *Journal of Social Service Research*, 27, 3 (2001), p. 1.

36. Wes Shera and Lilian Wells, *Empowerment Practice in Social Work* (Toronto: Canadian Scholars' Press, 1999), p. x.

37. Haya Itzhaky and Pinchas Gerber, "The Connection between Universal Values and Empowerment," in Shera and Wells, *Empowerment Practice*, p. 427.

38. Ruth Parsons, "Assess Helping Processes and Client Outcomes in Empowerment Practice," in Shera and Wells, *Empowerment Practice*, pp. 390–411.

39. Eagleton, *After Theory*, p. 109.

40. Eagleton, *After Theory*, p. 190.

41. Eileen Gambrill, "Evidence-Based Practice," *Journal of Social Work Education,* 39 (2003), pp. 3–26.

42. Harris Chaiklin, "Policy, Politics, Sociology, and the Pragmatic Tradition," presented at the Eastern Sociology Meetings, Baltimore, MD, March 5, 2000, p. 6.

43. Charles Atherton and Kathleen Bolland, "The Multiculturalism Debate and Social Work Education," *Journal of Social Work Education*, 33, 1 (Winter 1977), p. 148.

44. Angela Dillard, "Multicultural Conservatism," *Chronicle of Higher Education* (March 2, 2001), p. B8.

45. David Brooks, "Lonely Campus Voices," *New York Times* (September 27, 2003), p. A27.

46. Yilu Zhao, "Taking the Liberalism Out of Liberal Arts," *New York Times* (April 3, 2004), p. A15.

47. David Horowitz, "In Defense of Intellectual Diversity," *Chronicle of Higher Education* (February 13, 2004), p. B12.

48. Eagleton, *After Theory*, pp. 15–16.

49. Phyllis Chesler and Donna Hughes, "Feminism in the 21st Century," *Washington Post* (February 22, 2004), p. B7.

50. Charles Noble, *The Collapse of Liberalism* (Lanham, Md.: Rowman & Littlefield, 2004), p. 163.

51. Harold Schonberg, *The Lives of the Great Composers* (New York: Norton, 1970), p. 418.

52. Quoted in Stephen Hilgartner, "The Sokal Affair in Context," *Science, Technology, & Human Values* 22, 4 (Autumn 1997), p. 506.

53. William Epstein, "The Sleeping Sentinels of Social Work," *Academic Questions* (Summer 1990), p. 41.

54. Hilgartner, "Sokal," p. 513.

55. William Epstein, "Confirmational Response Bias and the Quality of the Editorial Processes among American Social Work Journals," (Las Vegas: author, 2004), p. 16.

56. Epstein, "Confirmational Bias," p. 19.

57. David Remnick, "War Without End?" *New Yorker* (April 21 and 28, 2003), p. 61.

58. Louis Menand, "Patriot Games," *New Yorker* (May 17, 2004), p. 92.

59. Scott McLemee, "Hot Type," *Chronicle of Higher Education* (May 21, 2004), p. A18.

CHAPTER 5

1. Peter Edelman, "The Worst Thing Bill Clinton Has Done," *Atlantic Monthly* (March 1997), p. 53.

2. Maria Cancian and Daniel Meyer, "Alternative Measures of Economic Success among TANF Participants," *Journal of Policy Analysis and Management* 23, 3 (2004), p. 543.

3. Theda Skocpol, *Protecting Soldiers and Mothers* (Cambridge, Mass.: Harvard University Press, 1992).

4. Linda Gordon, *Pitied but not Entitled* (Cambridge, Mass.: Harvard University Press, 1994).

5. Quoted in Gordon, *Pitied but not Entitled*, p. 105.

6. Frances Fox Piven and Richard Cloward, *Regulating the Poor* (New York: Vintage, 1971).

7. David Dodenhoff, "Is Welfare Really about Social Control?" *Social Service Review* (September 1998), p. 324.

8. Fred Block, Richard Cloward, Barbara Enhrenreich, and Frances Fox Piven, *The Mean Season* (New York: Pantheon, 1987), p. ix.

9. Mimi Abramovitz, *Regulating the Lives of Women* (Boston: South End Press, 1996), p. 36.

10. Abramovitz, *Regulating the Lives of Women*, p. 32.

11. Mimi Abramovitz, *Under Attack, Fighting Back* (New York: Monthly Review Press, 2000).

12. Skocpol.

13. Gordon, *Pitied but Not Entitled.*

14. Terry Eagleton, *After Theory* (New York: Basic Books, 2003), p. 54.

15. Steve Farkas and Jean Johnson, "The Values We Live By," (New York: Public Agenda, 1996).

16. Lawrence Mead, "The New Welfare Debate," *Commentary* (March 1988), p. 46.

17. Alan Weil and Kenneth Finegold, eds. *Welfare Reform: The Next Act* (Washington, D.C.: Urban Institute, 2002), pp. 19–20.

18. Weil and Finegold, *Welfare Reform*, p. 190.

19. Committee on Ways and Means, House of Representatives, *Overview of Entitlement Programs* (Washington, D.C.: U.S. Government Printing Office, 1996), pp. 437–438; 446–448.

20. John Kasarda, "Industrial Restructuring and the Consequences of Changing Job Locations," in Reynolds Farley, ed., *Changes and Challenges: America 1990* (New York: Russell Sage Foundation, 1995), p. 156.

21. William Julius Wilson, *When Work Disappears* (New York: Knopf, 1996), pp. 29–30.

22. Edward Murphy, "Survival Strategies of Low-Income Young Men" (Boston: Heller School, Brandeis University, 1998), pp. 3,2.

23. Committee on Ways and Means, *Overview*, pp. 1170, 1184.

24. Jerome Miller, *Search and Destroy* (New York: Cambridge University Press, 1996), pp. 84, 54, 7–8.

25. Katherine Edin and Christopher Jencks, "Reforming Welfare," in Christopher Jencks, *Rethinking Social Policy* (Cambridge, Mass.: Harvard University Press, 1992), pp. 207, 208.

26. Jason DeParle, *American Dream* (New York: Viking, 2004), p. 282.

27. Katherine Edin and Laura Lein, *Making Ends Meet* (New York: Russell Sage Foundation, 1997).

28. Robert Merton, *Social Theory and Social Structure* (Glencoe, Ill.: Free Press, 1957), pp. 144, 160.

29. DeParle describes this in his comic account of Wisconsin's welfare reform effort, W-2, chs. 12–14.

30. Frederick Wiseman, *Welfare* (Cambridge, Mass.: Zipporah Films, 1975).

31. Michael Lipsky, *Street-Level Bureaucracy* (New York: Russell Sage Foundation, 1980), p. xiii.

32. Theresa Funiciello, *Tyranny of Kindness* (New York: Atlantic Monthly Press, 1993), p. 252; emphasis in original.

33. Michael Goodman, "Just Another Day in Paradise," *Los Angeles Times Magazine* (December 19, 1993), p. 30.

34. "It's Not Like They Say," (Washington, D.C.: Southport Institute for Policy Analysis, n.d.); Marcia Meyers, Bonnie Glaser, and Karin Macdonald, "On the Front Lines of Welfare Delivery," *Policy Analysis and Management* 17 (Winter 1998).

35. Irene Bush and Katherine Kraft, "Women on Welfare: What They Have to Say About Becoming Self-Sufficient," (New Brunswick, N.J.: Rutgers University School of Social Work, 1997), pp. vii, iii, emphasis in original.

36. "Inhuman Services," *Harpers* (June 1997), p. 16.

37. David Stoesz, *A Poverty of Imagination* (Madison: University of Wisconsin Press, 2000), p. 118.

38. David Shipler, *The Working Poor* (New York: Knopf, 2004), p. 229.

39. Philip AuClaire, ""Public Attitudes toward Social Welfare Expenditures," *Social Work* 29 (March/April 1984), p. 141.

40. Hugh Heclo, "The Political Foundations of Antipoverty Policy," in Sheldon Danziger and Daniel Weinberg, eds., *Fighting Poverty* (Cambridge, Mass.: Harvard University Press, 1986), p. 330, emphasis in original.

41. John Doble and Keith Melville, "The Public's Social Welfare Mandate," *Public Opinion* 11 (January/February 1989).

42. Steve Farkas and Jean Johnson, "The Values We Live By" (New York: Public Agenda, 1996).

43. Shelby Steele, *The Content of Our Character* (New York: Harper Perennial, 1990), pp. 16–17.

44. George Gilder, *Wealth and Poverty* (New York: Basic Books, 1981), p. 118.

45. Martin Anderson, "Welfare Reform," in Peter Duignan and Alvin Rabushka, eds., *The United States in the 1980s* (Stanford: Hoover Institution, 1980), p. 145.

46. Charles Murray, *Losing Ground* (New York: Basic Books, 1984), pp. 226–227.

47. Michael Novak, *The New Consensus on Family and Welfare* (Washington, D.C.: American Enterprise Institute, 1987), p. 45.

48. Lawrence Mead, "Are Welfare Employment Programs Effective?" in Jonathan Crane, ed., *Social Programs That Work* (New York: Russell Sage Foundation, 1997), pp. 14, 15.

49. Lawrence Mead, *The New Paternalism* (Washington, D.C.: Brookings Institution, 1997).

50. Lawrence Mead, *The New Politics of Poverty* (New York: Basic Books, 1992), p. 181.

51. Lawrence Mead, *Beyond Entitlement* (New York: Free Press, 1986).

52. Judith Gueron and Edward Pauley, *From Welfare to Work* (New York: Russell Sage Foundation, 1991).

53. "Charge to the Working Group on Welfare Reform, Family Support, and Independence" (Washington, D.C.: n.p., n.d.).

54. Quoted in Leon Ginsberg, *Conservative Social Welfare Policy* (Chicago: Nelson Hall, 1998), p. 122.

55. David Super, "The New Welfare Law," (Washington, D.C.: Center on Budget and Policy Priorities, 1996), p. 2.

56. Gayle Hamilton, et al., *National Evaluation of Welfare-to-Work Strategies* (Washington, D.C.: Department of Health and Human Services, 1997).

57. Dan Bloom, Mary Farrell, James Kemple, and Nandita Verma, *FTP: The Family Transition Program* (New York: Manpower Demonstration Research Corporation, 1997).

58. Dan Bloom, Veronica Fellerath, David Long, and Robert Wood, "LEAP; Interim Findings of a Welfare Initiative to Improve School Attendance among Teenage Prents," (New York: Manpower Demonstration Research Corporation, 1993).

59. Janet Quint, Johannes Bos, and Denise Polit, *New Chance: Final Report* (New York: Manpower Demonstration Research Corporation, 1997).

60. Sarah Archibald, "New Hope for Wisconsin Works," *LaFollette Policy Report* 9 (Spring/Summer 1998), p. 13.

61. Hans Bos et al., "New Hope for People with Low Income," (New York: Manpower Demonstration Research Corporation, 1999), pp. 3–4, 26.

62. Katheryn Edin, "Single Mothers and Child Support," *Social Service Review* 17 (1995), pp. 214–215.

63. Katheryn Edin and Laura Lein, *Making Ends Meet* (New York: Russell Sage Foundation, 1997).

64. Bradley Schiller, "State Welfare-Reform Impacts," (Washington, D.C.: School of Public Affairs, American University, February 1998), pp. 13–14.

65. Harry Holzer, "Black Employment Problems," *Journal of Policy Analysis and Management* 13 (1994), p. 715.

66. David Howell and Elizabeth Howell, "The Effects of Immigrants on African American Earnings," (New York: New School for Social Research, 1997), p. 23.

67. Daniel Meyer and Maria Cancian, "Economic Well-Being Following an Exit from AFDC," (Madison, Wisc.: Institute for Research on Poverty, 1997), p. iv.

68. Ann Rangarajan and Anne Gordon, "The Transition from Welfare to Work," (Princeton, N.J.: Mathematica Policy Research, 1997), pp. 8–10.

69. DeParle, *American Dream*, p. 168.

70. Robert Pear, "Panel on Social Security Urges Investing in Stocks But Is Split Over Methods," *New York Times* (January 7, 1997), p. 1.

CHAPTER 6

1. Colin Pritchard, "Re-Analysing Children's Homicide and Undetermined Death Rates as an Indication of Improved Children Protection," *British Journal of Social Work* 23 (1993): 648–51.

2. Jane Waldfogel, *The Future of Child Protection* (Cambridge, Mass.: Harvard University Press, 1998), pp. 60–61.

3. United Nations Development Program, *Human Development Report* (New York: Oxford University Press, 1995, 1996, 1997, 2003), p. 237.

4. Marjie Lundstrom and Rochelle Sharpe, "Getting Away with Murder," Gannett News Service (n.d.), p. 2.

5. Lundstrom and Sharpe, "Getting Away with Murder," p. 8.

6. Sari Horwitz, Scott Higham, and Sarah Cohen, "'Protected' Children Died as Government Did Little," *Washington Post* (n.d.).

7. Sewell Chan, "Md. Threatens to Return D.C. Foster Children," *Washington Post* (April 18, 2002), p. B2.

8. Scott Higham, "District Says It's Not Liable in Girl's Death," *Washington Post* (March 28, 2002), p. B5.

9. Sue Pressley, "5-year-old Missing 15 Months, and No One Noticed," *Washington Post* (May 4, 2002), p. A1.

10. Carol Miller, "Miami Welfare Workers Held Off Notifying Police of Missing Child," *Washington Post* (May 6, 2002), p. A1.

11. Matthew Purdy, Andrew Jacobs, and Richard Jones, "Life Behind Basement Doors," *New York Times* (January 12, 2003), p. A1.

12. Richard Jones and Leslie Kaufman, "New Jersey Opens Files Showing Failures of Child Welfare System," *New York Times*. Available at http://query.nytimes.com/qst/abstract.html. [Accessed April 15, 2003].

13. Richard Jones and Leslie Kaufman, "Foster Care Secrecy Magnifies Suffering in New Jersey Cases," *New York Times* (May 4, 2003), pp. 1, 32.

14. Richard Jones, "For Family of Beaten Boy, Tears, Not Finger-Pointing," *New York Times* (August 20, 2003), p. 1.

15. Lydia Polgreen and Robert Worth, "New Jersey Couple Held in Abuse," *New York Times* (October 27, 2003), p. A1.

16. Richard Jones, "Adopted Boys Were Starved, and Caseworkers Did Little, Report Finds," *New York Times* (February 13, 2004), p. A21.

17. "Watching as the Children Starved," *New York Times* (June 24, 2004), p. A26.

18. Leslie Kaufman, "Cash Incentives for Adoptions Seen as Risk to Some Children," *New York Times* (October 29, 2003), p. A1.

19. Jones, "Adopted Boys," p. A21.

20. Richard Jones, "New Jersey Plan on Child Welfare," *New York Times* (February 19, 2004), p. A1.

21. Andrew Jacobs, "Lawsuit Challenges Mississippi's Short-of-Resources Child Protection System," *New York Times* (April 1, 2004), p. A14.

22. Duncan Lindsey, *The Welfare of Children* (New York: Oxford University Press, 1994), p. 116.

23. William Epstein, *Children Who Could Have Been* (Madison: University of Wisconsin Press, 1999).

24. Epstein, *Children Who Could Have Been,* pp. 121–22.

25. Alvin Schorr, "The Bleak Prospect for Public Child Welfare," *Social Service Review* (March 2000), p. 124.

26. Schorr, "Bleak Prospect," p. 125.

27. Schorr, "Bleak Prospect," p. 125.

28. Schorr, "Bleak Prospect," p. 127.

29. Schorr, "Bleak Prospect," p. 131.

30. *The Unsolved Challenge of System Reform* (Baltimore: Annie E. Casey Foundation, 2003), p. 2.

31. Paul Light, *The Health of the Human Services Workforce* (Washington, D.C.: Brookings Institution, 2003), p. 6.

32. Schorr, "Bleak Prospect," p. 131.

33. Arnold Sameroff, et al., reported in James Garbarino, *Raising Children in a Socially Toxic Environment* (San Francisco: Jossey-Bass, 1999), pp. 152–53.

34. Lindsey, *Welfare of Children,* p. 148.

35. James Garbarino, *Lost Boys,* (New York: Free Press, 1999), p. 14.

36. Daniel Bonevac, "Manifestations of Illiberalism in Philosophy," *Academic Questions* 12 (Winter 1998), p. 17.

37. In making this claim, advocates invoked the Indian Child Welfare Act (ICWA) of 1978, which forbade placement of Native American children outside of a tribe without the tribe's consent. A critical factor that differentiates ICWA from African American transracial adoption is one of cultural integrity, particularly the presence of a separate, viable language.

38. Leslie Doty Hollingsworth, "Promoting Same-Race Adoption for Children of Color," *Social Work* 43 (March 1998), pp. 104–16.

39. Rita Simon and Howard Altstein, "The Case for Transracial Adoption," *Children and Youth Service Review* 18, nos. 1–2 (1996), pp. 20–21.

40. Ellen Bass and Laura Davis, *The Courage to Heal* (New York: Harper&Row, 1988), p. 20.

41. Mark Pendergrast, *Victims of Memory* (Hinesburg, Vt.: Upper Access, 1996), ch. 9.

42. Frederick Crews, "The Trauma Trap," *New York Review of Books* (March 11, 2004), p. 37.

43. Erica Goode, "Defying Psychiatric Wisdom, These Skeptics Say 'Prove It,'" *New York Times* (March 9, 2004), p. D1.

44. Lela Costin, Howard Karger, and David Stoesz, *The Politics of Child Abuse in America* (New York: Oxford University Press, 1996), p. 137.

45. Renee Frederickson, *Repressed Memories* (New York: Fireside, 1992), p. 17.

46. Quoted in Pendergrast, *Victims of Memory*, p. 62.

47. Elizabeth Loftus and Katherine Kethcham, *The Myth of Repressed Memory* (New York: St. Martin's Griffin, 1994), p. 258.

48. Lawrence Wright, *Remembering Satan* (New York: Knopf, 1994).

49. Jim Okerblom and Mark Sauer, "Was Akiki Inquiry Rush to Judgment?" *San Diego Union-Tribune* (November 22, 1993), p. A13.

50. Michael Cranberry, "Case Illustrates Flaws in Child Abuse Trials," *Los Angeles Times* (November 29, 1993), p. A23.

51. Bill Callahan, "Gang of 6 Protected Akiki in Jail," *San Diego Union-Tribune* (November 24, 1993), p. A1; Jim Okerblom and Mark Sauer, "Akiki Cleared Completely," *San Diego Union-Tribune* (November 20, 1993), p. A1.

52. San Diego Child Abuse Coordinating Council, *Child Deaths in 1991* (San Diego: author, 1992), n.p.

53. Bruce Grierson, "A Bad Trip Down Memory Lane," *New York Times Sunday Magazine* (July 27, 2003).

54. Judith Marks Mishne, "Dilemmas in Provision of Urban Mental Health Services for Latency Age Children," *Child and Adolescent Social Work Journal* 10 (August 1993), p. 278.

55. Epstein, *Children Who Could Have Been*, p. 63.

56. John Schuerman, et al., "Evaluation of the Illinois Family First Placement Prevention Program: Final Report" (Chicago: Chapin Hall Center for Children, University of Chicago, June 1993).

57. Quoted in "This Week," *National Review*, 56, 12 (June 28, 2004), p. 8.

58. Anita Gates, "Foraging in the Mind, Where Slavery's Scars Linger," *New York Times* (September 14, 2001).

59. Holly Danks, "Judge Rejects Slave Trauma as a Defense for Killing," *The Oregonian* (May 31, 2004), pg. 1.

60. Danks, "Judge," p. 1.

61. Similarly, the incarceration of a child welfare professional as a result of taking a stand in the best interest of a child is unheard of, a contrast to journalists who with some regularity submit to imprisonment rather than breach professional ethics and reveal their sources.

62. Lindsey, *Welfare of Children*, p. 58.

63. Epstein, *Children Who Could Have Been*, p. 64.

64. Jerome Miller, *Last One Over the Wall* (Columbus: Ohio State University Press, 1991); Jason DeParle, *American Dream* (New York: Viking, 2004), p. 127.

65. *DeShaney v. Winnebago County Department of Social Services*, 489 U.S. 189 (1989).

66. This figure is derived from public support for youth development plus children's and youth services, assuming that 60 percent of such contributions are derived from private, nongovernmental sources, a figure roughly in line with the experience of the United

Way of America (conversation with Karen Brunn, United Way of America, November 9, 1999). Virginia Hodgkinson and Murray Weitzman, *Nonprofit Almanac* (Washington, D.C.: Independent Sector, 1997), p. 249.

67. Garbarino, *Lost Boys*, p. 180.

68. In this respect, it is worth noting that federal activity in children's services predates the establishment of the American welfare state in 1935 with the Social Security Act.

69. Shelley Boots, et al., *State Child Welfare Spending at a Glance* (Washington, D.C.: Urban Institute, 1999), pp. 4–5.

70. Costin, Karger, and Stoesz, *Politics of Child Abuse*, pp. 151–57.

71. U.S. House of Representatives, House Ways and Means Committee, *Overview of Entitlement Programs* (Washington, D.C.: U.S. Government Printing Office, 1998), p. 733.

72. House of Representatives *Overview*, p. 718.

73. Robert Pear, "U.S. Finds Fault in All 50 States' Child Welfare Programs, and Penalties May Follow," *New York Times* (April 26, 2004), p. A17.

74. Robert Pear, "Mental Care Poor for Some Children in State Custody," *New York Times* (September 1, 2003), p. A1, A11.

75. David Halbfinger, "Care of Juvenile Offenders in Mississippi is Faulted, *New York Times* (September 1, 2003), p. A11.

76. Terry Eagleton, *After Theory* (New York: Basic Books, 2003), p. 142.

77. C. Wright Mills, "The Professional Ideology of Social Pathologists," *American Journal of Sociology*, 49 (September 1942), p. 171.

78. William J. Goode, "The Protection of the Inept," *American Sociological Review*, 32, 1 (February 1967), p. 6, 7.

79. Goode, "Protection of the Inept," p. 8.

80. Goode, "Protection of the Inept," p. 11.

81. Goode, "Protection of the Inept," p. 11.

82. Goode, "Protection of the Inept," p. 11.

83. Goode, "Protection of the Inept," p. 11.

84. Quoted in Michael Ignatieff, "The Era of Error," *The New Republic*, 221 (August 9, 1999), p. 39.

CHAPTER 7

1. Arthur Schlesinger, Jr., *The Cycles of History* (Boston: Houghton Mifflin, 1986).

2. Milton and Rose Friedman, "The Tide in the Affairs of Men," in Annelise Anderson and Dennis Bark, eds., *Thinking about American: The United States in the 1990s* (Stanford: Hoover Institution, 1988).

3. Fay Cook and Edith Barrett, *Support for the American Welfare State* (New York: Columbia University Press, 1992).

4. Albert O. Hirschman, *The Rhetoric of Reaction* (Cambridge, Mass.: Harvard University Press, 1991).

5. Charles Murray, *Losing Ground* (New York: Basic Books, 1984).

6. Bruce Jansson, *The Reluctant Welfare State* (Pacific Grove, Calif.: Brooks/Cole, 1993).

7. Katherine Newman, *Declining Fortunes* (New York: Basic Books, 1993).

8. David Stoesz, *Small Change: Domestic Policy Under the Clinton Presidency* (White Plains, N.Y.: Longman, 1996), pp. 8–9.

9. T. Marmor, J. Mashaw, and P. Harvey, *America's Misunderstood Welfare State* (New York: Basic Books, 1990).

10. Murray, *Losing Ground*, pp. 227–28.

11. Lawrence Mead, *The New Politics of Poverty* (New York: Basic Books, 1992).

12. Lawrence Mead, *Beyond Entitlement* (New York: Basic Books, 1986).

13. David Stoesz and Howard Karger, "When Welfare Reform Fails," *Tikkun* (March/April 1989).

14. David Stoesz, *A Poverty of Imagination: Bootstrap Capitalism, Sequel to Welfare Reform* (Madison: University of Wisconsin Press, 2000).

15. George Gilder, *Wealth and Poverty* (New York: Basic Books, 1981), p. 118.

16. Richard Hernstein and Charles Murray, *The Bell Curve* (New York: Free Press, 1994).

17. Hirschman suggested that conservatives opposed Progressive initiatives out of a fear that they would subvert earlier achievements—already secured civil and political rights. I would argue that the issue is more profound; that conservatives fear that nothing less than civilization is at stake.

18. Marvin Olasky, "Beyond the Stingy Welfare State," *Policy Review* (Fall 1990), p. 14.

19. Michael Tanner, *The End of Welfare* (Washington, D.C.: CATO Institute, 1996).

20. Stoesz, *Poverty of Imagination.*

21. Randall Eberts, "Welfare to Work," (Kalamazoo, Mich.: Upjohn Institute, 1995), p. 4.

22. L. M. Quinn and R. S. Magill, "Politics versus Research in Social Policy," *Social Service Review* (Winter 1994).

23. R. Spalter-Roth, et al., *Welfare that Works* (Washington, D.C.: Institute for Women's Policy Research, 1995).

24. L. Pavetti, "Questions and Answers on Welfare Dynamics," (Washington, D.C.: Urban Institute, 1995).

25. K. Edin and L. Lein, *Making Ends Meet* (New York: Russell Sage, 1997).

26. David Brooks, "A Nation of Grinders," *New York Times Magazine* (June 29, 2003), p. 16.

27. G. Borjas, *Friends and Strangers* (New York: Basic Books, 1990).

28. J. Simon, *The Economic Consequences of Immigration* (Oxford: Basil Blackwell, 1989); M. Fix and J. Passel, *Immigration and Immigrants* (Washington, D.C.: Urban Institute, 1994).

29. Michael Sherraden, *Assets and the Poor* (Armonk, N.Y.: M.E. Sharpe, 1991).

30. K. Edwards and M. Sherraden, *Individual Development Accounts* (St. Louis. Mo.: Center for Social Development, 1994).

31. Larry Brown and Larry Beeferman, "From New Deal to New Opportunity," *The American Prospect* (February 12, 2001), p. 26.

32. Charles Noble, *The Collapse of Liberalism* (Lanham, Md.: Rowman & Littlefield, 2004), pp. 143–44.

33. David Osborne, *Laboratories of Democracy* (Cambridge, Mass.: Harvard Business School Press, 1988).

34. David Osborne and Ted Gaebler, *Reinventing Government* (Reading, Pa.: Addison Wesley, 1992).

35. Al Gore, *Creating a Government that Works Better and Costs Less* (Washington, D.C.: U.S. Government Printing Office, 1993).

36. Newt Gingrich, "The Challenges We Must Meet to Achieve Our Destiny," *Los Angeles Times* (January 27, 1995), p. A1.

37. Quoted by David Broder, "Reagan's Policies Are Standard for Would-Be Successors," *Omaha World-Herald* (January 24, 1988), p. 12.

38. M. Kelly, "You Say You Want a Revolution," *New Yorker* (November 21, 1994), p. 17.

39. Terry Eagleton, *After Theory* (New York: Basic Books, 2003), p. 87.

40. Jacob Hacker, *The Divided Welfare State* (New York: Cambridge University Press, 2002).

41. *CDFIs Side by Side* (Philadelphia: National Community Capital Association, 2001).

42. R. Baker, "The Ecumenist," *American Prospect* 17 (January 2000), p. 28.

43. David Stoesz, "It's Time to Charter Welfare Departments," *Families in Society*, 83, 4 (July-August 2002), pp. 398–99.

44. L. Solomon, *Microenterprise: Human Reconstruction of America's Inner Cities* (Washington, D.C.: Progressive Policy Institute, 1991).

45. Howard Karger, *Shortchanged: Life and Debt in the Fringe Economy* (San Francisco: Berrett-Koehler, 2006).

46. "CDFIs Side-by-Side" (Philadelphia: National Community Capital Association, 2001), p.48.

47. Committee on Ways and Means, *Overview of Entitlement Programs* (Washington, D.C.: U.S. Government Printing Office, 2000), pp. 646–47.

48. Pew Commission on Foster Care, "Report," Pew Charitable Trust, p. 4. Available at http://www.pewfostercare.org/. [Accessed June 8, 2004]

49. Quoted in Gerard Wallace, "Foster Care Plus Love," *Washington Post* (June 19, 2004), p. A21.

50. "Fixing Foster Care," *Washington Post* (June 23, 2004), p. A20.

51. Lela Costin, Howard Karger, and David Stoesz, *The Politics of Child Abuse in America* (New York: Oxford University Press, 1996), ch. 6.

52. "Ten Year Report," Youth Futures Authority (Savannah, Ga., 1999).

53. Paul Tough, "The Harlem Project," *New York Times Magazine* (June 20, 2004), p. 66.

54. Rutledge Hutson, A Vision for Eliminating Poverty and Family Violence (Washington, D.C.: Center for Law and Social Policy, 2003), pp. 5–6.

55. Hutson, Vision, pp. 5–6.

56. "Annual Report 2003" (El Paso County, Co.: Department of Human Services, 2003), p.1.

57. Rutledge Hutson, "Providing Comprehensive, Integrated Social Services to Vulnerable Children and Families" (Washington, D.C.: Center for Law and Social Policy, 2004), p.18.

58. Emilie Stoltzfus, "Child Welfare: The Chafee Foster Care Independence Program," (Washington, D.C.: Congressional Research Service, 2004).

59. Laura Steff, "Baby Steps Made in Well-Being of Children, Data Show," *Washington*

Post (March 25, 2004), p. A1; Ann Hulbert, "Are the Kids All Right?" *New York Times Magazine* (April 11, 2004), p. 9.

60. Brown and Beeferman, "New Deal," p. 27.

CHAPTER 8

1. James Surowiecki, "A Cut Too Far," *New Yorker* (April 21 and 28, 2003), p. 68.

2. Jeff Madrick, "The Iraqi Time Bomb," *New York Times Magazine* (April 6, 2003), p. 50.

3. Roger Altman, "Which Democrat Will Speak Fiscal Truth," *Washington Post* (May 25, 2003), p. B7.

4. "Deficit Delusions," *Washington Post* (August 29, 2003), p. A22.

5. John Cassidy, "Goodbye to All That," *New Yorker* (September 15, 2003), p. 95.

6. Jonathan Rauch, "The Accidental Radical," *National Journal* 35, 30 (July 26, 2003), p. 1.

7. Dana Milbank and Dan Balz, "GOP Eyes Tax Cuts as Annual Events," *Washington Post* (May 11, 2003), p. A1.

8. Adam Clymer, "Buoyed by Resurgence, G.O.P. Strives for an Era of Dominance," *New York Times* (May 25, 2003), p. A1.

9. Bill Keller, "Reagan's Son," *New York Times Magazine* (January 26, 2003).

10. Adam Clymer, "Democrats Seek a Stronger Focus, and Money," *New York Times* (May 26, 2003), p. A12.

11. John Micklethwait and Adrian Wooldridge, *The Right Nation* (New York: Penguin, 2004), p. 383.

12. Micklethwait and Woodridge, *Right Nation*, p. 383.

13. William Sullivan, "Reconstructing Public Philosophy," (Berkeley: University of California Press, 1986), pp. 159, 223.

14. Barbara Ehrenreich, *Fear of Falling* (New York: HarperCollins, 1989), p. 191.

15. David Stoesz, *A Poverty of Imagination: Bootstrap Capitalism, Sequel to Welfare Reform* (Madison: University of Wisconsin Press, 2000), pp. 69–70.

16. Karlyn Bowman, "Optimism Spreads Regarding Equal Pay for Equal Work," (Washington, D.C.: American Enterprise Institute, 1999).

17. Christina Hoff Summers, *The War Against Boys* (New York: Touchstone, 2000).

18. Claudia Deane, "Computer-Assisted Influence?" *Washington Post* (April 19, 2002), p. A23.

19. Quoted in Randall Rothenberg, *The Neoliberals* (New York: Simon and Schuster, 1984), pp. 68–69.

20. Charles Peters, "A New Politics," *Public Welfare*, 18 (1983), p. 36.

21. Neil Gilbert, *Welfare Justice* (New Haven, Conn.: Yale University Press, 1995), ch. 6.

22. Neil Gilbert, *The Transformation of the Welfare State* (New York: Oxford University Press, 2002), p. 171.

23. Amitai Etzioni, *The Spirit of Community* (New York: Touchstone, 1991).

24. Gilbert, *Transformation*, p. 189.

25. Anthony Giddens, *The Third Way*, (Cambridge, Mass.: Polity Press, 1999), p. 100.

26. Giddens, *Third Way*, p. 117.

27. Tony Blair, et al., "The Third, Better Way," *Washington Post* (September 27, 1998), p. A19.

28. Quoted in E. J. Dionne, Jr., "Reinventing the Third Way," *Washington Post* (May 28, 2002), p. A17.

29. Miguel de Cervantes Saavadra, *The Adventures of Don Quixote,* trans. J. M. Cohen (New York: Penguin, 1950), p. 477.

30. Robert K. Merton, *On Social Structure and Science* (Chicago: University of Chicago Press, 1996), p. 153.

31. Merton, *On Social Structure*, p. 149.

32. Merton, *On Social Structure*, p. 145.

33. Amartya Sen, *Development as Freedom* (New York: Knopf, 1999), p. 18.

34. Sen, *Development as Freedom*, pp. 48–49.

35. Martha Nussbaum, *Women and Human Development* (New York: Cambridge University Press, 2000), p. 72.

36. Nussbaum, *Women*, pp. 78–80.

37. Craig Calhoun, *The Dictionary of the Social Sciences* (New York: Oxford University Press, 2002), p. 379.

38. C. Wright Mills, *The Power Elite* (New York: Oxford University Press, 1956), pp. 275, 273.

39. Arnold Relman, "The New Medical-Industrial Complex," *New England Journal of Medicine* 303, 17 (1980), pp. 1–5.

40. Pierre Bourdieu and Loic Wacquant, *An Invitation to Reflexive Sociology* (Chicago: University of Chicago Press, 1992), p. 14.

41. Pierre Bourdieu, *Acts of Reisistance* (New York: New Press, 1998), p. 58.

42. Bourdieu, *Acts*, pp. 53–54.

43. Bourdieu and Wacquant, *Reflexive Sociology,* p. 41.

44. Michael Kaufman, *Soros* (New York: Vintage, 2002).

45. Terry Eagleton, *After Theory* (New York: Basic Books, 2003), p. 60.

46. George Soros, *Open Society, Reforming Global Capitalism (*New York: Public Affairs, 2000), p. 12.

47. Soros, *Open Society*, p. 26.

48. Soros, *Open Society*, p. 47.

49. David Brooks, "One Nation, Slightly Divisible," *Atlantic Monthly* (December 2001), p. 57.

50. Brooks, "One Nation," p. 58.

51. Brooks, "One Nation," p. 64.

52. Roger Kimball, *Tenured Radicals* (Chicago: Elephant Paperbacks, 1998), p. 218.

53. Russell Jacoby, *Dogmatic Wisdom* (New York: Doubleday, 1994), p. 195.

54. Michael Weiss, *The Clustered World* (New York: Little Brown, 2000), p. 178.

55. Weiss, *Clustered World*, p. 15.

56. Mike Davis, *Magical Urbanism* (New York: Verso, 2001), p. 115.

57. Davis, *Magical Urbanism*, p. 117.

58. Walter Michaels, "Diversity's False Solace," *New York Times Magazine* (April 11, 2004), p. 14.

59. Eagleton, *After Theory*, p. 109.

60. Daniel Patrick Moynihan, *Came the Revolution* (New York: Harcourt Brace Jovanovich, 1988), p. 291.

61. E. J. Dionne, Jr., *They Only Look Dead* (New York: Simon & Schuster, 1996).

EPILOGUE

1. " 'I See a Great Day Coming,' " *Washington Post* (November 4, 2004), p. A30.

2. Jim Hoagland, "Second-Term Opitons," *Washington Post* (November 4, 2004), p. A25.

3. Peter Beinart, "What Went Wrong?" *The New Republic* (November 15, 2004), p. 6.

4. Tom Toles, "Good Closer," *Washington Post* (November 4, 2004), p. A24.

5. John Harris, "New Group to Tout Democrats' Centrist Values," *Washington Post* (November 11, 2004), p. A20.

6. Bruce Reed, "Ending Our Losing Ways," *Washington Post* (November 7, 2004), p. B1.

7. Richard Cohen, "The Once and Future Hope?" *Washington Post* (November 4, 2004), p. A25.

8. "Executive Summary," *Scientific Integrity in Policymaking* (Union of Concerned Scientists) Available at http://www. ucsusa.org/global_environment/rsi/page. [Accessed November 11, 2004]

9. Brian Faler, "A 51 Percent Mandate," *Washington Post* (November 11, 2004), p. A6.

10. David Rosenbaum, "If a Tax Overhaul Has Winners, It Will Also Have Losers," *New York Times* (November 14, 2004), p. WK5.

11. Peter Wehner, "Some Thoughts on Social Security" Available at http://www.j-bradford-delong.net [Accessed January 11, 2005].

12. Michael Fletcher, "Bush Promotes Plan for Social Security," Washington Post (January 12, 2005), p. A4.

13. Jim Vandettei and Mike Allen, "In GOP, Resistance on Social Security," Washington Post (January 11, 2005), p. A4.

14. Wehner, "Some Thoughts."

INDEX

Note: The letter *t* following a page number indicates a table.